The Lives of the Poets of Great Britain and Ireland (1753)
Vol.- II

by

Theophilus Cibber

The Lives of the Poets of Great Britain and Ireland (1753)
Vol.- II
by Theophilus Cibber

ISBN: 978-93-60468-22-4

Published by

DOUBLE 9 BOOKS
2/13-B, Ansari Road
Daryaganj, New Delhi – 110002
info@double9books.com
www.double9books.com
Tel. 011-40042856

ABOUT THE AUTHOR

An English actor, writer, and author named Theophilus Cibber was born on November 25 or 26 or 1703 and died in October 1758. He was the son of actor-manager Colley Cibber. He started playing when he was young and then became a theater manager like his father. Alex Pope made fun of Theophilus Cibber in his 1727 work The Dunciad by calling him a young man who "thrusts his person full into your face" (III 132). He was famous on stage for playing Pistol in Henry IV, Part 2 and some of the comedic roles his father had played when he was younger, but some harsh critics said he put too much stress on certain parts. Theophilus got a bad name and was involved in a scandal because of his private life. He was on his way to Ireland and a season in Dublin when his ship sank. Theophilus Cibber was born during the Great Storm of 1703 and started playing at the Drury Lane Theatre when he was 16 years old, in 1721. Cibber was a notorious rake when he was younger, and he hung out with other young men of the same mind and character, like the Duke of Wharton.

CONTENTS

Anthony Brewer..7

Thomas May..10

John Taylour, Water-Poet..13

William Habington...15

Francis Goldsmith..17

John Cleveland...19

Dr. Barten Holyday..23

Thomas Nabbes...26

James Shirley...28

James Howel, Esq;...33

Sir Richard Fanshaw..36

Abraham Cowley..40

Sir William Davenant...55

Henry King, Bishop of Chichester..................................72

Philip Massinger..78

Sir Robert Stapleton...81

Dr. Jasper Main...83

John Milton...86

Mrs. Katherine Philips..112

Margaret, Duchess of Newcastle..................................122

William Cavendish..127

Sir John Birkenhead 133

Roger Boyle, Earl of Orrery 136

Richard Head...146

Thomas Hobbs...149

Sir Aston Cokaine 159

Sir George Wharton..162

Anne Killegrew 165

Nat. Lee 168

Samuel Butler 173

Edmund Waller Esq;...178

John Ogilby 195

Wilmot, Earl of Rochester..198

George Villiers, Duke of Buckingham 219

Matthew Smith, Esquire...234

Thomas Otway 235

John Oldham..244

(Dillon) (Wentworth) Earl of Roscommon 250

Anthony Brewer

A poet who flourished in the reign of Charles I. but of whose birth and life we can recover no particulars. He was highly esteemed by some wits in that reign, as appears from a Poem called Steps to Parnassus, which pays him the following well turned compliment.

> Let Brewer take his artful pen in hand,
> Attending muses will obey command,
> Invoke the aid of Shakespear's sleeping clay,
> And strike from utter darkness new born day.

Mr. Winstanley, and after him Chetwood, has attributed a play to our author called Lingua, or the Contention of the Tongue and the Five Senses for Superiority, a Comedy, acted at Cambridge, 1606; but Mr. Langbaine is of opinion, that neither that, Love's Loadstone, Landagartha, or Love's Dominion, as Winstanley and Philips affirm, are his; Landagartha being written by Henry Burnel, esquire, and Love's Dominion by Flecknoe. In the Comedy called Lingua, there is a circumstance which Chetwood mentions, too curious, to be omitted here. When this play was acted at Cambridge, Oliver Cromwel performed the part of Tactus, which he felt so warmly, that it first fired his ambition, and, from the possession of an imaginary crown, he stretched his views to a real one; to accomplish which, he was content to wade through a sea of blood, and, as Mr. Gray beautifully expresses it, shut the Gates of Mercy on Mankind; the speech with which he is said to have been so affected, is the following,

> Roses, and bays, pack hence: this crown and robe,
> My brows, and body, circles and invests;
> How gallantly it fits me! sure the slave
> Measured my head, that wrought this coronet;
> They lie that say, complexions cannot change!
> My blood's enobled, and I am transform'd
> Unto the sacred temper of a king;
> Methinks I hear my noble Parasites
> Stiling me Cæsar, or great Alexander,
> Licking my feet,—&c.

Mr. Langbaine ascribes to Brewer the two following plays,

Country Girl, a Comedy, often acted with applause, printed in 4to. 1647. This play has been revived since the Restoration, under the title of Country Innocence, or the Chamber-maid turned Quaker.

Love-sick King, an English Tragical History, with the Life and Death of Cartesmunda, the Fair Nun of Winchester; printed in 4to. London, 1655; this play was likewise revived 1680, and acted by the name of the Perjured Nun. The historical part of the plot is founded upon the Invasion of the Danes, in the reign of King Ethelred and Alfred.

This last play of Anthony Brewer's, is one of the best irregular plays, next to those of Shakespear, which are in our language. The story, which is extremely interesting, is conducted, not so much with art, as spirit; the characters are animated, and the scene busy. Canutus King of Denmark, after having gained the city of Winchester, by the villainy of a native, orders all to be put to the sword, and at last enters the Cloister, raging with the thirst of blood, and panting for destruction; he meets Cartesmunda, whose beauty stops his ruffian violence, and melts him, as it were, into a human creature. The language of this play is as modern, and the verses as musical as those of Rowe; fire and elevation run through it, and there are many strokes of the most melting tenderness. Cartesmunda, the Fair Nun of Winchester, inspires the King with a passion for her, and after a long struggle between honour and love, she at last yields to the tyrant, and for the sake of Canutus breaks her vestal vows. Upon hearing that the enemy was about to enter the Cloister, Cartesmunda breaks out into the following beautiful exclamation:

> The raging foe pursues, defend us Heaven!
> Take virgin tears, the balm of martyr'd saints
> As tribute due, to thy tribunal throne;
> With thy right hand keep us from rage and murder;
> Let not our danger fright us, but our sins;
> Misfortunes touch our bodies, not our souls.

When Canutus advances, and first sees Cartesmunda, his speech is poetical, and conceived in the true spirit of Tragedy.

> Ha! who holds my conquering hand? what power unknown,
> By magic thus transforms me to a statue,
> Senseless of all the faculties of life?
> My blood runs back, I have no power to strike;
> Call in our guards and bid 'em all give o'er.
> Sheath up your swords with me, and cease to kill:

Her angel beauty cries, she must not die,
Nor live but mine: O I am strangely touch'd!
Methinks I lift my sword, against myself,
When I oppose her—all perfection!
O see! the pearled dew drops from her eyes;
Arise in peace, sweet soul.

In the same scene the following is extremely beautiful.

I'm struck with light'ning from the torrid zone;
Stand all between me, and that flaming sun!
Go Erkinwald, convey her to my tent.
Let her be guarded with more watchful eyes
Than heaven has stars:
If here she stay I shall consume to death,
'Tis time can give my passions remedy,
Art thou not gone! kill him that gazeth on her;
For all that see her sure must doat like me,
And treason for her, will be wrought against us.
Be sudden—to our tents—pray thee away,
The hell on earth is love that brings delay.

Thomas May

A Poet and historian of the 17th century, was descended of an ancient, but decayed family in the county of Sussex, in the reign of Queen Elizabeth[1], and was educated a fellow commoner in Sidney Sussex College in Cambridge. He afterwards removed to London, and lived about the court, where he contracted friendships with several gentlemen of fashion and distinction, especially with Endymion Porter esquire, one of the gentlemen of the bedchamber to King Charles I. While he resided at court he wrote five plays, which are extant under his name. In 1622, he published at London, in 8vo. a translation of Virgil's Georgics with annotations; and in 1635, a Poem on King Edward III. It was printed under the title of the Victorious Reign of Edward III. written in seven books, by his Majesty's command. In the dedication to Charles I. our author writes thus; "I should humbly have craved your Majesty's pardon for my omission of the latter part of King Edward's reign, but that the sense of mine own defects hath put me in mind of a most necessary suit, so beg forgiveness for that part which is here written. Those great actions of Edward III. are the arguments of this poem, which is here ended, where his fortune began to decline, where the French by revolts, and private practices regained that which had been won from them by eminent and famous victories; which times may afford fitter observations for an acute historian in prose, than strains of heighth for an heroic poem." The poem thus begins,

> The third, and greatest Edward's reign we sing,
> The high atchievements of that martial King,
> Where long successful prowesse did advance,
> So many trophies in triumphed France,
> And first her golden lillies bare; who o're
> Pyrennes mountains to that western shore,
> Where Tagus tumbles through his yellow sand
> Into the ocean; stretch'd his conquering hand.

From the lines quoted, the reader will be able to judge what sort of versifier our author was, and from this beginning he has no great reason to expect an entertaining poem, especially as it is of the historical kind; and he who begins a poem thus insipidly, can never expect his readers to accompany him to the third page. May likewise translated Lucan's Pharsalia, which poem he continued down to the death of Julius Cæsar, both in Latin and English verse.

Dr. Fuller says, that some disgust was given to him at court, which alienated his affections from it, and determined him, in the civil wars to adhere to the Parliament.

Mr. Philips in his Theatrum Poetarum, observes, that he stood candidate with Sir William Davenant for the Laurel, and his ambition being frustrated, he conceived the most violent aversion to the King and Queen. Sir William Davenant, besides the acknowledged superiority of his abilities, had ever distinguished himself for loyalty, and was patronized and favoured by men of power, especially the Marquis of Newcastle: a circumstance which we find not to have happened to May: it is true, they were both the friends of the amiable Endymion Porter, esq; but we are not informed whether that gentleman interested himself on either side.

In the year 1647, was published in London in folio, The History of the Parliament of England, which began November 3, 1640, with a Short and Necessary View of some precedent Years, written by Thomas May, Esq; Secretary to the Parliament, and published by their authority. In 1650 he published in 8vo. A Breviary of the History of the Parliament of England. Besides these works, Mr. Philips tells us, he wrote a History of Henry IV. in English verse, the Comedy of the Old Wives Tale, and the History of Orlando Furioso; but the latter, Mr. Langbaine, who is a higher authority than Philips, assures us was written before May was able to hold a pen, much less to write a play, being printed in 4to. London, 1594. Mr. Winstanley says, that in his history, he shews all the spleen of a mal-content, and had he been preferred to the Bays, as he happened to be disappointed, he would have embraced the Royal interest with as much zeal, as he did the republican: for a man who espouses a cause from spite only, can be depended upon by no party, because he acts not upon any principles of honour or conviction.

Our author died suddenly in the year 1652, and was interred near the tomb of Camden, on the West side of the North isle of Westminster Abbey, but his body, with several others, was dug up after the restoration, and buried in a pit in St. Margaret's church yard[2]. Mr. May's plays are,

> 1. Agrippina, Empress of Rome, a Tragedy, printed in 12mo. London, 1639. Our author has followed Suetonius and Tacitus, and has translated and inserted above 30 lines from Petronius Arbiter; this circumstance we advance on the authority of Langbaine, whose extensive reading has furnished him with the means of tracing the plots of most

part of our English plays; we have heard that there is a Tragedy on this subject, written by Mr. Gray of Cambridge, the author of the beautiful Elegy in a Country Church Yard; which play Mr. Garrick has sollicited him to bring upon the stage; to which the author has not yet consented.

2. Antigone, the Theban Princess, a Tragedy, printed in 8vo. London, 1631, and dedicated to Endymion Porter, Esq; Our author in the contexture of this Tragedy, has made use of the Antigone of Sophocles, and the Thebais of Seneca.

3. Cleopatra, Queen of Egypt, a Tragedy, acted 1626, and printed in 12mo. London, 1639, and dedicated to Sir Kenelme Digby: The author has followed the historians of those times. We have in our language two other plays upon the same subject, one by Shakespear, and the other by Dryden.

4. Heir, a Comedy, acted by the company of revels, 1620; this play is much commended by Mr. Thomas Carew, in a copy of verses prefixed to the play, where, amongst other commendations bestowed on the stile, and natural working up of the passions, he says thus of the oeconomy of the play.

> The whole plot doth alike itself disclose,
> Thro' the five Acts, as doth a lock, that goes
> With letters, for 'till every one be known,
> The lock's as fast, as if you had found none.

If this comedy, is no better than these wretched commendatory lines, it is miserable indeed.

5. Old Couple, a Comedy, printed in 4to; this play is intended to expose the vice of covetousness.

Footnotes:

1. Langbaine's Lives of the Poets.

2. Wood's Fasti Oxon. vol. i. p. 205.

John Taylour, Water-Poet

Was born in Gloucestershire, where he went to school with one Green, and having got into his accidence, was bound apprentice to a Waterman in London, which, though a laborious employment, did not so much depress his mind, but that he sometimes indulged himself in poetry. Taylour relates a whimsical story of his schoolmaster Mr. Green, which we shall here insert upon the authority of Winstanley. "Green loved new milk so well, that in order to have it new, he went to the market to buy a cow, but his eyes being dim, he cheapened a bull, and asking the price of the beast, the owner and he agreed, and driving it home, would have his maid to milk it, which she attempting to do, could find no teats; and whilst the maid and her master were arguing the matter, the bull very fairly pissed into the pail;" whereupon his scholar John Taylour wrote these verses,

> Our master Green was overseen
> In buying of a bull,
> For when the maid did mean to milk,
> He piss'd the pail half full.

Our Water-poet found leisure to write fourscore books, some of which occasioned diversion enough in their time, and were thought worthy to be collected in a folio volume. Mr. Wood observes, that had he had learning equal to his natural genius, which was excellent, he might have equalled, if not excelled, many who claim a great share in the temple of the muses. Upon breaking out of the rebellion, 1642, he left London, and retired to Oxford, where he was much esteemed for his facetious company; he kept a common victualling house there, and thought he did great service to the Royal cause, by writing Pasquils against the round-heads. After the garrison of Oxford surrendered, he retired to Westminster, kept a public house in Phænix Alley near Long Acre, and continued constant in his loyalty to the King; after whose death, he set up a sign over his door, of a mourning crown, but that proving offensive, he pulled it down, and hung up his own picture[1], under which were these words,

> There's many a head stands for a sign,
> Then gentle reader why not mine?

On the other side,

> Tho' I deserve not, I desire
> The laurel wreath, the poet's hire.

He died in the year 1654, aged 74, and was buried in the church yard of St. Paul's Covent-Garden; his nephew, a Painter at Oxford, who lived in Wood's time, informed him of this circumstance, who gave his picture to the school gallery there, where it now hangs, shewing him to have had a quick and smart countenance. The following epitaph was written upon him,

> Here lies the Water-poet, honest John,
> Who row'd on the streams of Helicon;
> Where having many rocks and dangers past,
> He at the haven of Heaven arrived at last.

Footnote:

1. Athen. Oxon. vol. ii. p. 393.

William Habington

Son of Thomas Habington, Esq; was born at Hendlip in Worcestershire, on the 4th of November 1605, and received his education at St. Omers and Paris, where he was earnestly pressed to take upon him the habit of a Jesuit; but that sort of life not suiting with his genius, he excused himself and left them[1]. After his return from Paris, he was instructed by his father in history, and other useful branches of literature, and became, says Wood, a very accomplished gentleman. This author has written,

1. Poems, 1683, in 8vo. under the title of Castara: they are divided into three parts under different titles, suitable to their subject. The first, which was written when he was courting his wife, Lucia, the beautiful daughter of William Lord Powis, is introduced by a character, written in prose, of a mistress. The second are copies to her after marriage, by the character of a wife; after which is a character of a friend, before several funeral elegies. The third part consists of divine poems, some of which are paraphrases on several texts out of Job, and the book of psalms.

2. The Queen of Arragon, a Tragi-Comedy, which play he shewed to Philip Earl of Pembroke, who having a high opinion of it, caused it to be acted at court, and afterwards to be published, the contrary to the author's inclination.

3. Observations on History, Lond. 1641, 8vo.

4. History of Edward IV. Lond. 1640, in a thin folio, written and published at the desire of King Charles I. which in the opinion of some critics of that age, was too florid for history, and fell short of that calm dignity which is peculiar to a good historian, and which in our nation has never been more happily attained than by the great Earl of Clarendon and Bishop Burnet. During the civil war, Mr. Habington, according to Wood, temporized with those in power, and was not unknown to Oliver Cromwell; but there is no account of his being raised to any preferment during the Protector's government. He died the 30th of November, 1654.

We shall present the readers with the prologue to the Queen of Arragon, acted at Black-Fryars, as a specimen of this author's poetry.

> Ere we begin that no man may repent,
> Two shillings, and his time, the author sent
> The prologue, with the errors of his play,
> That who will, may take his money and away.
> First for the plot, 'tis no way intricate
> By cross deceits in love, nor so high in state,
> That we might have given out in our play-bill
> This day's the Prince, writ by Nick Machiavil.
> The language too is easy, such as fell
> Unstudied from his pen; not like a spell
> Big with mysterious words, such as inchant
> The half-witted, and confound the ignorant.
> Then, what must needs, afflict the amourist,
> No virgin here, in breeches casts a mist
> Before her lover's eyes; no ladies tell
> How their blood boils, how high their veins do swell.
> But what is worse no baudy mirth is here;
> (The wit of bottle-ale, and double beer)
> To make the wife of citizen protest,
> And country justice swear 'twas a good jest.
> Now, Sirs, you have the errors of his wit,
> Like, or dislike, at your own perils be't.

Footnote:

1. Wood Athen. Oxon. v. 1, p, 100.

Francis Goldsmith

Was the son of Francis Goldsmith, of St. Giles in the Fields in Middlesex, Esq; was educated under Dr. Nicholas Grey, in Merchant-Taylor's School, became a gentleman commoner in Pembroke-College in the beginning of 1629, was soon after translated to St. John's College, and after he had taken a degree in arts, to Grey's-Inn, where he studied the common law several years, but other learning more[1]. Mr. Langbaine says, that he could recover no other memoirs of this gentleman, but that he lived in the reign of King Charles the First, and obliged the World with a translation of a play out of Latin called, Sophompaneas, or the History of Joseph, with Annotations, a Tragedy, printed 4to. Lond. 1640, and dedicated to the Right Hon. Henry Lord Marquis of Dorchester. This Drama was written by the admirable Hugo Grotius, published by him at Amsterdam 1635, and dedicated to Vossius, Professor of History and Civil Arts in Amsterdam. He stiles it a Tragedy, notwithstanding it ends successfully, and quotes for his authority in so doing, Æschilus, Euripides, and even Vossius, in his own Art of Poetry. Some make it a Question, whether it be lawful to found a dramatic Poem on any sacred subject, and some people of tender consciences have murmured against this Play, and another of the same cast called Christ's Passion; but let us hear the opinion of Vossius himself, prefixed to this Play. "I am of opinion, (says he) it is better to chuse another argument than sacred. For it agrees not with the majesty of sacred things, to be made a play and a fable. It is also a work of very dangerous consequence, to mingle human inventions with things sacred; because the poet adds uncertainties of his own, sometimes falsities; which is not only to play with holy things, but also to graft in men's minds opinions, now and then false. These things have place, especially when we bring in God, or Christ speaking, or treating of the mysteries of religion. I will allow more where the history is taken out of the sacred scriptures; but yet in the nature of the argument is civil, as the action of David flying from his son Absolom; or of Joseph sold by his brethren, advanced by Pharaoh to the government of Egypt, and that dignity adored by, and made known unto his brethren. Of which argument is Sophompaneas, written by Hugo Grotius, embassador from the Queen of Sweden to the King of France; which tragedy, I suppose, may be set for a pattern to him, that would handle an argument from the holy scriptures." This is the opinion of Vossius, and with him all must agree who admire the truly admirable Samson Agonistes of Milton.

As we have frequently mentioned Grotius, the short account of so great a man, which is inserted in Langbaine, will not be unpleasing to the reader.

"Hugo Grotius, says he, was an honour to his country: he was born in the year 1583, and will be famous to posterity, in regard of those many excellent pieces he has published. In some of his writings he defended Arminianism, for which he suffered imprisonment in the castle of Louverstein, in the year 1618; at which time his associate Barnevelt lost his head on the same account. Afterwards Grotius escaped out of prison, by means of Maria Reigersberg his wife, and fled into Flanders; and thence into France, where he was kindly received by Lewis XIII. He died at Rostock in Mecclebourg, Sept. 1, 1645. His life is written at large by Melchoir Adamus, in Latin."

As to our author's translation, which is in heroic verse, it is much commended by verses from four of his friends.

He also translated Grotius's consolatory oration to his father, with epitaphs; and also his Catechism into English verse.

Mr. Goldsmith died at Ashton in Northamptonshire, in September 1655, and was buried there, leaving behind him an only daughter named Katherine, afterwards the wife of Sir Henry Dacres.

Footnote:

1. Wood Athen. Oxon. v. 2. p. 194.

John Cleveland

Was the son of a vicar of Hinkley, in Leicestershire, where he was born, and received his grammatical education, under one Mr. Richard Vines, a zealous Puritan. After he had compleated his school education, he was sent to Christ's College in Cambridge, and in a short time distinguishing himself for his knowledge of the Latin tongue, and for Oratory, he was preferred to a fellowship in St. John's-College, in the said university. He continued there about nine years, and made during that time some successful attempts in poetry. At length, upon the eruption of the civil war, he was the first who espoused the Royal cause in verse, against the Presbyterians, who persecuted him in their turn with more solid severity; for he was ejected, as soon as the reins of power were in their hands. Dr. Fuller bestows upon our author the most lavish panegyric: He was (says he) a general artist, pure latinist, an exquisite orator, and what was his masterpiece, an eminent poet. Dr. Fuller thus characterizes him, but as Cleveland has not left remains behind him sufficient to convey to posterity so high an idea of his merit, it may be supposed that the Doctor spoke thus in his favour, meerly on account of their agreement in political principles. He addressed an oration, says Winstanley, to Charles I. who was so well pleased with it, that he sent for him, and gave him his hand to kiss, with great expressions of kindness. When Oliver Cromwell was in election to be member for the town of Cambridge, as he engaged all his friends and interests to oppose it; so when it was carried but by one vote, he cried out with much passion, that, that single vote had ruined church and kingdom[1], such fatal events did he presage from the success of Oliver. Mr. Cleveland was no sooner forced from the College, by the prevalence of the Parliament's interest, but he betook himself to the camp, and particularly to Oxford the head quarters of it, as the most proper sphere for his wit, learning and loyalty. Here he began a paper war with the opposite party, and wrote some smart satires against the Rebels, especially the Scots. His poem called the Mixt Assembly; his character of a London Diurnal, and a Committee-man, are thought to contain the true spirit of satire, and a just representation of the general confusion of the times. From Oxford he went to the garrison of Newark, where he acted as judge advocate till that garrison was surrendered, and by an excellent temperature, of both, says Winstanley, he was a just and prudent judge for the King, and a faithful advocate for the Country.

Here he drew up a bantering answer and rejoinder to a Parliament officer, who had written to him on account of one Hill, that had deserted their side, and carried off with him to Newark, the sum of 133 l. and 8 d. We shall give part of Mr. Cleveland's answer to the officer's first letter, by which an estimate may be formed of the rest.

Sixthly Beloved!

"It is so, that our brother and fellow-labourer in the gospel, is start aside; then this may serve for an use of instruction, not to trust in man, or in the son of man. Did not Demas leave Paul? Did not Onesimus run from his master Philemon? Also this should teach us to employ our talents, and not to lay them up in a napkin; had it been done among the cavaliers, it had been just, then the Israelite had spoiled the Egyptian; but for Simeón to plunder Levi, that—that, &c."

The garrison of Newark defended themselves with much courage and resolution against the besiegers, and did not surrender but by the King's special command, after he had thrown himself into the hands of the Scots; which action of his Majesty's Cleveland passionately resented, in his poem called, the King's Disguise: Upon some private intelligence, three days before the King reached them, he foresaw, that the army would be bribed to surrender him, in which he was not mistaken. As soon as this event took place, Cleveland, who warmly adhered to the regal party, was obliged to atone for his loyalty by languishing in a jail, at Yarmouth, where he remained for some time under all the disadvantages of poverty, and wretchedness: At last being quite spent with the severity of his confinement, he addressed Oliver Cromwell in a petition for liberty, in such pathetic and moving terms, that his heart was melted with the prisoner's expostulation, and he ordered him to be set at liberty. In this address, our author did not in the least violate his loyalty, for he made no concessions to Oliver, but only a representation of the hardships he suffered, without acknowledging his sovereignty, tho' not without flattering his power. Having thus obtained his liberty, he settled himself in Gray's-Inn, and as he owed his releasement to the Protector, he thought it his duty to be passive, and not at least to act against him: But Cleveland did not long enjoy his state of unenvied ease, for he was seized with an intermitting fever, and died the 29th of April, 1685.

[2]On the first of May he was buried, and his dear friend Dr. John Pearson, afterwards lord bishop of Chester, preached his funeral sermon, and gave this reason, why he declined commending the deceased, "because such praising of him would not be adequate to the expectation of the audience, seeing some who knew him must think it far below him."—

There were many who attempted to write elegies upon him, and several performances of this kind, in Latin and English, are prefixed to the edition of Cleveland's works, in verse and prose, printed in 8vo, in 1677, with his effigies prefixed.

From the verses of his called Smectymnuus, we shall give the following specimen, in which the reader will see he did not much excel in numbers.

> Smectymnuus! the goblin makes me start,
> I'th' name of Rabbi-Abraham, what art?
> Syriack? or Arabick? or Welsh? what skilt?
> Up all the brick-layers that Babel built?
> Some conjurer translate, and let me know it,
> 'Till then 'tis fit for a West Saxon Poet.
> But do the brotherhood then play their prizes?
> Like murmurs in religion with disguises?
> Out-brave us with a name in rank and file,
> A name, which if 'twere trained would spread a mile;
> The Saints monopoly, the zealous cluster,
> Which like a porcupine presents a muster.

The following lines from the author's celebrated satire, entitled, the Rebel-Scot, will yet more amply shew his turn for this species of poetry.

> "Nature herself doth Scotchmen beasts confess,
> Making their country such a wilderness;
> A land that brings in question and suspence
> God's omnipresence; but that Charles came thence;
> But that Montrose and Crawford's loyal band
> Aton'd their sin, and christen'd half their land.—
> A land where one may pray with curst intent,
> O may they never suffer banishment!
> Had Cain been Scot, God would have chang'd his doom,
> Not forc'd him wander, but confin'd him home.—
>
> "Lord! what a goodly thing is want of shirts!
> How a Scotch stomach and no meat converts!
> They wanted food and rayment, so they took
> Religion for their temptress and their cook.—
> Hence then you proud impostors get you gone,
> You Picts in gentry and devotion.
> You scandal to the stock of verse, a race
> Able to bring the gibbet in disgrace.—

"The Indian that heaven did forswear,
Because he heard some Spaniards were there,
Had he but known what Scots in Hell had been,
He would, Erasmus-like, have hung between."

It is probable that this bitterness against our brethren of North-Britain, chiefly sprang from Mr. Cleveland's resentment of the Scots Army delivering up the King to the Parliament.

Footnotes:

1. Wood fasti Oxon

2. Winst. Lives of the Poets

3 .Winst. Lives of the Poets.

Dr. Barten Holyday

Son of Thomas Holyday, a taylor, was born at All Saints parish, within the city of Oxford, about the latter end of Queen Elizabeth's reign; he was entered early into Christ Church, in the time of Dr, Ravis, his relation and patron, by whom he was chosen student, and having taken his degrees of batchelor and master of arts, he became archdeacon of Oxfordshire. In 1615, he entered into holy orders[1], and was in a short time taken notice of as an eloquent or rather popular preacher, by which he had two benefices confered on him both in the diocese of Oxford.

In the year 1618 he went as chaplain to Sir Francis Stewart, when he accompanied to Spain the Count Gundamore, after he had continued several Years at our court as embassador, in which journey Holyday behaved in a facetious and pleasant manner, which ingratiated him in the favour of Gundamore[2].

Afterwards our author became chaplain to King Charles I. and succeeded Dr. Bridges in the archdeaconry of Oxon, before the year 1626. In 1642 he was by virtue of the letters of the said King, created, with several others, Dr. of divinity. When the rebellion broke out, he sheltered himself near Oxford; but when he saw the royal party decline so much that their cause was desperate, he began to tamper with the prevailing power; and upon Oliver Cromwell's being raised to the Protectorship, he so far coincided with the Usurper's interests, as to undergo the examination of the Friers, in order to be inducted into the rectory of Shilton in Berks, in the place of one Thomas Lawrence, ejected on account of his being non compos mentis. For which act he was much blamed and censured by his ancient friends the clergy, who adhered to the King, and who rather chose to live in poverty during the usurpation, than by a mean compliance with the times, betray the interest of the church, and the cause of their exiled sovereign.

After the King's restoration he quitted the living he held under Cromwell, and returned to Eisley near Oxon, to live on his archdeaconry; and had he not acted a temporizing part it was said he might have been raised to a see, or some rich deanery. His poetry however, got him a name in those days, and he stood very fair for preferment; and his philosophy discovered in his book de Anima, and well languaged sermons, (says Wood) speaks him eminent in his generation, and shew him to have traced the rough parts, as well as the pleasant paths of poetry.

His works are,

1 Three Sermons, on the Passion, Resurrection, and Ascension of our Saviour, Lond. 1626.

2. Two Sermons at Paul's Cross.

3. A Sermon on the Nature of Faith.

4. Motives to a godly Life, in Ten Sermons, Oxon, 1657.

5. Four Sermons against Disloyalty, Oxon, 1661.

Technogamia; or the Marriage of Arts, a Comedy, acted publicly in Christ's Church Hall, with no great applause 1617. But the Wits of those times being willing to distinguish themselves before the King, were resolved, with leave, to act the same comedy at Woodstock, whereupon (says Wood) the author making some foolish alterations in it, it was accordingly acted on Sunday night the 26th of August 1621, but it being too grave for the King, and too scholastic for the Audience, or as some said, that the actors in order to remove their timidity, had taken too much wine before, they began, his Majesty after two acts offered several times to withdraw; at length being persuaded by some of those who were near to him, to have patience till it was ended, lest the young men should be discouraged, he sat it out, tho' much against his will; upon which these Verses were made by a certain scholar;

> At Christ Church Marriage done before the King
> Lest that those Mates should want an offering,
> The King himself did offer; what I pray?
> He offered twice or thrice to go away.

6. Survey of the World in Ten Books, a Poem, Oxon, 1661, which was judged by Scholars to be an inconsiderable piece, and by some not to be his. But being published just before his death, it was taken for a posthumous work, which had been composed by him in his younger Days[3].

He translated out of Latin into English the Satires of Persius, Oxon. 1616, in apologizing for the defects of this work, he plays upon the word *translate*: To have committed no faults in this translation, says he, would have been to translate myself, and put off man. Wood calls this despicable pun, an elegant turn.

7. Satires of Juvenal illustrated with Notes, Oxon. folio 1673. At the end of which is the Fourth Edition of Persius, before mentioned.

8. Odes of Horace, Lond. 1652; this Translation Wood says, is so near that of Sir Thomas Hawkins, printed 1638, or that of Hawkins so near this, that to whom to ascribe it he is in doubt.

Dr. Holyday, who according to the same author was highly conceited of his own worth, especially in his younger Days, but who seems not to have much reason for being so, died at a Village called Eisley on the 2d day of October 1661, and was three days after buried at the foot of Bishop King's monument, under the south wall of the aisle joining on the south side to the choir of Christ Church Cathedral, near the remains of William Cartwright, and Jo. Gregory.

Footnotes:

1. Athen. Oxon. 259. Ed. 1721.

2. Wood ubi supra.

3. Athen. Oxon. p. 260.

Thomas Nabbes

A writer, in the reign of Charles I, whom we may reckon, says Langbaine, among poets of the third rate, but who in strict justice cannot rise above a fifth. He was patronized by Sir John Suckling. He has seven plays and masks extant, besides other poems, which Mr. Langbaine says, are entirely his own, and that he has had recourse to no preceding author for assistance, and in this respect deserves pardon if not applause from the critic. This he avers in his prologue to Covent-Garden.

> He justifies that 'tis no borrowed strain,
> From the invention of another's brain.
> Nor did he steal the fancy. 'Tis the fame
> He first intended by the proper name.
> 'Twas not a toil of years: few weeks brought forth,
> This rugged issue, might have been more worth,
> If he had lick'd it more. Nor doth he raise
> From the ambition of authentic plays,
> Matter or words to height, nor bundle up
> Conceits at taverns, where the wits do sup;
> His muse is solitary, and alone
> Doth practise her low speculation.

The reader from the above specimen may see what a poet he was; but as he was in some degree of esteem in his time, we thought it improper to omit him.

The following are his plays;

1.   The Bride, a Comedy; acted in the Year 1638 at a private House in Drury-Lane by their Majesty's Servants, printed 4to. 1640.

2.   Covent Garden, a Comedy; acted in the Year 1632.

3.   Hannibal and Scipio, an Historical Tragedy, acted in the year 1635.

4.   Microcosmus, a Moral Masque, represented at a private house in Salisbury Court, printed 1637.

5. Spring's Glory, Vindicating Love by Temperance, against the Tenet, Sine Cerere & Baccho friget Venus; moralized in a Masque. With other Poems, Epigrams, Elegies, and Epithalamiums of the author's, printed in 4to, London, 1638. At the end of these poems is a piece called A Presentation, intended for the Prince's Birth day, May 29, 1638, annually celebrated.

6. Tottenham-Court, a Comedy, acted in the year 1633, at a private house in Salisbury Court, printed in 4to. 1638.

7. Unfortunate Lovers, a Tragedy, never acted, printed in 4to. London, 1640.

Mr. Philips and Mr. Winstanley, according to their old custom, have ascribed two other anonymous plays to our author: The Woman Hater Arraigned, a Comedy, and Charles the First, a Tragedy, which Langbaine has shewn not to be his.

James Shirley

A very voluminous dramatic author, was born in the city of London, and: was descended from the Shirleys in Suffex or Warwickshire; he was educated in grammar learning in Merchant Taylors school, and transplanted thence to St. John's College, but in what station he lived there, we don't find.

Dr. William Laud, afterwards archbishop of Canterbury, presiding over that house, conceived a great affection for our author, and was willing to cherish and improve those promising abilities early discoverable in him. Mr. Shirley had always an inclination to enter into holy orders, but, for a very particular reason, was discouraged from attempting it by Dr. Laud; this reason to some may appear whimsical and ridiculous, but has certainly much weight and force in it.

Shirley had unfortunately a large mole upon his left cheek, which much disfigured him, and gave him a very forbidding appearance. Laud observed very justly, that an audience can scarce help conceiving a prejudice against a man whose appearance shocks them, and were he to preach with the tongue of an angel, that prejudice could never be surmounted; besides the danger of women with child fixing their eyes on him in the pulpit, and as the imagination of pregnant women has strange influence on the unborn infants, it is somewhat cruel to expose them to that danger, and by these means do them great injury, as ones fortune in some measure depends upon exterior comeliness[1]. But Shirley, who was resolute to be in orders, left that university soon after, went to Cambridge, there took the degrees in arts, and became a minister near St. Alban's in Hertfordshire; but never having examined the authority, and purity of the Protestant Church, and being deluded by the sophistry of some Romish priests, he changed his religion for theirs[2], quitted his living, and taught a grammar school in the town of St. Alban's; which employment he finding an intolerable drudgery, and being of a fickle unsteady temper, he relinquished it, came up to London, and took lodgings in Gray's Inn, where he commenced a writer for the stage with tolerable success. He had the good fortune to gain several wealthy and beneficent patrons, especially Henrietta Maria the Queen Consort, who made him her servant.

When the civil war broke out, he was driven from London, and attended upon his Royal Mistress, while his wife and family were left in a deplorable condition behind him. Some time after that, when the Queen of England was forced, by the fury of opposition, to sollicit succours from France, in order to reinstate her husband; our author could no longer wait upon her, and was received into the service of William Cavendish, marquis of Newcastle, to take his fortune with him in the wars. That noble spirited patron had given him such distinguishing marks of his liberality, as Shirley thought himself happy in his service, especially as by these means he could at the same time serve the King.

Having mentioned Henrietta Maria, Shirley's Royal Mistress, the reader will pardon a digression, which flows from tenderness, and is no more than an expression of humanity. Her life-time in England was embittered with a continued persecution; she lived to see the unhappy death of her Lord; she witnessed her exiled sons, not only oppressed with want, but obliged to quit France, at the remonstrance of Cromwel's ambassador; she herself was loaded with poverty, and as Voltaire observes, "was driven to the most calamitous situation that ever poor lady was exposed to; she was obliged to sollicit Cromwel to pay her an allowance, as Queen Dowager of England, which, no doubt, she had a right to demand; but to demand it, nay worse, to be obliged to beg it of a man who shed her Husband's blood upon a scaffold, is an affliction, so excessively heightened, that few of the human race ever bore one so severe."

After an active service under the marquis of Newcastle, and the King's cause declining beyond hope of recovery, Shirley came again to London, and in order to support himself and family, returned his former occupation of teaching a school, in White Fryars, in which he was pretty successful, and, as Wood says, 'educated many ingenious youths, who, afterwards in various faculties, became eminent.' After the Restoration, some of the plays our author had written in his leisure moments, were represented with success, but there is no account whether that giddy Monarch ever rewarded him for his loyalty, and indeed it is more probable he did not, as he pursued the duke of Lauderdale's maxim too closely, of making friends of his enemies, and suffering his friends to shift for themselves, which infamous maxim drew down dishonour on the administration and government of Charles II. Wood further remarks, that Shirley much assisted his patron, the duke of Newcastle, in the composition of his plays, which the duke afterwards published, and was a drudge to John Ogilby in his translation of Homer's Iliad and Odysseys, by writing annotations on them. At length, after Mr. Shirley had lived to the age of 72, in various conditions, having been much agitated in the world, he, with his second wife, was driven by the dismal conflagration that happened in London, Anno 1666, from his habitation in

Fleet-street, to another in St. Giles's in the Fields. Where, being overcome with miseries occasioned by the fire, and bending beneath the weight of years, they both died in one day, and their bodies were buried in one grave, in the churchyard of St. Giles's, on October 29, 1666.

The works of this author

1. Changes, or Love in a Maze, a Comedy, acted at a private house in Salisbury Court, 1632.

2. Contention for Honour and Riches, a Masque, 1633.

3. Honoria and Mammon, a Comedy; this Play is grounded on the abovementioned Masque.

4. The Witty Fair One, a Comedy, acted in Drury Lane, 1633.

5. The Traitor, a Tragedy, acted by her Majesty's servants, 1635. This Play was originally written by Mr. Rivers, a jesuit, but altered by Shirley.

6. The Young Admiral, a Tragi-Comedy, acted at a private house in Drury Lane, 1637.

7. The Example, a Tragi-Comedy, acted in Drury Lane by her Majesty's Servants, 1637.

8. Hyde Park, a Comedy, acted in Drury Lane, 1637.

9. The Gamester, a Comedy, acted in Drury Lane, 1637; the plot is taken from Queen Margate's Novels, and the Unlucky Citizen.

10. The Royal Master, a Tragi-Comedy, acted at the Theatre in Dublin, 1638.

11. The Duke's Mistress, a Tragi-Comedy, acted by her Majesty's servants, 1638.

12. The Lady of Pleasure, a Comedy, acted at a private house in Drury Lane, 1638.

13. The Maid's Revenge, a Tragedy, acted at a private house in Drury Lane, with applause, 1639.

14. Chabot Admiral of France, a Tragedy, acted in Drury Lane, 1639; Mr. Chapman joined in this play; the story may be found in the histories of the reign of Francis I.

15. The Ball, a Comedy, acted in Drury Lane, 1639; Mr. Chapman likewise assisted in this Comedy.

On the Author's Valentine, Mrs. Metcalf.

Could I charm the queen of love,
To lend a quill of her white dove;
Or one of Cupid's pointed wings
Dipt in the fair Caftalian Springs;
Then would I write the all divine
Perfections of my Valentine.

As 'mongst, all flow'rs the Rose excells,
As Amber 'mongst the fragrant'st smells,
As 'mongst all minerals the Gold,
As Marble 'mongst the finest mold,
As Diamond 'mongst jewels bright
As Cynthia 'mongst the lesser lights[3]:
So 'mongst the Northern beauties shine,
So far excels my Valentine.

In Rome and Naples I did view
Faces of celestial hue;
Venetian dames I have seen many,
(I only saw them, truck'd not any)
Of Spanish beauties, Dutch and French,
I have beheld the quintessence[3]:
Yet saw I none that could out-shine,
Or parallel my Valentine.

Th' Italians they are coy and quaint.
But they grosly daub and paint;
The Spanish kind, and apt to please,
But fav'ring of the same disease:
Of Dutch and French some few are comely,
The French are light, the Dutch are homely.
Let Tagus, Po, the Loire and Rhine
Then veil unto my Valentine.

Footnotes:

1. Langbaine's Lives of the Poets.

2. Athen. Oxon. p. 281. vol. ii.

3. Bad rhimes were uncommon with the poets of Howel's time.

16. Arcadia, a Dramatic Pastoral, performed at the Phænix in Drury Lane by the Queen's servants, 1649.

17. St. Patrick for Ireland, an Historical Play, 1640; for the plot see Bedes's Life of St. Patrick, &c.

18. The Humorous Courtier, a Comedy, presented at a private house in Drury Lane, 1640.

19. Love's Cruelty, a Tragedy, acted by the Queen's servants, 1640.

20. The Triumph of Beauty, a Masque, 1646; part of this piece seems to be taken from Shakespear's Midsummer's Night's Dream, and Lucian's Dialogues.

21. The Sisters, a Comedy, acted at a private house in Black Fryars, 1652.

22. The Brothers, a Comedy, 1652.

23. The Doubtful Heir, a Tragi-Comedy, acted at Black Fryars, 1652.

24. The Court Secret, a Tragi-Comedy, acted at a private house in Black Fryars, 1653, dedicated to the Earl of Strafford; this play was printed before it was acted.

25. The Impostor, a Tragi-Comedy, acted at a private house in Black Fryars, 1653.

26. The Politician, a Tragedy, acted in Salisbury Court, 1655; part of the plot is taken from the Countess of Montgomery's Urania.

27. The Grateful Servant, a Tragi-Comedy, acted at a private house in Drury Lane, 1655.

28. The Gentleman of Venice, a Tragi-Comedy, acted at a private house in Salisbury Court. Plot taken from Gayron's Notes on Don Quixote.

29. The Contention of Ajax and Ulysses for Achilles's Armour, a Masque, 1658. It is taken from Ovid's Metamorphosis, b. xiii.

30. Cupid and Death, a Masque, 1658.

31. Love Tricks, or the School Of Compliments, a Comedy, acted by the Duke of York's servants in little Lincoln's-Inn-Fields, 1667.

32. The Constant Maid, or Love will find out the Way, a Comedy, acted at the New House called the Nursery, in Hatton Garden, 1667.

33. The Opportunity, a Comedy, acted at the private house in Drury Lane by her Majesty's servants; part of this play is taken from Shakespear's Measure for Measure.

34. The Wedding, a Comedy, acted at the Phænix in Drury Lane.

35. A Bird in a Cage, a Comedy, acted in Drury Lane.

36. The Coronation, a Comedy. This play is printed with Beaumont's and Fletcher's.

37. The Cardinal, a Tragedy, acted at a private house in Black Fryars.

38. The Triumph of Peace, a Masque, presented before the King and Queen at Whitehall, 1633, by the Gentlemen of the Four Inns of Court.

We shall present the reader with a quotation taken from a comedy of his, published in Dodsley's collection of old plays, called A Bird in a Cage, p. 234. Jupiter is introduced thus speaking,

> Let the music of the spheres,
> Captivate their mortal ears;
> While Jove descends into this tower,
> In a golden streaming shower.
> To disguise him from the eye
> Of Juno, who is apt to pry
> Into my pleasures: I to day
> Have bid Ganymede go to play,
> And thus stole from Heaven to be
> Welcome on earth to Danae.
> And see where the princely maid,
> On her easy couch is laid,
> Fairer than the Queen of Loves,
> Drawn about with milky doves.

Footnotes:

1 .Athen. Oxon. p 376

2. Wood, ubi supra.

James Howel, Esq;

Was born at Abernant in Carmarthenshire, the place where his father was minister, in the year 1594[1]. Howel himself, in one of his familiar epistles, says, that his ascendant was that hot constellation of Cancer about the middle of the Dog Days. After he was educated in grammar learning in the free school of Hereford, he was sent to Jesus College in the beginning of 1610, took a degree in arts, and then quitted the university. By the help of friends, and a small sum of money his father assisted him with, he travelled for three years into several countries, where he improved himself in the various languages; some years after his return, the reputation of his parts was so great, that he was made choice of to be sent into Spain, to recover of the Spanish monarch a rich English ship, seized by the Viceroy of Sardinia for his master's use, upon some pretence of prohibited goods being found in it.

During his absence, he was elected Fellow of Jesus College, 1623, and upon his return, was patronized by Emanuel, lord Scroop, Lord President of the North, and by him was made his secretary[2]. As he resided in York, he was, by the Mayor and Aldermen of Richmond, chose a Burgess for their Corporation to sit in that Parliament, that began at Westminster in the year 1627. Four years after, he went secretary to Robert, earl of Leicester, ambassador extraordinary from England to the King of Denmark, before whom he made several Latin speeches, shewing the occasion of their embassy, viz. to condole the death of Sophia, Queen Dowager of Denmark, Grandmother to Charles I. King of England.

Our author enjoyed many beneficial employments, and at length, about the beginning of the civil war, was made one of the clerks of the council, but being extravagant in his temper, all the money he got was not sufficient to preserve him from a Jail. When the King was forced from the Parliament, and the Royal interest declined, Howel was arrested; by order of a certain committee, who owed him no good-will, and carried prisoner to the Fleet; and having now nothing to depend upon but his wits, he was obliged to write and translate books for a livelihood, which brought him in, says Wood, a comfortable subsistance, during his stay there; he is the first person we have met with, in the course of this work, who may be said to have made a trade of authorship, having written no less than 49 books on different subjects.

In the time of the rebellion, we find Howel tampering with the prevailing power, and ready to have embraced their measures; for which reason, at the reiteration, he was not continued in his place of clerk to the council, but was only made king's historiographer, being the first in England, says Wood, who bore that title; and having no very beneficial employment, he wrote books to the last.

He had a great knowledge in modern histories, especially in those of the countries in which he had travelled, and he seems, by his letters, to have been no contemptible politician: As to his poetry, it is smoother, and more harmonious, than was very common with the bards of his time.

As he introduced the trade of writing for bread, so he also is charged with venal flattery, than which nothing can be more ignoble and base. To praise a blockhead's wit because he is great, is too frequently practised by authors, and deservedly draws down contempt upon them. He who is favoured and patronized by a great man, at the expence of his integrity and honour, has paid a dear price for the purchase, a miserable exchange, patronage for virtue, dependance for freedom.

Our author died the beginning of November, 1666, and was buried on the North side of the Temple church.

We shall not trouble the reader with an enumeration of all the translations and prose works of this author; the occasion of his being introduced here, is, his having written

Nuptials of Peleus and Thetis, consisting of a Masque and a Comedy, for the Great Royal Ball, acted in Paris six times by the King in person, the Duke of Anjou, the Duke of York, with other Noblemen; also by the Princess Royal, Henrietta Maria, Princess of Conti, &c. printed in 4to. 1654, and addressed to the Marchioness of Dorchester. Besides this piece, his Dodona's Grove, or Vocal Forest, is in the highest reputation.

His entertaining letters, many of whom were written to the greatest personages in England, and some in particular to Ben Johnson, were first published in four volumes; but in 1737, the tenth edition of them was published in one volume, which is also now become scarce. They are interspersed with occasional verses; from one of these little pieces we shall select the following specimen of this author's poetical talent.

Sir Richard Fanshaw

Was the youngest, and tenth son of Sir Henry Fanshaw of Ware-park in Hertfordshire; he was born in the year 1607, and was initiated in learning by the famous Thomas Farnaby. He afterwards compleated his studies in the university of Cambridge, and from thence went to travel into foreign countries, by which means he became a very accomplished gentleman. In 1635 he was patronized by King Charles I. on account of his early and promising abilities; he took him into his service, and appointed him resident at the court of Spain[1]. During his embassy there, his chief business was, to demand reparation and punishment of some free-booters, who had taken ships from the English, and to endeavour the restoration of amity, trade and commerce.

When the civil war broke out, he returned to England, having accomplished the purposes of his embassy abroad, and attached himself with the utmost zeal to the Royal Standard; and during those calamitous times was intrusted with many important matters of state.

In 1644, attending the court at Oxford, the degree of Doctor of Civil Laws was conferred upon him[2], and the reputation of his parts every day increasing, he was thought a proper person to be secretary to Charles, Prince of Wales, whom he attended into the Western parts of England, and from thence into the Isles of Scilly and Jersey.

In 1648 he was appointed treasurer of the navy, under the command of Prince Rupert, in which office he continued till the year 1650, when he was created a baronet by King Charles II. and sent envoy extraordinary to the court of Spain. Being recalled thence into Scotland, where the King then was, he served there in quality of secretary of state, to the satisfaction of all parties, notwithstanding he refused to take the covenant engagements, which Charles II. forced by the importunity of the Presbyterians, entered into, with a resolution to break them. In 1651 he was made prisoner at the battle of Worcester and committed to close custody in London, where he continued, 'till his confinement introduced a very dangerous sickness; he then had liberty granted him, upon giving bail, to go for the recovery of his health, into any place he should chuse, provided he stirred not five miles from thence, without leave from the Parliament. ·

In February, 1659, he repaired to the King at Breda, who knighted him the April following. Upon his Majesty's reiteration, it was expected, from his great services, and the regard the King had for him, that he would have been made secretary of state, but at that period there were so many people's merits to repay, and so great a clamour for preferment, that Sir Richard was disappointed, but had the place of master of requests conferred on him, a station, in those times, of considerable profit and dignity.

On account of his being a good Latin scholar, he was also made a secretary for that tongue[3]. In 1661, being one of the burgesses for the university of Cambridge, he was sworn a privy counsellor for Ireland, and having by his residence in foreign parts, qualified himself for public employment, he was sent envoy extraordinary to Portugal, with a dormant commission to the ambassador, which he was to make use of as occasion should require. Shortly after, he was appointed ambassador to that court, where he negotiated the marriage between his master King Charles II. and the Infanta Donna Catharina, daughter to King John VI. and towards the end of the same year he returned to England. We are assured by Wood, that in the year 1662, he was sent again ambassador to that court, and when he had finished his commission, to the mutual satisfaction of Charles II. and Alphonso King of Portugal, being recalled in 1663, he was sworn one of his Majesty's Privy Council. In the beginning of the year 1644 he was sent ambassador to Philip IV. King of Spain, and arrived February 29 at Cadiz, where he met with a very extraordinary and unexpected salutation, and was received with some circumstances of particular esteem. It appears from one of Sir Richard's letters, that this distinguishing respect was paid him, not only on his own, but on his master's account; and in another of his letters he discovers the secret why the Spaniard yielded him, contrary to his imperious proud nature, so much honour, and that is, that he expected Tangier and Jamaica to be restored to him by England, which occasioned his arrival to be so impatiently longed for, and magnificently celebrated. During his residence at this court King Philip died, September 17, 1665, leaving his son Charles an infant, and his dominions under the regency of his queen, Mary Anne, daughter of the emperor Ferdinand III. Sir Richard taking the advantage of his minority, put the finishing hand to a peace with Spain, which was sufficiently tired and weakened with a 25 years war, for the recovery of Portugal, which had been dismembered from the Spanish crown in 1640; the treaty of peace was signed at Madrid December 6, 1665. About the 14th of January following, his excellency took a journey into Portugal, where he staid till towards the end of March; the design of his journey certainly was to effect an accommodation between that crown and Spain, which however was not produced till 1667, by the interposition of his Britannic Majesty. Our author having finished his commission was preparing for his return to

England, when June 4, 1666, he was seized at Madrid with a violent fever, which put an end to his valuable life, the 16th of the same month, the very day he intended to set out for England: his body being embalmed, it was conveyed by his lady, and all his children, then living, by land to Calais, and so to London, whence being carried to All Saints church in Hertford, it was deposited in the vault of his father-in-law, Sir John Harrison. The Author of the Short Account of his Life, prefixed to his letters, says, 'that he was remarkable for his meekness, sincerity, humanity and piety, and also was an able statesman and a great scholar, being in particular a compleat master of several modern languages, especially the Spanish, which he spoke and wrote with as much advantage, as if he had been a native.' By his lady, eldest daughter of Sir John Harrison, he had six sons, and eight daughters, whereof only one son and four daughters survived him.

The following is an account of his works,

> 1. An English Translation in Rhyme, of the celebrated Italian Pastoral, called Il Pastor Fido, or the Faithful Shepherd, written originally by Battista Guarini, printed in London, 1644 in 4to. and 1664 8vo.

> 2. A Translation from English into Latin Verse, of the Faithful Shepherders, a Pastoral, written originally by John Fletcher, Gent. London, 1658.

> 3. In the octavo edition of the Faithful Shepherd, Anno 1664, are inserted the following Poems of our author, viz. 1st, An Ode upon the Occasion of his Majesty's Proclamation, 1630, commanding the Gentry to reside upon their Estates in the Country. 2d, A Summary Discourse of the Civil Wars of Rome, extracted from the best Latin Writers in Prose and Verse. 3d, An English Translation of the Fourth Book of Virgil's Æneid on the Loves of Dido and Æneas. 4th, Two Odes out of Horace, relating to the Civil Wars of Rome, against covetous, rich Men.

> 4. He translated out of Portuguese into English, The Lusiad, or Portugal's Historical Poem, written originally by Luis de Camoens, London, 1655, &c. folio.

After his decease, namely, in 1671, were published these two posthumous pieces of his in 4to, Querer per solo Querer, To Love only for Love's sake, a Dramatic Romance, represented before the King and Queen of Spain, and Fiestas de Aranjuez, Festivals at Aranjuez: both written originally in Spanish, by Antonio de Mendoza, upon occasion of celebrating the Birth-day of King Philip IV. in 1623, at Aranjuez; they were translated by our author in 1654, during his confinement at Taukerley-park in Yorkshire, which uneasy situation induced him to write the following stanzas on this work, which are here inserted, as a specimen of his versification.

> Time was, when I, a pilgrim of the seas,
> When I 'midst noise of camps, and courts disease,
> Purloin'd some hours to charm rude cares with verse,
> Which flame of faithful shepherd did rehearse.

> But now restrain'd from sea, from camp, from court,
> And by a tempest blown into a port;
> I raise my thoughts to muse on higher things,
> And eccho arms, and loves of Queens and Kings.

> Which Queens (despising crowns and Hymen's band)
> Would neither men obey, nor men command:
> Great pleasure from rough seas to see the shore
> Or from firm land to hear the billows roar.

We are told that he composed several other things remaining still in manuscript, which he had not leisure to compleat; even some of the printed pieces have not all the finishing so ingenious an author could have bestowed upon them; for as the writer of his Life observes, 'being, for his loyalty and zeal to his Majesty's service, tossed from place to place, and from country to country, during the unsettled times of our anarchy, some of his Manuscripts falling into unskilful hands, were printed and published without his knowledge, and before he could give them the last finishing strokes.' But that was not the case with his Translation of the Pastor Fido, which was published by himself, and applauded by some of the best judges, particularly Sir John Denham, who after censuring servile translators, thus goes on,

> A new and nobler way thou dost pursue
> To make translations and translators too.
> They but preserve the ashes, these the flame,
> True to his sense, but truer to his fame.

Footnotes:

1. Short Account of Sir Richard Fanshaw, prefixed to his Letters.

2. Wood, Fast. ed. 1721, vol. ii. col. 43, 41.

3. Wood, ubi supra.

Abraham Cowley

Was the son of a Grocer, and born in London, in Fleet-street, near the end of Chancery Lane, in the year 1618. His mother, by the interest of her friends, procured him to be admitted a King's scholar in Westminster school[1]; his early inclination to poetry was occasioned by reading accidentally Spencer's Fairy Queen, which, as he himself gives an account, 'used to lye in his mother's parlour, he knew not by what accident, for she read no books but those of devotion; the knights, giants, and monsters filled his imagination; he read the whole over before he was 12 years old, and was made a poet, as immediately as a child is made an eunuch.'

In the 16th year of his age, being still at Westminster school, he published a collection of poems, under the title of Poetical Blossoms, in which there are many things that bespeak a ripened genius, and a wit, rather manly than puerile. Mr. Cowley himself has given us a specimen in the latter end of an ode written when he was but 13 years of age. 'The beginning of it, says he, is boyish, but of this part which I here set down, if a very little were corrected, I should not be much ashamed of it.' It is indeed so much superior to what might be expected from one of his years, that we shall satisfy the reader's curiosity by inserting it here.

IX.

This only grant me, that my means may lye,
Too low for envy, for contempt too high:
Some honour I would have;
Not from great deeds, but good alone,
The unknown are better than ill known,
Rumour can ope the grave:
Acquaintance I would have, but when 't depends
Not on the number, but the choice of friends.

X.

Books should, not business, entertain the light
And sleep, as undisturbed as death, the night:
My house a cottage, more

Than palace, and should fitting be
For all my use, no luxury:
My garden painted o'er
With nature's hand, not art, and pleasures yield,
Horace might envy in his Sabine Field.

XI.

Thus would I double my life's fading space,
For he that runs it well, twice runs his race;
And in this true delight,
These unbought sports, that happy state,
I could not fear; nor wish my fate;
But boldly say, each night,
To-morrow let my sun his beams display,
Or in clouds hide them: I have lived to-day.

It is remarkable of Mr. Cowley, as he himself tells us, that he had this defect in his memory, that his teachers could never bring him to retain the ordinary rules of grammar, the want of which, however, he abundantly supplied by an intimate acquaintance with the books themselves, from whence those rules had been drawn. In 1636 he was removed to Trinity College in Cambridge, being elected a scholar of that house[2]. His exercises of all kinds were highly applauded, with this peculiar praise, that they were fit, not only for the obscurity of an academical life, but to have made their appearance on the true theatre of the world; and there he laid the designs, and formed the plans of most of the masculine, and excellent attempts he afterwards happily finished. In 1638 he published his Love's Riddle, written at the time of his being a scholar in Westminster school, and dedicated by a copy of verses to Sir Kenelm Digby. He also wrote a Latin Comedy entitled Naufragium Joculare, or the Merry Shipwreck. The first occasion of his entering into business, was, an elegy he wrote on the death of Mr. William Harvey, which introduced him to the acquaintance of Mr. John Harvey, the brother of his deceased friend, from whom he received many offices of kindness through the whole course of his life[3]. In 1643, being then master of arts, he was, among many others, ejected his college, and the university; whereupon, retiring to Oxford, he settled in St. John's College, and that same year, under the name of a scholar of Oxford, published a satire entitled the Puritan and the Papist. His zeal in the Royal cause, engaged him in the service of the King, and he was present in many of his Majesty's journies and expeditions; by this means he gained an acquaintance and familiarity with the personages of the court and of the gown, and particularly had the entire friendship of my lord Falkland, one of the principal secretaries of state.

During the heat of the civil war, he was settled in the family of the earl of St. Alban's, and accompanied the Queen Mother, when she was obliged to retire into France. He was absent from his native country, says Wood, about ten years, during which time, he laboured in the affairs of the Royal Family, and bore part of the distresses inflicted upon the illustrious Exiles: for this purpose he took several dangerous journies into Jersey, Scotland, Flanders, Holland, and elsewhere, and was the principal instrument in maintaining a correspondence between the King and his Royal Consort, whose letters he cyphered and decyphered with his own hand.

His poem called the Mistress was published at London 1647, of which he himself says, "That it was composed when he was very young. Poets (says he) are scarce thought free men of their company, without paying some duties and obliging themselves to be true to love. Sooner or later they must all pass through that trial, like some Mahometan monks, who are bound by their order once at least in their life, to make a pilgrimage to Mecca. But we must not always make a judgment of their manners from their writings of this kind, as the Romanists uncharitably do of Beza for a few lascivious sonnets composed by him in his youth. It is not in this sense that poetry is said to be a kind of painting: It is not the picture of the poet, but of things, and persons imagined by him. He may be in his practice and disposition a philosopher, and yet sometimes speak with the softness of an amorous Sappho. I would not be misunderstood, as if I affected so much gravity as to be ashamed to be thought really in love. On the contrary, I cannot have a good opinion of any man who is not at least capable of being so."

What opinion Dr. Sprat had of Mr. Cowley's Mistress, appears by the following passage extracted from his Life of Cowley. "If there needed any excuse to be made that his love-verses took up so great a share in his works, it may be alledged that they were composed when he was very young; but it is a vain thing to make any kind of apology for that sort of writing. If devout or virtuous men will superciliously forbid the minds of the young to adorn those subjects about which they are most conversant, they would put them out of all capacity of performing graver matters, when they come to them: for the exercise of all men's wit must be always proper for their age, and never too much above it, and by practice and use in lighter arguments, they grow up at last to excell in the most weighty. I am not therefore ashamed to commend Mr. Cowley's Mistress. I only except one or two expressions, which I wish I could have prevailed with those that had the right of the other edition to have left out; but of all the rest, I dare boldly pronounce, that never yet was written so much on a subject so delicate, that can less offend the severest rules of morality. The whole passion of love is intimately described by all its mighty train of hopes, joys and disquiets. Besides this amorous tenderness, I know not how in every copy there is something of more useful knowledge gracefully insinuated; and every where there is something feigned to inform the minds of wise men, as well as to move the hearts of young men or women."

Our author's comedy, named the Guardian, he afterwards altered, and published under the title of the Cutter of Coleman-Street. Langbaine says, notwithstanding Mr. Cowley's modest opinion of this play, it was acted not only at Cambridge, but several times afterwards privately, during the prohibition of the stage, and after the King's return publickly at Dublin; and always with applause. It was this probably that put the author upon revising it; after which he permitted it to appear publickly on the stage under a new title, at his royal highness the Duke of York's theatre. It met with opposition at first from some who envied the author's unshaken loyalty; but afterwards it was acted with general applause, and was esteemed by the critics an excellent comedy.

In the year 1656 it was judged proper by those on whom Mr. Cowley depended, that he should come over into England, and under pretence of privacy and retirement, give notice of the situation of affairs in this nation. Upon his return he published a new edition of all his poems, consisting of four parts, viz.

1. Miscellanies.

2. The Mistress; or several copies of love-verses.

3. Pindarique Odes, written in imitation of the stile and manner of Pindar.

4. Davedeis, a sacred poem of the troubles of David in four books.

"Which, says Dr. Sprat, was written in so young an age, that if we shall reflect on the vastness of the argument, and his manner of handling it, he may seem like one of the miracles that he there adorns; like a boy attempting Goliah. This perhaps, may be the reason, that in some places, there may be more youthfulness and redundance of fancy, than his riper judgement would have allowed. But for the main of it I will affirm, that it is a better instance and beginning of a divine poem, than ever I yet saw in any language. The contrivance is perfectly ancient, which is certainly the true form of an heroic poem, and such as was never yet done by any new devices of modern wits. The subject was truly divine, even according to God's own heart. The matters of his invention, all the treasures of knowledge and histories of the bible. The model of it comprehended all the learning of the East. The characters lofty and various; the numbers firm and powerful; the digressions beautiful and proportionable. The design, to submit mortal wit to heavenly truths. In all, there is an admirable mixture of human virtues and passions with religious raptures. The truth is, continues Dr. Sprat, methinks in other matters his wit exceeded all other men's, but in his moral and divine works it out-did itself; and no doubt it proceeded from this cause, that in the lighter kinds of poetry he chiefly represented the humours and affections of others; but in these he sat to himself, and drew the figure of his own mind. We have the first book of the Davideis translated out of English into very elegant Latin by Mr. Cowley himself." Dr. Sprat says of his Latin poetry, "that he has expressed to admiration all the numbers of verse and figures of poetry, that are scattered up and down amongst the ancients; and that there is hardly to be found in them any good fashion of speech, or colour of measure; but he has comprehended it, and given instances of it, according as his several arguments required either a majestic spirit, or passionate, or pleasant. This he observes, is the more extraordinary, in that it was never yet performed by any single poet of the ancient Romans themselves."

The same author has told us, that the occasion of Mr. Cowley's falling on the pindarique way of writing, was his accidentally meeting with Pindar's works in a place where he had no other books to direct him. Having thus considered at leisure the heighth of his invention, and the majesty of his stile, he tried immediately to imitate it in English, and he performed it, says the Dr. without the danger that Horace presaged to the man that should attempt it. Two of our greatest poets, after allowing Mr. Cowley to have been a successful imitator of Pindar, yet find fault with his numbers. Mr. Dryden having told us, that our author brought Pindaric verse as near perfection as possible in so short a time, adds, "But if I may be allowed to speak my mind modestly, and without injury to his sacred ashes, somewhat of the purity of English, somewhat of more sweetness in the numbers, in a word, somewhat of a finer turn and more lyrical verse is yet wanting;" and Mr. Congreve having excepted against the irregularity of the measure of the English Pindaric odes, yet observes, "that the beauty of Mr. Cowley's verses are an attonement for the irregularity of his stanzas; and tho' he did nor imitate Pindar in the strictness of his numbers, he has very often happily copied him in the force of his figures, and sublimity of his stile and sentiments."

Soon after his return to England, he was seized upon thro' mistake; the search being intended after another gentleman of considerable note in the King's party. The Republicans, who were sensible how much they needed the assistance and coalition of good men, endeavoured sometimes by promises, and sometimes by threatning, to bring our author over to their interest; but all their attempts proving fruitless, he was committed to a severe confinement, and with some difficulty at last obtained his liberty, after giving a thousand pounds bail, which Dr. Scarborough in a friendly manner took upon himself. Under these bonds he continued till Cromwell's death, when he ventured back into France, and there remained, as Dr. Sprat says, in the same situation as before, till near the time of the King's return. This account is a sufficient vindication of Mr. Cowley's unshaken loyalty, which some called in question; and as this is a material circumstance in the life of Cowley, we shall give an account of it in the words of the elegant writer of his life just now mentioned, as it is impossible to set it in a fairer, or more striking light than is already done by that excellent prelate. "The cause of his loyalty being called in question, he tells us, was a few lines in a preface to one of his books; the objection, says he, I must not pass in silence, because it was the only part of his life that was liable to misinterpretation, even by the confession of those that envied his fame.

"In this case it were enough to alledge for him to men of moderate minds, that what he there said was published before a book of poetry; and so ought rather to be esteemed as a problem of his fancy and invention, than as a real image of his judgement; but his defence in this matter may be laid on a surer foundation. This is the true reason to be given of his delivering that opinion: Upon his coming over he found the state of the royal party very desperate. He perceived the strength of their enemies so united, that till it should begin to break within itself, all endeavours against it were like to prove unsuccessful. On the other side he beheld their zeal for his Majesty's cause to be still so active, that often hurried them into inevitable ruin. He saw this with much grief; and tho' he approved their constancy as much as any man living, yet he found their unreasonable shewing it, did only disable themselves, and give their adversaries great advantages of riches and strength by their defeats. He therefore believed it would be a meritorious service to the King, if any man who was known to have followed his interest, could insinuate into the Usurper's minds, that men of his principles, were now willing to be quiet, and could persuade the poor oppressed Royalists to conceal their affections for better occasions. And as for his own particular, he was a close prisoner when he writ that against which the exception is made; so that he saw it was impossible for him to pursue the ends for which he came hither, if he did not make some kind of declaration of his peaceable intentions. This was then his opinon; and the success of the thing seems to prove that it was not ill-grounded. For certainly it was one of the greatest helps to the King's affairs about the latter end of that tyranny, that many of his best friends dissembled their counsels, and acted the same designs under the disguises and names of other parties. The prelate concludes this account with observing, that, that life must needs be very unblameable, which had been tried in business of the highest consequence, and practised in the hazardous secrets of courts and cabinets, and yet there can nothing disgraceful be produced against it, but only the error of one paragraph, and single metaphor."

About the year 1662, his two Books of Plants were published, to which he added afterwards four more, and all these together, with his Latin poems, were printed in London, 1678; his Books on Plants was written during his residence in England, in the time of the usurpation, the better to distinguish his real intention, by the study of physic, to which he applied.

It appears by Wood's Fasti Oxon. that our poet was created Dr. of Physic at Oxford, December 2, 1657, by virtue of a mandamus from the then government. After the King's restoration, Mr. Cowley, being then past the 40th year of his age, the greatest part of which had been spent in a various and tempestuous condition, resolved to pass the remainder of his life in a studious retirement: In a letter to one of his friends, he talks of making a voyage to America, not from a view of accumulating wealth, but there to chuse a habitation, and shut himself up from the busy world for ever. This scheme was wildly romantic, and discovered some degree of vanity, in the author; for Mr. Cowley needed but retire a few miles out of town, and cease from appearing abroad, and he might have been sufficiently secured against the intrusion of company, nor was he of so much consequence as to be forced from his retirement; but this visionary scheme could not be carried into execution, by means of Mr. Cowley's want of money, for he had never been much on the road of gain. Upon the settlement of the peace of the nation, he obtained a competent estate, by the favour of his principal patrons, the duke of Buckingham, and the earl of St. Albans. Thus furnished for a retreat, he spent the last seven or eight years of his life in his beloved obscurity, and possessed (says Sprat) that solitude, which from his very childhood he so passionately desired. This great poet, and worthy man, died at a house called the Porch-house, towards the West end of the town of Chertsey in Surry, July 28, 1667, in the 49th year of his age. His solitude, from the very beginning, had never agreed so well with the constitution of his body, as his mind: out of haste, to abandon the tumult of the city, he had not prepared a healthful situation in the country, as he might have done, had he been more deliberate in his choice; of this, he soon began to find the inconvenience at Barn-elms, where he was afflicted with a dangerous and lingring fever. Shortly after his removal to Chertsey, he fell into another consuming disease: having languished under this for some months, he seemed to be pretty well cured of its ill symptoms, but in the heat of the summer, by staying too long amongst his labourers in the meadows, he was taken with a violent defluxion, and stoppage in his breast and throat; this he neglected, as an ordinary cold, and refused to send for his usual physicians, 'till it was past all remedy, and so in the end, after a fortnight's sickness, it proved mortal to him.

He was buried in Westminster Abbey, the 3d of August following, near the ashes of Chaucer and Spenser. King Charles II. was pleased to bestow upon him the best character, when, upon the news of his death, his Majesty declared, that Mr. Cowley had not left a better man behind him in England. A monument was erected to his memory in May 1675, by George, duke of Buckingham, with a Latin inscription, written by Dr. Sprat, afterwards lord bishop of Rochester.

Besides Mr. Cowley's works already mentioned, we have, by the fame hand, A Proposition for the advancement of Experimental Philosophy. A Discourse, by way of Vision, concerning the Government of Oliver Cromwel, and several Discourses, by way of Essays, in Prose and Verse. Mr. Cowley had designed a Discourse on Stile, and a Review of the Principles of the Primitive Christian Church, but was prevented by death. In Mr. Dryden's Miscellany Poems, we find a poem on the Civil War, said to be written by our author, but not extant in any edition of his works: Dr. Sprat mentions, as very excellent in their kind, Mr. Cowley's Letters to his private friends, none of which were published. As a poet, Mr. Cowley has had tribute paid him from the greatest names in all knowledge, Dryden, Addison, Sir John Denham, and Pope. He is blamed for a redundance of wit, and roughness of verification, but is allowed to have possessed a fine understanding, great reading, and a variety of genius. Let us see how Mr. Addison characterizes him in his Account of the great English Poets.

> Great Cowley then (a mighty genius) wrote,
> O'errun with wit, and lavish of his thought;
> His turns too closely on the readers press,
> He more had pleased us, had he pleased us less:
> One glittering thought no sooner strikes our eyes,
> With silent wonder, but new wonders rise.
> As in the milky way, a shining white
> O'erflows the heavens with one continued light;
> That not a single star can shew his rays,
> Whilst jointly all promote the common blaze.
> Pardon, great poet, that I dare to name,
> Th' uncumber'd beauties of thy verse with blame;
> Thy fault is only wit in its' excess,
> But wit like thine, in any shape will please.

In his public capacity, he preserved an inviolable honour and loyalty, and exerted great activity, with discernment: in private life, he was easy of access, gentle, polite, and modest; none but his intimate friends ever discovered, by his discourse, that he was a great poet; he was generous in his disposition, temperate in his life, devout and pious in his religion, a warm friend, and a social companion. Such is the character of the great Mr. Cowley, who deserves the highest gratitude from posterity, as well for his public as private conduct. He never prostituted his muse to the purposes of lewdness and folly, and it is with pleasure we can except him from the general, and too just, charge brought against the poets, That they have abilities to do the greatest service, and by misdirecting them, too frequently fawn the harlot face of loose indulgence, and by dressing up pleasure in an elegant attire, procure votaries to her altar, who pay too dear for gazing at the shewy phantom by loss of their virtue. It is no compliment to the taste of the present age, that the works of Mr. Cowley are falling into disesteem; they certainly contain more wit, and good sense, than the works of many other poets, whom it is now fashionable to read; that kind of poetry, which is known by the name of Light, he succeeds beyond any of his cotemporaries, or successors; no love verses, in our language, have so much true wit, and expressive tenderness, as Cowley's Mistress, which is indeed perfect in its kind. What Mr. Addison observes, is certainly true, 'He more had pleased us, had he pleased us less.' He had a soul too full, an imagination too fertile to be restrained, and because he has more wit than any other poet, an ordinary reader is somehow disposed to think he had less. In the particular of wit, none but Shakespear ever exceeded Cowley, and he was certainly as cultivated a scholar, as a great natural genius. In that kind of poetry which is grave, and demands extensive thinking, no poet has a right to be compared with Cowley: Pope and Dryden, who are as remarkable for a force of thinking, as elegance of poetry, are yet inferior to him; there are more ideas in one of Cowley's pindaric odes, than in any piece of equal length by those two great genius's (St. Cæcilia's ode excepted) and his pindaric odes being now neglected, can proceed from no other cause, than that they demand too much attention for a common reader, and contain sentiments so sublimely noble, as not to be comprehended by a vulgar mind; but to those who think, and are accustomed to contemplation, they appear great and ravishing. In order to illustrate this, we shall quote specimens in both kinds of poetry; the first taken from his Mistress called Beauty, the other is a Hymn to Light, both of which, are so excellent in their kind, that whoever reads them without rapture, may be well assured, that he has no poetry in his soul, and is insensible to the flow of numbers, and the charms of sense.

BEAUTY.

I.

Beauty, thou wild fantastic ape,
Who dost in ev'ry country change thy shape!
Here black, there brown, here tawny, and there white;

Thou flatt'rer which compli'st with every sight!
Thou Babel which confound'st the eye
With unintelligible variety!
Who hast no certain what nor where,
But vary'st still, and dost thy self declare
Inconstant, as thy she-professors are.

II.

Beauty, love's scene and masquerade,
So gay by well-plac'd lights, and distance made;
False coin, and which th' impostor cheats us still;
The stamp and colour good, but metal ill!
Which light, or base, we find when we
Weigh by enjoyment and examine thee!
For though thy being be but show,
'Tis chiefly night which men to thee allow:
And chuse t'enjoy thee, when thou least art thou.

III.

Beauty, thou active, passive ill!
Which dy'st thy self as fast as thou dost kill!
Thou Tulip, who thy stock in paint dost waste,
Neither for physic good, nor smell, nor taste.
Beauty, whose flames but meteors are,
Short-liv'd and low, though thou would'st seem a star,
Who dar'st not thine own home descry,
Pretending to dwell richly in the eye,
When thou, alas, dost in the fancy lye.

IV.

Beauty, whose conquests still are made
O'er hearts by cowards kept, or else betray'd;
Weak victor! who thy self destroy'd must be
When sickness, storms, or time besieges thee!
Thou unwholesome thaw to frozen age!
Thou strong wine, which youths fever dost enrage,
Thou tyrant which leav'st no man free!
Thou subtle thief, from whom nought safe can be!
Thou murth'rer which hast kill'd, and devil which would
damn me.

HYMN to LIGHT.

I.

First born of Chaos, who so far didst come,
From the old negro's darksome womb!
Which when it saw the lovely child,
The melancholly mass put on kind looks and smiled.

II.

Thou tide of glory, which no rest dost know,
But ever ebb, and ever flow!
Thou golden shower of a true Jove!
Who does in thee descend, and Heaven to earth make love!

III.

Hail active nature's watchful life, and health!
Her joy, her ornament and wealth!
Hail to thy husband heat, and thee!
Thou the world's beauteous bride, the lusty bridegroom he!

IV.

Say from what golden quivers of the sky,
Do all thy winged arrows fly?
Swiftness and power by birth are thine,
From thy great fire they came, thy fire the word divine.

V.

'Tis I believe this archery to shew
That so much cost in colours thou,
And skill in painting dost bestow,
Upon thy ancient arms, the gaudy heav'nly bow.

VI.

Swift as light, thoughts their empty career run,
Thy race is finish'd, when begun;
Let a Post-Angel start with thee,
And thou the goal of earth shall reach as soon as he.

VII.

Thou in the moon's bright chariot proud and gay,
Dost thy bright wood of stars survey;
And all the year doth with thee bring
O thousand flowry lights, thine own nocturnal spring.

VIII.

Thou Scythian-like dost round thy lands above
The sun's gilt tent for ever move,
And still as thou in pomp dost go,
The shining pageants of the world attend thy show.

IX.

Nor amidst all these triumphs dost thou scorn
The humble Glow-Worms to adorn,
And with those living spangles gild,
(O greatness without pride!) the blushes of the Field.

X.

Night, and her ugly subjects thou dost fright,
And sleep, the lazy Owl of night;
Asham'd and fearful to appear,
They skreen their horrid shapes, with the black
hemisphere.

XI.

With 'em there hastes, and wildly takes th' alarm,
Of painted dreams, a busy swarm,
At the first opening of thine eye,
The various clusters break, the antick atoms fly.

XII.

The guilty serpents, and obscener beasts,
Creep conscious to their secret rests:
Nature to thee doth reverence pay,
Ill omens, and ill sights removes out of thy way.

XIII.

At thy appearance, grief itself is said,
To shake his wings, and rouze his head;
And cloudy care has often took
A gentle beamy smile, reflected from thy look.

XIV.

At thy appearance, fear itself grows bold;
Thy sun-shine melts away his cold:
Encourag'd at the sight of thee,
To the cheek colour comes, and firmness to the knee.

XV.

Even lust, the master of a harden'd face,
Blushes if thou be'st in the place,
To darkness' curtains he retires,
In sympathizing nights he rolls his smoaky fires.

XVI.

When, goddess, thou lift'st up thy waken'd head,
Out of the morning's purple bed,
Thy choir of birds about thee play,
And all the joyful world salutes the rising day.

XVII.

The ghosts, and monster spirits, that did presume
A body's priv'lege to assume,
Vanish again invisibly,
And bodies gain again their visibility.

XVIII.

All the world's bravery that delights our eyes,
Is but thy sev'ral liveries,
Thou the rich dye on them bestow'st,
Thy nimble pencil paints this landskip as thou go'st.

XIX.

A crimson garment in the rose thou wear'st;
A crown of studded gold thou bear'st,
The virgin lillies in their white,
Are clad but with the lawn of almost naked light.

XX.

The Violet, spring's little infant, stands,
Girt in thy purple swadling-bands:
On the fair Tulip thou dost dote;
Thou cloath'st it in a gay and party-colour'd coat.

XXI.

With flame condens'd thou dost the jewels fix,
And solid colours in it mix:
Flora herself, envies to see
Flowers fairer than her own, and durable as she.

XXII.

Ah, goddess! would thou could'st thy hand with-hold,
And be less liberal to gold;
Didst thou less value to it give,
Of how much care (alas) might'st thou poor man relieve!

XXIII.

To me the sun is more delightful far,
And all fair days much fairer are;
But few, ah wondrous few there be,
Who do not Gold prefer, O goddess, ev'n to thee.

XXIV.

Thro' the soft ways of Heav'n, and air, and sea,
Which open all their pores to thee,
Like a clear river thou dost glide,
And with thy living stream through the close channels
slide.

XXV.

But where firm bodies thy free course oppose,
Gently thy source the land overflows;
Takes there possession, and does make,
Of colours mingled light, a thick and standing lake.

XXVI.

But the vast ocean of unbounded day
In th'Empyræan heav'n does stay;
Thy rivers, lakes, and springs below,
From thence took first their rise, thither at last must flow.

Footnotes:

1. Wood's Fasti Oxon, vol. ii. col. 120.

2. Essay on himself.

3. Sprat's Account of Cowley.

Sir William Davenant

Few poets have been subjected to more various turns of fortune, than the gentleman whose memoirs we are now about to relate. He was amongst the first who refined our poetry, and did more for the interest of the drama, than any who ever wrote for the stage. He lived in times of general confusion, and was no unactive member of the state, when its necessities demanded his assistance; and when, with the restoration, politeness and genius began to revive, he applied himself to the promotion of these rational pleasures, which are fit to entertain a cultivated people. This great man was son of one Mr. John Davenant, a citizen of Oxford, and was born in the month of February, 1605; all the biographers of our poet have observed, that his father was a man of a grave disposition, and a gloomy turn of mind, which his son did not inherit from him, for he was as remarkably volatile, as his father was saturnine. The same biographers have celebrated our author's mother as very handsome, whose charms had the power of attracting the admiration of Shakespear, the highest compliment which ever was paid to beauty. As Mr. Davenant, our poet's father, kept a tavern, Shakespear, in his journies to Warwickshire, spent some time there, influenced, as many believe, by the engaging qualities of the handsome landlady. This circumstance has given rise to a conjecture, that Davenant was really the son of Shakespear, as well naturally as poetically, by an unlawful intrigue, between his mother and that great man; that this allegation is founded upon probability, no reader can believe, for we have such accounts of the amiable temper, and moral qualities of Shakespear, that we cannot suppose him to have been guilty of such an act of treachery, as violating the marriage honours; and however he might have been delighted with the conversation, or charmed with the person of Mrs. Davenant, yet as adultery was not then the fashionable vice, it would be injurious to his memory, so much as to suppose him guilty.

Our author received the first rudiments of polite learning from Mr. Edward Sylvester, who kept a grammar school in the parish of All Saints in Oxford. In the year 1624, the same in which his father was Mayor of the city, he was entered a member of the university of Oxford, in Lincoln's-Inn College, under the tuition of Mr. Daniel Hough, but the Oxford antiquary is of opinion, he did not long remain there, as his mind was too much addicted to gaiety, to bear the austerities of an academical life, and being encouraged by some gentlemen, who admired the vivacity of his genius, he repaired to court, in hopes of making his fortune in that pleasing, but dangerous element. He became first page to Frances, duchess of Richmond, a lady much celebrated in those days, as well for her beauty, as the influence she had at court, and her extraordinary taste for grandeur, which excited her to keep a kind of private court of her own, which, in our more fashionable æra, is known by the name of Drums, Routs, and Hurricanes. Sir William afterwards removed into the family of Sir Fulk Greville, lord Brooke, who being himself a man of taste and erudition, gave the most encouraging marks of esteem to our rising bard. This worthy nobleman being brought to an immature fate, by the cruel hands of an assassin, 1628, Davenant was left without a patron, though not in very indigent circumstances, his reputation having increased, during the time he was in his lordship's service: the year ensuing the death of his patron, he produced his first play to the world, called Albovino, King of the Lombards, which met with a very general, and warm reception, and to which some very honourable recommendations were prefixed, when it was printed, in several copies of verses, by men of eminence, amongst whom, were, Sir Henry Blount, Edward Hyde, afterwards earl of Clarendon, and the honourable Henry Howard. Our author spent the next eight years of his life in a constant attendance upon court, where he was highly caressed by the most shining characters of the times, particularly by the earl of Dorset, Edward Hyde, and Lord Treasurer Weston: during these gay moments, spent in the court amusements, an unlucky accident happened to our author, which not a little deformed his face, which, from nature, was very handsome. Wood has affirmed, that this accident arose from libidinous dalliance with a handsome black girl in Axe-yard, Westminster. The plain fact is this, Davenant was of an amorous complexion, and was so unlucky as to carry the marks of his regular gallantries in the depression of his nose; this exposed him to the pleasant raillery of cotemporary wits, which very little affected him, and to shew that he was undisturbed by their merriment, he wrote a burlesque copy of verses upon himself. This accident happened pretty early in his life, since it gave occasion to the following stanzas in Sir John Suckling's Sessions of the Poets, which we have transcribed from a correct copy of Suckling's works.

> Will Davenant ashamed of a foolish mischance,
> That he had got lately travelling in France,
> Modestly hop'd the handsomness of his muse,
> Might any deformity about him excuse.

> Surely the company had been content,
> If they cou'd have found any precedent,
> But in all their records in verse, or prose,
> There was none of a laureat, who wanted a nose.

Suckling here differs from the Oxford historian, in saying that Sir William's disorder was contracted in France, but as Wood is the highest authority, it is more reasonable to embrace his observation, and probably, Suckling only mentioned France, in order that it might rhime with mischance.

Some time after this, Davenant was rallied by another hand, on account of this accident, as if it had been a jest that could never die; but what is more extraordinary, is, that Sir William himself could not forget the authoress of this misfortune, but has introduced her in his Gondibert, and, in the opinion of some critics, very improperly. He brings two friends, Ulfinore the elder, and Goltho the younger, on a journey to the court of Gondibert, but in this passage to shew, as he would insinuate the extream frailty of youth, they were arrested by a very unexpected accident, notwithstanding the wife councils, which Ulfinore had just received from his father[1]. The lines which have an immediate reference to this fair enchantress, are too curious to be here omitted.

I.

The black-ey'd beauty did her pride display,
Thro' a large window, and in jewels shone,
As if to please the world, weeping for day,
Night had put all her starry jewels on.

II.

This, beauty gaz'd on both, and Ulfinore
Hung down his head, but yet did lift his eyes
As if he fain would see a little more,
For much, tho' bashful, he did beauty prize.

III.

Goltho did like a blushless statue stare,
Boldly her practis'd boldness did outlook;
And even for fear she would mistrust her snare,
Was ready to cry out, that he was took.

IV.

She, with a wicked woman's prosp'rous art,
A seeming modesty, the window clos'd;
Wisely delay'd his eyes, since of his heart
She thought she had sufficiently dispos'd.

V.

Nicely as bridegroom's was her chamber drest,
Her bed as brides, and richer than a throne;
And sweeter seem'd than the Circania's nest.
Though built in Eastern groves of Cinnamon.

VI.

The price of princes pleasure, who her love,
(Tho'! but false were) at rates so costly bought,
The wealth of many, but many hourly prove
Spoils to some one, by whom herself is caught.

VII.

She sway'd by sinful beauty's destiny,
Finds her tyrannic power must now expire,
Who meant to kindle Goltho in her eye,
But to her breast has brought the raging fire.

VIII.

Yet even in simple love she uses art,
Tho' weepings are from looser eyes, but leaks;
Yet eldest lovers scarce would doubt her heart,
So well she weeps, as she to Goltho speaks.

During our author's attendance at court, he wrote several plays, and employed his time in framing masques, which were acted by the principal nobility of both sexes; the Queen herself condescended to take a share in one of them, which gave very great offence to the scrupulous moralists, which sprung up in those days; the particular account of this dramatic piece we shall give in the conclusion of his life, and now proceed in enumerating the incidents of it.

Upon the death of Ben Johnson, which happened in the year 1637, our poet succeeded to his laurel, notwithstanding the violent opposition of his competitor Thomas May, who was so extremely affected with his disappointment, though he had been a zealous courtier, yet from resentment to the Queen, by whose interest Davenant was preferred, he commenced an enemy to the King's party, and became both an advocate and historian for the Parliament.

As soon as the civil war broke out, Mr. Davenant had an early share in them and demonstrated his loyalty by speaking and acting for the King. He was accused by the Parliament for being embarked in a design in May 1641, of seducing the army from their adherence to the parliamentary authority, and bringing it again under the subjection of the King, and defence of his person. In this scheme many of Sir William's friends were engaged, viz. Mr. Henry Piercy, afterwards lord Piercy, Mr. Goring, Mr. Jermyn, Mr. Ashburnham, Sir John Suckling, and others: most of these persons, upon their design being discovered, placed their security in flight, and Mr. Davenant amongst the rest; but a proclamation being published for apprehending him, he was stopped at Feversham, sent up to town, and put into the custody of a sergeant at arms[2]. In the month of July following, our author was bailed, and not long after finding it necessary, on account of the violence of the times, to withdraw to France, he had the misfortune to be seized again in Kent by the Mayor of Canterbury; how he escaped the present danger, none of his biographers have related, but it appears that he did not, upon this occasion, suffer long confinement; he at last retired beyond sea, where he continued for some time, but the Queen sending over a considerable quantity of military stores, for the use of the earl of Newcastle's army, Mr. Davenant returned again to England, offered his service to that noble peer, who was his old friend and patron, and by him made lieutenant-general of his ordnance: this promotion gave offence to many, who were his rivals in his lordship's esteem: they remonstrated, that Sir William Davenant, being a poet, was, for that very reason, unqualified for a place of so much trust, and which demanded one of a solid, and less volatile turn of mind, than the sons of Parnassus generally are. In this complaint they paid but an indifferent compliment to the General himself, who was a poet, and had written, and published several plays. That Davenant behaved well in his military capacity is very probable, since, in the month of September, 1643, he received the honour of knighthood from the King, at the siege of Gloucester, an acknowledgment of his bravery, and signal services, which bestowed at a time when a strict scrutiny was made concerning the merit of officers, puts it beyond doubt, that Davenant, in his martial character, was as deserving as in his poetical. During these severe contentions, and notwithstanding his public character, our author's muse sometimes raised her voice, in the composition of several plays, of which we shall give some account when we enumerate his dramatic performances. History is silent as to the means which induced Davenant to quit the Northern army, but as soon as the King's affairs so far declined, as to afford no hopes of a revival, he judged it necessary to retire into France, where he was extremely well received by the Queen, into whose confidence he had the honour to be taken, and was intrusted with the negotiation of matters of the highest importance, in the summer of the year 1646. Before this time Sir William had embraced the popish religion, which circumstance might so far ingratiate him with the queen, as to trust him with the most important concerns. Lord Clarendon, who had a particular esteem for him, has given a full account of this affair, though not much to his advantage, but yet with all the tenderness due to Sir William's good intentions, and of that long and intimate acquaintance that had subsisted between them; which is the more worthy the reader's notice, as it has entirely escaped the observation of all those, who have undertaken to write this gentleman's Memoirs, though the most remarkable passage in his whole life.

The King, in retiring to the Scots, had followed the advice of the French ambassador, who had promised on their behalf, if not more than he had authority to do, at least, more than they were inclined to perform; to justify, however, his conduct at home, he was inclined to throw the weight, in some measure, upon the King, and with this view, he, by an express, informed cardinal Mazarine, that his Majesty was too reserved in giving the Parliament satisfaction, and therefore desired that some person might be sent over, who had a sufficient degree of credit with the English Monarch, to persuade him to such compliances, as were necessary for his interest. 'The Queen, says the noble historian, who was never advised by those, who either understood, or valued her Husband's interest, consulted those about her, and sent Sir William Davenant, an honest man, and a witty, but in all respects unequal to such a trust, with a letter of credit to the King, who knew the person well enough under another character than was likely to give him much credit upon the argument, with which he was entrusted, although the Queen had likewise otherwise declared her opinion to his Majesty, that he should part with the church for his peace and security.' Sir William had, by the countenance of the French ambassador, easy admission to the King, who heard patiently all he had to say, and answered him in a manner, which demonstrated that he was not pleased with the advice. When he found his Majesty unsatisfied, and not disposed to consent to what was earnestly desired by those by whom he had been sent, who undervalued all those scruples of conscience, with which his Majesty was so strongly possessed, he took upon himself the liberty of offering some reasons to the king, to induce him to yield to what was proposed, and among other things said, it was the opinion and advice of all his friends; his Majesty asked, what friends? to which Davenant replied, lord Jermyn, and lord Colepepper; the King upon this observed, that lord Jermyn did not understand any thing of the church, and that Colepepper was of no religion; but, says his Majesty, what is the opinion of the Chancellor of the Exchequer? to which Davenant answered, he did not know, that he was not there, and had deserted the Prince, and thereupon mentioned the Queen's displeasure against the Chancellor; to which the King said, 'The Chancellor was an honest man, and would never desert him nor the Prince, nor the Church; and that he was sorry he was not with his son, but that his wife was mistaken.'

Davenant then offering some reasons of his own, in which he treated the church with indignity, his Majesty was so transported with anger, that he gave him a sharper rebuke than he usually gave to any other man, and forbad him again, ever to presume to come into his presence; upon which poor Davenant was deeply affected, and returned into France to give an account of his ill success to those who sent him.

Upon Davenant's return to Paris, he associated with a set of people, who endeavoured to alleviate the distresses of exile by some kind of amusement. The diversion, which Sir William chose was of the literary sort, and having long indulged an inclination of writing an heroic poem, and having there much leisure, and some encouragement, he was induced to undertake one of a new kind; the two first books of which he finished at the Louvre, where he lived with his old friend Lord Jermyn; and these with a preface, addressed to Mr. Hobbs, his answer, and some commendatory poems, were published in England; of which we shall give some further account in our animadversions upon Gondibert.

While he employed himself in the service of the muses, Henrietta Maria, the queen dowager of England whose particular favourite he was found out business for him of another nature. She had heard that vast improvements might be made in the loyal colony of Virginia, in case proper artificers were sent there; and there being many of these in France who were destitute of employment, she encouraged Sir William to collect these artificers together, who accordingly embarked with his little colony at one of the ports in Normandy; but in this expedition he was likewise unfortunate; for before the vessel was clear of the French coast, she was met by one of the Parliament ships of war, and carried into the Isle of Wight, where our disappointed projector was sent close prisoner to Cowes Castle, and there had leisure enough, and what is more extraordinary, wanted not inclination to resume his heroic poem, and having written about half the third book, in a very gloomy prison, he thought proper to stop short again, finding himself, as he imagined under the very shadow of death. Upon this occasion it is reported of Davenant, that he wrote a letter to Hobbes, in which he gives some account of the progress he made in the third book of Gondibert, and offers some criticisms upon the nature of that kind of poetry; but why, says he, should I trouble you or myself, with these thoughts, when I am pretty certain I shall be hanged next week. This gaiety of temper in Davenant, while he was in the most deplorable circumstances of distress, carries something in it very singular, and perhaps could proceed from no other cause but conscious innocence; for he appears to have been an inoffensive good natured man. He was conveyed from the Isle of Wight to the Tower of London, and for some time his life was in the utmost hazard; nor is it quite certain by what means he was preserved from falling a sacrifice to the prevailing fury. Some conjecture that two aldermen of York, to whom he had been kind when they were prisoners, interposed their influence for him; others more reasonably conjecture that Milton was his friend, and prevented the utmost effects of party rage from descending on the head of this son of the muses. But by whatever means his life was saved, we find him two years after a prisoner of the Tower, where he obtained some indulgence by the favour of the Lord Keeper Whitlocke; upon receiving which he wrote him a letter of thanks, which as it serves to illustrate how easily and politely he wrote in prose, we shall here insert. It is far removed either from meanness or bombast, and has as much elegance in it as any letters in our language.

MY LORD,

"I am in suspense whether I should present my thankfulness to your lordship for my liberty of the Tower, because when I consider how much of your time belongs to the public, I conceive that to make a request to you, and to thank you afterwards for the success of it, is to give you no more than a succession of trouble; unless you are resolved to be continually patient, and courteous to afflicted men, and agree in your judgment with the late wise Cardinal, who was wont to say, If he had not spent as much time in civilities, as in business, he had undone his master. But whilst I endeavour to excuse this present thankfulness, I should rather ask your pardon, for going about to make a present to you of myself; for it may argue me to be incorrigible, that, after so many afflictions, I have yet so much ambition, as to desire to be at liberty, that I may have more opportunity to obey your lordship's commands, and shew the world how much I am,

MY LORD,

Your lordship's most

Obliged, most humble,

And obedient servant,

WM. DAVENANT."

Our author was so far happy as to obtain by this letter the favour of Whitlocke, who was, perhaps, a man of more humanity and gentleness of disposition, than some other of the covenanters. He at last obtained his liberty entirely, and was delivered from every thing but the narrowness of his circumstances, and to redress these, encouraged by the interest of his friends, he likewise made a bold effort. He was conscious that a play-house was entirely inconsistent with the gloominess, and severity of these times; and yet he was certain that there were people of taste enough in town, to fill one, if such a scheme could be managed; which he conducted with great address, and at last brought to bear, as he had the countenance of lord Whitlocke, Sir John Maynard, and other persons of rank, who really were ashamed of the cant and hypocrisy which then prevailed. In consequence of this, our poet opened a kind of theatre at Rutland House, where several pieces were acted, and if they did not gain him reputation, they procured him what is more solid, and what he then more wanted, money. Some of the people in power, it seems, were lovers of music, and tho' they did not care to own it, they were wise enough to know that there was nothing scandalous or immoral in the diversions of the theatre. Sir William therefore, when he applied for a permission called what he intended to represent an opera; but when he brought it on the stage, it appeared quite another thing, which when printed had the following title:

First day's entertainment at Rutland House by declamation and music, after the manner of the ancients.

This being an introductory piece, it demanded all the author's wit to make it answer different intentions; for first it was to be so pleasing as to gain applause; and next it was to be be so remote from the very appearance of a play, as not to give any offence to that pretended sanctity that was then in fashion. It began with music, then followed a prologue, in which the author rallies the oddity of his own performance. The curtain being drawn up to the sound of slow and solemn music, there followed a grave declamation by one in a guilded rostrum, who personated Diogenes, and shewed the use and excellency of dramatic entertainments. The second part of the entertainment consisted of two lighter declamations; the first by a citizen of Paris, who wittily rallies the follies of London; the other by a citizen of London, who takes the same liberty with Paris and its inhabitants. To this was tacked a song, and after that came a short epilogue. The music was composed by Dr. Coleman, Capt. Cook, Mr. Henry Laws, and Mr. George Hudson.

There were several other pieces which Sir William introduced upon this stage of the same kind, which met with as much success, as could be expected from the nature of the performances themselves, and the temper and disposition of the audience. Being thus introduced, he at last grew a little bolder, and not only ventured to write, but to act several new plays, which were also somewhat in a new taste; that is, they were more regular in their structure, and the language generally speaking, smoother, and more correct than the old tragedies. These improvements were in a great measure owing to Sir William's long residence in France, which gave him an opportunity of reading their best writers, and hearing the sentiments of their ablest critics upon dramatic entertainments, where they were as much admired and encouraged, as at that time despised in England. That these were really improvements, and that the public stood greatly indebted to Sir William Davenant as a poet, and master of a theatre, we can produce no less an authority than that of Dryden, who, beyond any of his predecessors, contemporaries, or those who have succeeded him, understood poetry as an art. In his essay on heroic plays, he thus speaks, "The first light we had of them, on the English theatre (says he) was from Sir William Davenant. It being forbidden him in the religious times to act tragedies or comedies, because they contained some matter of scandal to those good people, who could more easily dispossess their lawful sovereign, than endure a wanton jest, he was forced to turn his thoughts another way, and to introduce the examples of moral virtue written in verse, and performed in recitative music. The original of this music, and of the scenes which adorned his works, he had from the Italian opera's; but he heightened his characters, as I may probably imagine, from the examples of Corneille, and some French poets. In this condition did this part of poetry remain at his Majelty's return, when grown bolder as now owned by public authority, Davenant revived the Siege of Rhodes, and caused it to be acted as a just drama. But as few men have the happiness to begin and finish any new project, so neither did he live to make his design perfect. There wanted the fulness of a plot, and the variety of characters to form it as it ought; and perhaps somewhat might have been added to the beauty of the stile: all which he would have performed with more exactness, had he pleased to have given us another work of the fame nature. For myself and others who came after him, we are bound with all veneration to his memory, to acknowledge what advantage we received from that excellent ground work, which is laid, and since it is an easy thing to add to what is already invented, we ought all of us, without envy to him, or partiality to ourselves, to yield him the precedence in it."

Immediately after the restoration there were two companies of players formed, one under the title of the King's Servants, the other, under that of the Duke's Company, both by patents, from the crown; the first granted to Henry Killigrew, Esq; and the latter to Sir William Davenant. The King's company acted first at the Red Bull in the upper end of St. John's Street, and after a year or two removing from place to place, they established themselves in Drury-Lane. It was some time before Sir William Davenant compleated his company, into which he took all who had formerly played under Mr. Rhodes in the Cock-Pit in Drury-Lane, and amongst these the famous Mr. Betterton, who appeared first to advantage under the patronage of Sir William Davenant. He opened the Duke's theatre in Lincoln's-Inn-Fields with his own dramatic performance of the Siege of Rhodes, the house being finely decorated, and the stage supplied with painted scenes, which were by him introduced at least, if not invented, which afforded certainly an additional beauty to the theatre, tho' some have insinuated, that fine scenes proved the ruin of acting; but as we are persuaded it will be an entertaining circumstance to our Readers, to have that matter more fully explained, we shall take this opportunity of doing it.

In the reign of Charles I, dramatic entertainments were accompanied with rich scenery, curious machines, and other elegant embellishments, chiefly condufted by the wonderful dexterity of that celebrated English, architect Inigo Jones. But these were employed only in masques at court, and were too expensive for the little theatres in which plays were then acted. In them there was nothing more than a ouftain of very coarse stuff, upon the drawing up of which, the stage appeared either with bare walls on the sides, coarsly matted, or covered with tapestry; so that for the place originally represented, and all the successive changes in which the poets of those times freely indulged themselves, there was nothing to help the spectator's understanding, or to assist the actor's performance, but bare imagination. In Shakespear's time so undecorated were the theatres, that a blanket supplied the place of a curtain; and it was a good observation of the ingenious Mr. Chitty, a gentleman of acknowledged taste in dramatic excellence, that the circumstance of the blanket, suggested to Shakespear that noble image in Macbeth, where the murderer invokes

> Thick night to veil itself in the dunnest smoke of Hell,
> Nor Heaven peep thro' the blanket of the dark
> To cry hold, hold.

It is true, that while things continued in this situation, there were a great many play-houses, sometimes six or seven open at once. Of these some were large, and in part open, where they acted by day light; others smaller, but better fitted up, where they made use of candles. The plainness of the theatre made the prices small, and drew abundance of company; yet upon the whole it is doubtful, whether the spectactors in all these houses were really superior in number, to those who have frequented the theatres in later times. If the spirit and judgment of the actors supplied all deficiencies, and made as some would insinuate, plays more intelligible without scenes, than they afterwards were with them, it must be very astonishing; neither is it difficult to assign another cause, why those who were concerned in play-houses, were angry at the introduction of scenes and decorations, which was, that notwithstanding the advanced prices, their profits from that time were continually sinking; and an author, of high authority in this case, assures us, in an historical account of the stage, that the whole sharers in Mr. Hart's company divided a thousand pounds a year a-piece, before the expensive decorations became fashionable. Sir William Davehant considered things in another light: he was well acquainted with the alterations which the French theatre had received, under the auspice of cardinal Richelieu, who had an excellent taste; and he remembered the noble contrivances of Inigo Jones, which were not at all inferior to the designs of the best French masters. Sir William was likewise sensible that the monarch he served was an excellent judge of every thing of this kind; and these considerations excited in him a passion for the advancement of the theatre, to which the great figure it has since made is chiefly owing. Mr. Dryden has acknowledged his admirable talents in this way, and gratefully remembers the pains taken by our poet, to set a work of his in the fairest light possible, and to which, he ingenuously ascribes the success with which it was received. This is the hislory of the life and progress of scenery on our stage; which, without doubt, gives greater life to the entertainment of a play; but as the best purposes may be prostituted, so there is some reason to believe that the excessive fondness for decorations, which now prevails, has hurt the true dramatic taste. Scenes are to be considered as secondary in a play, the means of setting it off with lustre, and ought to engross but little attention; as it is more important to hear what a character speaks, than to observe the place where he stands; but now the case is altered. The scenes in a Harlequin Sorcerer, and other unmeaning pantomimes, unknown to our more elegant and judging forefathers, procure crowded houses, while the noblest strokes of Dryden, the delicate touches of Otway and Rowe, the wild majesty of Shakespear, and the heart-felt language of Lee, pass neglected, when put in competition with those gewgaws of the stage, these feasts of the eye; which as they can communicate no ideas, so they can neither warm nor reform the heart, nor answer one moral purpose in nature.

We ought not to omit a cirrumstance much in favour of Sir William Davenant, which proves him to have been as good a man as a poet. When at the Restoration, those who had been active in disturbing the late reign, and secluding their sovereign from the throne, became obnoxious to the royal party, Milton was likely to feel the vengeance of the court, Davenant actuated by a noble principle of gratitude, interposed all his influence, and saved the greatest ornament of the world from the stroke of an executioner. Ten years before that, Davenant had been rescued by Milton, and he remembered the favour; an instance, this, that generosity, gratitude, and nobleness of nature is confined to no particular party; but the heart of a good man will still discover itself in acts of munificence and kindness, however mistaken he may be in his opinion, however warm in state factions. The particulars of this extraordinary affair are related in the life of Milton.

Sir William Davenant continued at the head of his company of actors, and at last transferred them to a new and magnificent theatre built in Dorset-Gardens, where some of his old plays were revived with very singular circumstances of royal kindness, and a new one when brought upon the stage met with great applause.

The last labour of his pen was in altering a play of Shakespear's, called the Tempest, so as to render it agreeable to that age, or rather susceptible of those theatrical improvements he had brought into fashion. The great successor to his laurel, in a preface to this play, in which he was concerned with Davenant, 'says, that he was a man of quick and piercing imagination, and soon found that somewhat might be added to the design of Shakespear, of which neither Fletcher nor Suckling had ever thought; and therefore to put the last hand to it, he designed the counterpart to Shakespear's plot, namely, that of a man who had never seen a woman, that by this means, these two characters of innocence and love might the more illustrate and commend each other. This excellent contrivance he was pleased to communicate to me, and to defire my assistance in it. I confess that from the first moment it so pleased me, that I never wrote any thing with so much delight. I might likewise do him that justice to acknowledge that my writing received daily amendments, and that is the reason why it is not so faulty, as the rest that I have done, without the help or correction of so judicious a friend. The comical parts of the sailors were also of his invention and Writing, as may easily be discovered from the stile.'

This great man died at his house in little Lincoln's-Inn-Fields, April 17, 1668, aged 63, and two days afterwards was interred in Westminster-Abbey. On his gravestone is inscribed, in imitation of Ben Johnson's short epitaph,

O RARE SIR WILLIAM DAVENANT!

It may not be amiss to observe, that his remains rest very near the place out of which those of Mr. Thomas May, who had been formerly his rival for the bays, and the Parliament's historian, were removed, by order of the ministry. As to the family our author left behind him, some account of it will be given in the life of his son Dr. Charles Davenant, who succeeded him as manager of the theatre. Sir William's works entire were published by his widow 1673, and dedicated to James Duke of York.

After many storms of adversity, our author spent the evening of his days in ease and serenity. He had the happiness of being loved by people of all denominations, and died lamented by every worthy good man. As a poet, unnumbered evidences may be produced in his favour. Amongst these Mr. Dryden is the foremost, for when his testimony can be given in support of poetical merit, we reckon all other evidence superfluous, and without his, all other evidences deficient. In his words then we shall sum up Davenant's character as a poet, and a man of genius.

'I found him, (says he) in his preface to the Tempest, of so quick a fancy, that nothing was proposed to him on which he could not quickly produce a thought extreamly pleasant and surprizing, and these first thoughts of his, contrary to the old Latin proverb, were not always the least happy, and as his fancy was quick, so likewise were the products of it remote and new. He borrowed not of any other, and his imaginations were such as could not easily enter into any other man. His corrections were sober and judicious, and he corrected his own writings much more severely than those of another man, bestowing twice the labour and pain in polishing which he used in invention.'

Before we enumerate the dramatic works of Sir William Davenant, it will be but justice to his merit, to insert some animadversions on his Gondibert; a poem which has been the subject of controversy almost a hundred years; that is, from its first appearance to the present time. Perhaps the dispute had been long ago decided, if the author's leisure had permitted him to finish it. At present we see it to great disadvantage; and if notwithstanding this it has any beauties, we may fairly conclude it would have come much nearer perfection, if the story, begun with so much spirit, had been brought to an end upon the author's plan.

Mr. Hobbes, the famous philosopher of Malmsbury, in a letter printed in his works, affirms, 'that he never yet saw a poem that had so much shape of art, health of morality and vigour, and beauty of expression, as this of our author; and in an epistle to the honourable Edward Howard, author of the British Princes, he thus speaks. My judgment in poetry has been once already censured by very good wits for commending Gondibert; but yet have they not disabled my testimony. For what authority is there in wit? a jester may have it; a man in drink may have it, and be fluent over night, and wise and dry in the morning: What is it? and who can tell whether it be better to have it or no? I will take the liberty to praise what I like as well as they, and reprehend what they like.'—Mr. Rymer in his preface to his translation of Rapin's Reflexions on Aristotle's Treatise of Poetry, observes, that our author's wit is well known, and in the preface to that poem, there appears some strokes of an extraordinary judgment; that he is for unbeaten tracts, and new ways of thinking, but certainly in the untried seas he is no great discoverer. One design of the Epic poets before him was to adorn their own country, there finding their heroes and patterns of virtue, where example, as they thought, would have the greater influence and power over posterity; "but this poet, says Rymer, steers a different course; his heroes are all foreigners; he cultivates a country that is nothing a-kin to him, and Lombardy reaps the honour of all. Other poets chose some action or hero so illustrious, that the name of the poem prepared the reader, and made way for its reception; but in this poem none can divine what great action he intended to celebrate, nor is the reader obliged to know whether the hero be Turk or Christian; nor do the first lines give any light or prospect into the design. Altho' a poet should know all arts and sciences, yet ought he discreetly to manage his knowledge. He must have a judgment to select what is noble and beautiful, and proper for the occasion. He must by a particular chemistry, extract the essence of things; without soiling his wit with dross or trumpery. The sort of verse Davenant makes choice of in his Gondibert might contribute much to the vitiating his stile; for thereby he obliges himself to stretch every period to the end of four lines: Thus the sense is broken perpetually with parentheses, the words jumbled in confusion, and darkness spread over all; but it must be acknowledged, that Davenant had a particular talent for the manners; his thoughts are great, and there appears something roughly noble thro' the whole." This is the substance of Rymer's observations on Gondibert. Rymer was certainly a scholar, and a man of discernment; and tho' in some parts of the criticisms he is undoubtedly right, yet in other parts he is demonstrably wrong. He complains that Davenant has laid the scene of action in Lombardy, which Rymer calls neglecting his own country; but the critic should have considered, that however well it might have pleased the poet's countrymen, yet as an epic poem is supposed to be read in every nation enlightened by science, there can no objections arise from that quarter by any but those who were of the same country with the author. His not making choice of a pompous name, and introducing his poem with an exordium, is rather a beauty than a fault; for by these means he leaves room for surprize, which is the first excellency in any poem, and to strike out beauties where they are not expected, has a happy influence upon the reader. Who would think from Milton's introduction, that so stupendous a work would ensue, and simple dignity is certainly more noble, than all the efforts and colourings which art and labour can bestow.

The ingenious and learned Mr. Blackwall, Professor of Greek in the university of Aberdeen, in his enquiry into the life and writings of Homer, censures the structure of the poem; but, at the same time pays a compliment to the abilities of the author. "It was indeed (says he) a very extraordinary project of our ingenious countryman, to write an epic poem without mixing allegory, or allowing the smallest fiction throughout the composure. It was like lopping off a man's limb, and then putting him upon running races; tho' it must be owned that the performance shews, with what ability he could have acquitted himself, had he been sound and entire."

Such the animadversions which critics of great name have made on Gondibert, and the result is, that if Davenant had not power to begin and consummate an epic poem, yet by what he has done, he has a right to rank in the first class of poets, especially when it is considered that we owe to him the great perfection of the theatre, and putting it upon a level with that of France and Italy; and as the theatrical are the most rational of all amusements, the latest posterity should hold his name in veneration, who did so much for the advancement of innocent pleasures, and blending instruction and gaiety together.

The dramatic works of our author are,

1.   Albovine King of the Lombards, a tragedy. This play is commended by eight copies of verses. The story of it is related at large, in a novel, by Bandello, and is translated by Belleforest[3].

2.   Cruel Brother, a tragedy.

3.   Distresses, a tragi-comedy, printed in folio, Lond. 1673.

4.   First Day's Entertainment at Rutland-House, by declamation and music, after the manner of the ancients. Of this we have already given some account.

5.   The Fair Favourite, a tragi-comedy, printed in folio, 1673.

6.   The Just Italian, a tragi-comedy.

7.   Law against Lovers, a tragi-comedy, made up of two plays by Shakespear, viz. Measure for Measure, and Much Ado about Nothing.

8.   Love and Honour, a tragi-comedy; which succeeded beyond any other of our author's plays, both on the theatre at Lincoln's-Inn, and Dorset-Garden.

9.   Man's the Master, a tragi-comedy, acted upon the Duke of York's theatre.

10. Platonic Lovers, a tragi-comedy.

11. Play House to be Let. It is difficult to say, under what species this play should be placed, as it consists of pieces of different kinds blended together, several of which the author wrote in Oliver's time, that were acted separately by stealth.—The History of Sir Francis Drake, expressed by instrumental and vocal music, and by art of perspective scenes, and the cruelty of the Spaniards in Peru, were first printed in 4to. and make the third and fourth acts of this play. The second act consists of a French farce, translated from Molliere's Ganarelle, ou le Cocu Imaginaire, and purposely by our author put into a sort of jargon, common to Frenchmen newly come over. The fifth act consists of tragedy travestie; or the actions of Cæsar, Anthony and Cleopatra in burlesque verse.

12. Siege of Rhodes in two parts. These plays, during the civil war, were acted in Stilo Recitativo, but afterwards enlarged, and acted with applause at the Duke's theatre. Solyman the second took this famous city in the year 1522, which is circumstantially related by Knolles in his History of the Turks, from whence our author took the story.

13. Siege, a tragi-comedy.

14. News from Plymouth, a comedy.

15. Temple of Love, presented by Queen Henrietta, wife to King Charles I and her ladies at Whitehall, viz. The Marchioness of Hamilton; Lady Mary Herbert; Countess of Oxford; Berkshire; Carnarvon: The noble Persian Youths were represented by the Duke of Lenox, and the Earls of Newport and Desmond.

16. Triumphs of the Prince d'Amour, presented by his Highness the Prince Elector, brother-in-law to Charles I. at his palace in the Middle Temple. This masque, at the request of this honourable society, was devised and written by the author in three days, and was presented by the members thereof as an entertainment to his Highness. A list of the Masquers names, as they were ranked according to their antiquity, is subjoined to the Masque.

17. Wits, a comedy; first acted at Black-Fryars, and afterwards at the Duke of York's theatre. This piece appeared on the stage with remarkable applause.

These pieces have in general been received with applause on the stage, and have been read with pleasure by people of the best taste: The greatest part of them were published in the author's life-time in 4to. and all since his death, collected into one volume with his other works, printed in folio, Lond. 1673; and dedicated by his widow to the late King James, as has been before observed.

Footnotes:

1. Gond. b. iii. cant. 3. stanz. 31.

2. Athen. Oxon. vol. ii, col. 412.

3. Histories Tragiques, Tom. IV. No. XIX.

Henry King, Bishop of Chichester

The eldest son of Dr. John King lord bishop of London, whom Winstanley calls a person well fraught with episcopal qualities, was born at Wornal in Bucks, in the month of January 1591. He was educated partly in grammar learning in the free school at Thame in Oxfordshire, and partly in the College school at Westminster, from which last he was elected a student in Christ Church 1608[1], being then under the tuition of a noted tutor. Afterwards he took the degrees in arts, and entered into holy orders, and soon became a florid preacher, and successively chaplain to King James I. archdeacon of Colchester, residentiary of St. Paul's cathedral, canon and dean of Rochester, in which dignity he was installed the 6th of February 1638. In 1641, says Mr. Wood, he was made bishop of Chichester, being one of those persons of unblemished reputation, that his Majesty, tho' late, promoted to that honourable office; which he possessed without any removal, save that by the members of the Long Parliament, to the time of his death.

When he was young he delighted much in the study of music and poetry, which with his wit and fancy made his conversation very agreeable, and when he was more advanced in years he applied himself to oratory, philosophy, and divinity, in which he became eminent.

It happened that this bishop attending divine service in a church at Langley in Bucks, and hearing there a psalm sung, whose wretched expression, far from conveying the meaning of the Royal Psalmist, not only marred devotion, but turned what was excellent in the original into downright burlesque; he tried that evening if he could not easily, and with plainness suitable to the lowest understanding, deliver it from that garb which rendered it ridiculous. He finished one psalm, and then another, and found the work so agreeable and pleasing, that all the psalms were in a short time compleated; and having shewn the version to some friends of whose judgment he had a high opinion, he could not resist their importunity (says Wood) of putting it to the press, or rather he was glad their sollicitations coincided with his desire to be thought a poet.

He was the more discouraged, says the antiquary, as Mr. George Sandys's version and another by a reformer had failed in two different extremes; the first too elegant for the vulgar use, changing both metre and tunes, wherewith they had been long acquainted; the other as flat and poor, and as lamely executed as the old one. He therefore ventured in a middle way, as he himself in one of his letters expresses it, without affectation of words, and endeavouring to leave them not disfigured in the sense. This version soon after was published with this title;

The Psalms of David from the New Translation of the Bible, turned into Metre, to be sung after the old tunes used in churches, Lond. 1651, in 12mo.

There is nothing more ridiculous than this notion of the vulgar of not parting with their old versions of the psalms, as if there were a merit in singing hymns of nonsense. Tate and Brady's version is by far the most elegant, and best calculated to inspire devotion, because the language and poetry are sometimes elevated and sublime; and yet for one church which uses this version, twenty are content with that of Sternhold and Hopkins, the language and poetry of which, as Pope says of Ogilvy's Virgil, are beneath criticism. —

After episcopacy was silenced by the Long Parliament, he resided in the house of Sir Richard Hobbart (who had married his sister) at Langley in Bucks. He was reinstated in his See by King Charles II. and was much esteemed by the virtuous part of his neighbours, and had the blessings of the poor and distressed, a character which reflects the highest honour upon him.

Whether from a desire of extending his beneficence, or instigated by the restless ambition peculiar to the priesthood, he sollicited, but in vain, a higher preferment, and suffered his resentment to betray him into measures not consistent with his episcopal character. He died on the first day of October 1669[2], and was buried on the south side of the choir, near the communion table, belonging to the cathedral church in Chichester. Soon after there was a monument put over his grave, with an inscription, in which it is said he was,

> Antiquâ, eáque regia Saxonium apud Danmonios in agro Devoniensi, prosapia oriundus,

That he was,

> Natalium Splendore illustris, pietate, Doctrina, et virtutibus illustrior, &c.

This monument was erected at the charge of his widow, Anne daughter of Sir William Russel of Strensham in Worcestershire, knight and baronet.

Our author's works, besides the version of the Psalms already mentioned, are as follows;

A Deep Groan fetched at the Funeral of the incomparable and glorious Monarch King Charles I. printed 1649.

Poems, Elegies, Paradoxes, Sonnets, &c. Lond. 1657.

Several Letters, among which are extant, one or more to the famous archbishop Usher, Primate of Ireland, and another to Isaac Walton, concerning the three imperfect books of Richard Hooker's Ecclesiastical Polity, dated the 13th of November 1664, printed at London 1665.

He has composed several Anthems, one of which is for the time of Lent. Several Latin and Greek Poems, scattered in several Books.

He has likewise published several Sermons,

1.   Sermon preached at Paul's Cross 25th of November 1621, upon occasion of a report, touching the supposed apostasy of Dr. John King—late bishop of London, on John xv. 20, Lond. 1621; to which is also added the examination of Thomas Preston, taken before the Archbishop of Canterbury at Lambeth 20th of December 1621, concerning his being the author of the said Report.

2.   David's Enlargement, Morning Sermon on Psalm xxxii. 5. Oxon. 1625. 4to.

3.   Sermon of Deliverance, at the Spittal on Easter Monday, Psalm xc. 3. printed 1626, 4to.

4.   Two Sermons at Whitehall on Lent, Eccles. xii. 1, and Psalm lv. 6. printed 1627, in 4to.

5.   Sermon at St. Paul's on his Majesty's Inauguration and Birth, on Ezekiel xxi. 27. Lond. 1661. 4to.

6.   Sermon on the Funeral of Bryan Bishop of Winchester, at the Abbey Church of Westminster, April 24, 1662, on Psalm cxvi. 15. Lond. 1662. 4to.

7.   Visitation Sermon at Lewis, October 1662. on Titus ii. 1. Lond. 1663. 4to.

8.   Sermon preached the 30th of January, 1664, at Whitehall, being the Day of the late King's Martyrdom, on 2. Chron. xxxv. 24, 25. Lond. 1665, 4to.

To these Sermons he has added an Exposition of the Lord's Prayer, delivered in certain Sermons, on Matth. vi. 9. &c. Lond. 1628. 4to.

We shall take a quotation from his version of the 104th psalm.

My soul the Lord for ever bless:
O God! thy greatness all confess;
Whom majesty and honour vest,
In robes of light eternal drest.

He heaven made his canopy;
His chambers in the waters lye:
His chariot is the cloudy storm,
And on the wings of wind is born.

He spirits makes his angels quire,
His ministers a flaming fire.
He so did earth's foundations cast,
It might remain for ever fast:

Then cloath'd it with the spacious deep,
Whose wave out-swells the mountains steep.
At thy rebuke the waters fled,
And hid their thunder-frighted head.

They from the mountains streaming flow,
And down into the vallies go:
Then to their liquid center hast,
Where their collected floods are cast.

These in the ocean met, and joyn'd,
Thou hast within a bank confin'd:
Not suff'ring them to pass their bound,
Lest earth by their excess be drown'd.

He from the hills his chrystal springs
Down running to the vallies brings:
Which drink supply, and coolness yield,
To thirsting beasts throughout the field.

By them the fowls of heaven rest,
And singing in their branches nest.
He waters from his clouds the hills;
The teeming earth with plenty fills.

He grass for cattle doth produce,
And every herb for human use:
That so he may his creatures feed,
And from the earth supply their need.

He makes the clusters of the vine,
To glad the sons of men with wine.
He oil to clear the face imparts,
And bread, the strength'ner of their hearts.

The trees, which God for fruit decreed,
Nor sap, nor moistning virtue need.
The lofty cedars by his hand
In Lebanon implanted stand.

Unto the birds these shelter yield,
And storks upon the fir-trees build:
Wild goats the hills defend, and feed,
And in the rocks the conies breed.

He makes the changing moon appear,
To note the seasons of the year:
The sun from him his strength doth get,
And knows the measure of his set.

Thou mak'st the darkness of the night,
When beasts creep forth that shun the light,
Young lions, roaring after prey,
From God their hunger must allay.

When the bright sun casts forth his ray,
Down in their dens themselves they lay.
Man's labour, with the morn begun,
Continues till the day be done.

O Lord! what wonders hast thou made,
In providence and wisdom laid!
The earth is with thy riches crown'd,
And seas, where creatures most abound.

There go the ships which swiftly fly;
There great Leviathan doth lye,
Who takes his pastime in the flood:
All these do wait on thee for food.

Thy bounty is on them distill'd,
Who are by thee with goodness fill'd.
But when thou hid'st thy face, they die,
And to their dust returned lie.

Thy spirit all with life endues,
The springing face of earth renews,
God's glory ever shall endure,
Pleas'd in his works, from change secure.

Upon the earth he looketh down,
Which shrinks and trembles at his frown:
His lightnings touch, or thunders stroak,
Will make the proudest mountains smoak.

To him my ditties, whilst I live,
Or being have, shall praises give:
My meditations will be sweet,
When fixt on him my comforts meet.

Upon the earth let sinners rot,
In place, and memory forgot.
But thou, my soul, thy maker bless:
Let all the world his praise express;

Footnotes:

1. Athen. Oxon, vol. ii. p. 431. 1721 Ed.

2. Wood Athen. Oxon, p. 431, vol. 2.

Philip Massinger

A poet of no small eminence, was son of Mr. Philip Massinger, a gentleman belonging to the earl of Montgomery, in whose service he lived[1].

He was born at Salisbury, about the year 1585, and was entered a commoner in St. Alban's Hall in Oxford, 1601, where, though he was encouraged in his studies (says Mr. Wood) by the earl of Pembroke, yet he applied his mind more to poetry and romances, than to logic and philosophy. He afterwards quitted the university without a degree, and being impatient to move in a public sphere, he came to London, in order to improve his poetic fancy, and polite studies by conversation, and reading the world. He soon applied himself to the stage, and wrote several tragedies and comedies with applause, which were admired for the purity of their stile, and the oeconomy of their plots: he was held in the highest esteem by the poets of that age, and there were few who did not reckon it an honour to write in conjunction with him, as Fletcher, Middleton, Rowley, Field and Decker did[2]. He is said to have been a man of great modesty. He died suddenly at his house on the bank side in Southwark, near to the then playhouse, for he went to bed well, and was dead before morning. His body was interred in St. Saviour's church-yard, and was attended to the grave by all the comedians then in town, on the 18th of March, 1669. Sir Aston Cokaine has an epitaph on Mr. John Fletcher, and Mr. Philip Massinger, who, as he says, both lie buried in one grave. He prepared several works for the public, and wrote a little book against Scaliger, which many have ascribed to Scioppius, the supposed author of which Scaliger, uses with great contempt. Our author has published 14 plays of his own writing, besides those in which he joined with other poets, of which the following is the list,

1.   The Bashful Lover, a Tragi-Comedy, often acted at a private house in Black Fryars, by his Majesty's Servants, with success, printed in 8vo. 1655.

2.   The Bondman, an ancient Story, often acted at the Cockpit in Drury Lane, by the Lady Elizabeth's servants, printed in 4to. London, 1638, and dedicated to Philip, Earl of Montgomery.

3.   The City Madam, a Comedy, acted at a private house in Black-fryars, with applause, 4to. 1659, for Andrew Pennywick one of the actors, and dedicated by him to Anne, Countess of Oxford.

4. The Duke of Milan, a Tragedy printed in 4to. but Mr. Langbaine has not been able to find out when it was acted.

5. The Emperor of the East, a Tragi-Comedy, acted at the Black Fryars, and Globe Playhouse, by his Majesty's Servants, printed in 4to. London, 1632, and dedicated to John, Lord Mohune, Baron of Okehampton; this play is founded on the History of Theodosius the younger; see Socrates, lib. vii.

6. The Fatal Dowry, a Tragedy, often acted at private house in Black Fryars, by his Majesty's servants, printed in 4to. London, 1632; this play was written by our author, in conjunction with Nathaniel Field. The behaviour of Charlois in voluntarily chusing imprisonment to ransom his father's corpse, that it might receive the funeral rites, is copied from the Athenian Cymon, so much celebrated by Valerius Maximus, lib. v. c. 4. ex. 9. Plutarch and Cornelius Nepos, notwithstanding, make it a forced action, and not voluntary.

7. The Guardian, a comical History, often acted at a private house in Black Fryars, by the King's Servants, 1665. Severino's cutting off Calipso's nose in the dark, taking her for his wife Jolantre, is borrowed from the Cimerian Matron, a Romance, 8vo. the like story is related in Boccace. Day 8. Novel 7.

8. The Great Duke of Florence, a comical History, often presented with success, at the Phænix in Drury Lane, 1636; this play is taken from our English Chronicles, that have been written in the reign of Edgar.

9. The Maid of Honour, a Tragi-Comedy, often acted at the Phænix in Drury Lane, 1632.

10. A New Way to pay Old Debts, a Comedy, acted 1633; this play met with great success on its first representation, and has been revived by Mr. Garrick, and acted on the Theatre-Royal in Drury Lane, 1750.

11. Old Law, a New Way to please You, an excellent Comedy, acted before the King and Queen in Salisbury-house, printed in 4to. London, 1656. In this play our author was assisted by Mr. Middleton, and Mr. Rowley.

12. The Picture, a Tragi-Comedy, often presented at the Globe and Black Fryars Playhouse, by the King's servants, printed in London, 1636, and dedicated to his selected friends, the noble Society of the Inner-Temple; this play was performed by the most celebrated actors of that age, Lowin, Taylor, Benfield.

13. The Renegado, a Tragi-Comedy, often acted by the Queen's Servants, at the private Playhouse in Drury Lane, printed in 4to. London, 1630.

14. The Roman Actor, performed several times with success, at a private house in the Black-Fryars, by the King's Servants; for the plot read Suetonius in the Life of Domitian, Aurelius Victor, Eutropius, lib. vii. Tacitus, lib. xiii.

15. Very Woman, or the Prince of Tarent, a Tragi-Comedy, often acted at a private house in Black Fryars, printed 1655.

16. The Virgin Martyr, a Tragedy, acted by his Majesty's Servants, with great applause, London, printed in 4to. 1661. In this play our author took in Mr. Thomas Decker for a partner; the story may be met with in the Martyrologies, which have treated of the tenth persecution in the time of Dioclesian, and Maximian.

17. The Unnatural Combat, a Tragedy, presented by the King's Servants at the Globe, printed at London 1639. This old Tragedy, as the author tells his patron, has neither Prologue nor Epilogue, "it being composed at a time, when such by-ornaments were not advanced above the fabric of the whole work."

Footnotes:

1. Langbaine's Lives of the Poets.

2. Langbaine, ubi supra.

Sir Robert Stapleton

This gentleman was the third son of Richard Stapleton, esq; of Carleton, in Mereland in Yorkshire, and was educated a Roman Catholic, in the college of the English Benedictines, at Doway in Flanders, but being born with a poetical turn, and consequently too volatile to be confined within the walls of a cloister, he threw off the restraint of his education, quitted a recluse life, came over to England, and commenced Protestant[1]. Sir Robert having good interest, found the change of religion prepared the way to preferment; he was made gentleman usher of the privy chamber to King Charles II. then Prince of Wales; we find him afterwards adhering to the interest of his Royal Master, for when his Majesty was driven out of London, by the threatnings and tumults of the discontented rabble, he followed him, and on the 13th of September, 1642, he received the honour of knighthood. After the battle of Edgehill, when his Majesty was obliged to retire to Oxford, our author then attended him, and was created Dr. of the civil laws. When the Royal cause declined, Stapleton thought proper to addict himself to study, and to live quietly under a government, no effort of his could overturn, and as he was not amongst the most conspicuous of the Royalists, he was suffered to enjoy his solitude unmolested. At the restoration he was again promoted in the service of King Charles II. and held a place in that monarch's esteem 'till his death. Langbaine, speaking of this gentleman, gives him a very great character; his writings, says he, have made him not only known, but admired throughout all England, and while Musæus and Juvenal are in esteem with the learned, Sir Robert's fame will still survive, the translation of these two authors having placed his name in the temple of Immortality. As to Musæus, he had so great a value for him, that after he had translated him, he reduced the story into a dramatic poem, called Hero and Leander, a Tragedy, printed in 4to. 1669, and addressed to the Duchess of Monmouth. Whether this play was ever acted is uncertain, though the Prologue and Epilogue seem to imply that it appeared on the stage.

Besides these translations and this tragedy, our author has written

The slighted Maid, a Comedy, acted at the Theatre in Little Lincoln's-Inn-Fields, by the Duke of York's Servants, printed in London 1663, and dedicated to the Duke of Monmouth.

Pliny's Panegyric, a Speech in the Senate, wherein public Thanks are presented to the Emperor Trajan, by C. Plenius Cæcilius Secundus, Consul of Rome, Oxon, 1644.

Leander's Letter to Hero, and her Answer, printed with the Loves; 'tis taken from Ovid, and has Annotations written upon it by Sir Robert.

A Survey of the Manners and Actions of Mankind, with Arguments, Marginal Notes, and Annotations, clearing the obscure Places, out of the History of the Laws and Ceremonies of the Romans, London, 1647, 8vo. with the author's preface before it. It is dedicated to Henry, Marquis of Dorchester, his patron.

The History of the Low-Country War, or de bello Gallico, &c. 1650, folio, written in Latin by Famianus Strada. Our author paid the last debt to nature on the eleventh day of July, 1669, and was buried in the Abbey of St. Peter at Westminster. He was uncle to Dr. Miles Stapleton of Yorkshire, younger brother to Dr. Stapleton, a Benedictine Monk, who was president of the English Benedictines at Delaware in Lorraine, where he died, 1680.

Footnote:

1. Wood's Fasti, vol. ii. p. 23.

Dr. Jasper Main

This poet was born at Hatherleigh, in the Reign of King James I. He was a man of reputation, as well for his natural parts, as his acquired accomplishments. He received his education at Westminster school, where he continued 'till he was removed to Christ Church, Oxon, and in the year 1624 admitted student. He made some figure at the university, in the study of arts and sciences, and was sollicited by men of eminence, who esteemed him for his abilities, to enter into holy orders; this he was not long in complying with, and was preferred to two livings, both in the gift of the College, one of which was happily situated near Oxford.

Much about this time King Charles I. was obliged to keep his court at Oxford, to avoid being exposed to the resentment of the populace in London, where tumults then prevailed, and Mr. Main was made choice of, amongst others, to preach before his Majesty. Soon after he was created doctor of divinity, and resided at Oxford, till the time of the mock visitation, sent to the university, when, amongst a great many others, equally distinguished for their loyalty and zeal for that unfortunate Monarch, he was ejected from the college, and stript of both his livings. During the rage of the civil war, he was patronized by the earl of Devonshire, at whose house he resided till the restoration of Charles II. when he was not only put in possession of his former places, but made canon of Christ's Church, and arch-deacon of Chichester, which preferments he enjoyed till his death. He was an orthodox preacher, a man of severe virtue, a ready and facetious wit. In his younger years he addicted himself to poetry, and produced two plays, which were held in some esteem in his own time; but as they have never been revived, nor taken notice of by any of our critics, in all probability they are but second rate performances.

The Amorous War. a Tragedy, printed in 4to. Oxon. 1658.

The City Match, a Comedy, acted before the King and Queen in Whitehall, and afterwards on the stage in Black Fryars, with great applause, and printed in 4to. Oxon. 1658. These two plays have been printed in folio, 4to, and 8vo. and are bound together.

Besides these dramatic pieces, our author wrote a Poem upon the Naval Victory over the Dutch by the Duke of York, a subject which Dryden has likewise celebrated in his Annus Mirabilis. He published a translation of part of Lucian, said to be done by Mr. Francis Hicks, to which he added some dialogues of his own, though Winstanley is of opinion, that the whole translation is also his. In the year 1646, −47, −52, −62, he published several sermons, and entered into a controversy with the famous Presbyterian leader, Mr. Francis Cheynel, and his Sermon against False Prophets was particularly levelled at him. Cheynel's Life is written by a gentleman of great eminence in literature, and published in some of the latter numbers of of the Student, in which the character of that celebrated teacher is fully displayed. Dr. Main likewise published in the year 1647 a book called The People's War examined according to the Principles of Scripture and Reason, which he wrote at the desire of a person of quality. He also translated Dr. Donne's Latin Epigrams into English, and published them under the title of, A Sheaf of Epigrams.

On the 6th of December, 1642, he died, and his remains were deposited on the North side of the choir in Christ's Church. In his will he left several legacies for pious uses: fifty pounds for the rebuilding of St. Paul's; a hundred pounds to be distributed by the two vicars of Cassington and Burton, for the use of the poor in those parishes, with many other legacies.

He was a man of a very singular turn of humour, and though, without the abilities, bore some resemblance to the famous dean of St. Patrick's, and perhaps was not so subject to those capricious whims which produced so much uneasiness to all who attended upon dean Swift. It is said of Dr. Main, that his propension to innocent raillery was so great, that it kept him company even after death. Among other legacies, he bequeathed to an old servant an old trunk, and somewhat in it, as he said, that would make him drink: no sooner did the Dr. expire, than the servant, full of expectation, visited the trunk, in hopes of finding some money, or other treasure left him by his master, and to his great disappointment, the legacy, with which he had filled his imagination, proved no other than a Red Herring.

The ecclesiastical works of our author are as follow,

1. A Sermon concerning Unity and Agreement, preached at Carfax Church in Oxford, August 9, 1646. 1 Cor. i. 10.

2. A Sermon against False Prophets, preached in St. Mary's Church in Oxford, shortly after the surrender of that garrison, printed in 1697. Ezek. xxii. 28. He afterwards published a Vindication of this Sermon from the aspersions of Mr. Cheynel.

3. A Sermon preached at the Consecration of the Right Reverend Father in God, Herbert, Lord Bishop of Hereford, 1662. 1 Tim. iv. 14.

4. Concio ad Academiam Oxoniensem, pro more habita inchoante Jermino, Maii 27, 1662.

As a specimen of his poetry, we present a copy of verses addressed to Ben Johnson.

Scorn then, their censures, who gave't out, thy wit
As long upon a comedy did fit,
As elephants bring forth: and thy blots
And mendings took more time, than fortune plots;
That such thy draught was, and so great thy thirst,
That all thy plays were drawn at Mermaid[1] first:
That the King's yearly butt wrote, and his wine
Hath more right than those to thy Cataline.
Let such men keep a diet, let their wit,
Be rack'd and while they write, suffer a fit:
When th' have felt tortures, which outpain the gout;
Such as with less the state draws treason out;
Sick of their verse, and of their poem die,
Twou'd not be thy wont scene—

Footnote:

1. A tavern in Bread-street.

John Milton

The British nation, which has produced the greatest men in every profession, before the appearance of Milton could not enter into any competition with antiquity, with regard to the sublime excellencies of poetry. Greece could boast an Euripides, Eschylus, Sophocles and Sappho; England was proud of her Shakespear, Spenser, Johnson and Fletcher; but then the ancients had still a poet in reserve superior to the rest, who stood unrivalled by all succeeding times, and in epic poetry, which is justly esteemed the highest effort of genius, Homer had no rival. When Milton appeared, the pride of Greece was humbled, the competition became more equal, and since Paradise Lost is ours; it would, perhaps, be an injury to our national fame to yield the palm to any state, whether ancient or modern.

The author of this astonishing work had something very singular in his life, as if he had been marked out by Heaven to be the wonder of every age, in all points of view in which he can be considered. He lived in the times of general confusion; he was engaged in the factions of state, and the cause he thought proper to espouse, he maintained with unshaken firmness; he struggled to the last for what he was persuaded were the rights of humanity; he had a passion for civil liberty, and he embarked in the support of it, heedless of every consideration of danger; he exposed his fortune to the vicissitudes of party contention, and he exerted his genius in writing for the cause he favoured.

There is no life, to which it is more difficult to do justice, and at the same time avoid giving offence, than Milton's, there are some who have considered him as a regicide, others have extolled him as a patriot, and a friend to mankind: Party-rage seldom knows any bounds, and differing factions have praised or blamed him, according to their principles of religion, and political opinions.

In the course of this life, a dispassionate regard to truth, and an inviolable candour shall be observed. Milton was not without a share of those failings which are inseparable from human nature; those errors sometimes exposed him to censure, and they ought not to pass unnoticed; on the other hand, the apparent sincerity of his intentions, and the amazing force of his genius, naturally produce an extream tenderness for the faults with which his life is chequered: and as in any man's conduct fewer errors are seldom found, so no man's parts ever gave him a greater right to indulgence.

The author of Paradise Lost was descended of an ancient family of that name at Milton, near Abingdon in Oxfordshire. He was the son of John Milton a money-scrivener, and born the 9th of December, 1608. The family from which he descended had been long seated there, as appears by the monuments still to be seen in the church of Milton, 'till one of them, having taken the unfortunate side in the contests between the houses of York and Lancaster, was deprived of all his estate, except what he held by his wife[1]. Our author's grandfather, whose name was John Milton, was under-ranger, or reaper of the forest of Shotover, near Halton in Oxfordshire: but a man of Milton's genius needs not have the circumstance of birth called in to render him illustrious; he reflects the highest honour upon his family, which receives from him more glory, than the longest descent of years can give. Milton was both educated under a domestic tutor, and likewise at St. Paul's school under Mr. Alexander Gill, where he made, by his indefatigable application, an extraordinary progress in learning. From his 12th year he generally sat up all night at his studies, which, accompanied with frequent head-aches, proved very prejudicial to his eyes. In the year 1625 he was entered into Christ's College in Cambridge, under the tuition of Mr. William Chappel, afterwards bishop of Ross in Ireland, and even before that time, had distinguished himself by several Latin and English poems[2]. After he had taken the degree of master of arts, in 1632 he left the university, and for the space of five years lived with his parents at their house at Horton, near Colebrook in Buckinghamshire, where his father having acquired a competent fortune, thought proper to retire, and spend the remainder of his days. In the year 1634 he wrote his Masque of Comus, performed at Ludlow Castle, before John, earl of Bridgwater, then president of Wales: It appears from the edition of this Masque, published by Mr. Henry Lawes, that the principal performers were, the Lord Barclay, Mr. Thomas Egerton, the Lady Alice Egerton, and Mr. Lawes himself, who represented an attendant spirit.

The Prologue, which we found in the General Dictionary, begins with the following lines.

> Our stedfast bard, to his own genius true,
> Still bad his muse fit audience find, tho' few;
> Scorning the judgment of a trifling age,
> To choicer spirits he bequeath'd his page.
> He too was scorned, and to Britannia's shame,
> She scarce for half an age knew Milton's name;
> But now his fame by every trumpet blown,

We on his deathless trophies raise our own.
Nor art, nor nature, could his genius bound:
Heaven, hell, earth, chaos, he survey'd around.
All things his eye, thro' wit's bright empire thrown,
Beheld, and made what it beheld his own.

In 1637 Our author published his Lycidas; in this poem he laments the death of his friend Mr. Edward King, who was drowned in his passage from Chester on the Irish seas in 1637; it was printed the year following at Cambridge in 4to. in a collection of Latin and English poems upon Mr. King's death, with whom he had contracted the strongest friendship. The Latin epitaph informs us, that Mr. King was son of Sir John King, secretary for Ireland to Queen Elizabeth, James I. and Charles I. and that he was fellow in Christ's-College Cambridge, and was drowned in the twenty-fifth year of his age. But this poem of Lycidas does not altogether consist in elegiac strains of tenderness; there is in it a mixture of satire and severe indignation; for in part of it he takes occasion to rally the corruptions of the established clergy, of whom he was no favourer; and first discovers his acrimony against archbishop Laud; he threatens him with the loss of his head, a fate which he afterwards met, thro' the fury of his enemies; at least, says Dr. Newton, I can think of no sense so proper to be given to the following verses in Lycidas;

Besides what the grim wolf, with privy paw,
Daily devours apace, and nothing said;
But that two-handed engine at the door,
Stands ready to smite once, and smite no more.

Upon the death of his mother, Milton obtained leave of his father to travel, and having waited upon Sir Henry Wotton, formerly ambassador at Venice, and then provost of Eaton College, to whom he communicated his design, that gentleman wrote a letter to him, dated from the College, April 18, 1638, and printed among the Reliquiæ Wottonianæ, and in Dr. Newton's life of Milton. Immediately after the receipt of this letter our author set out for France, accompanied only with one man, who attended him thro' all his travels. At Paris Milton was introduced to the famous Hugo Grotius, and thence went to Florence, Siena, Rome, and Naples, in all which places he was entertained with the utmost civility by persons of the first distinction.

When our author was at Naples he was introduced to the acquaintance of Giovanni Baptista Manso, Marquis of Villa, a Neapolitan nobleman, celebrated for his taste in the liberal arts, to whom Tasso addresses his dialogue on friendship, and whom he likewise mentions in his Gierusalemme liberata, with great honour. This nobleman shewed extraordinary civilities to Milton, frequently visited him at his lodgings, and accompanied him when he went to see the several curiosities of the city. He was not content with giving our author these exterior marks of respect only, but he honoured him by a Latin distich in his praise, which is printed before Milton's Latin poems. Milton no doubt was highly pleased with such extreme condescension and esteem from a person of the Marquis of Villa's quality; and as an evidence of his gratitude, he presented the Marquis at his departure from Naples, his eclogue, entitled Mansus; which, says Dr. Newton, is well worth reading among his Latin poems; so that it may be reckoned a peculiar felicity in the Marquis of Villa's life to have been celebrated both by Tasso and Milton, the greatest poets of their nation. Having seen the finest parts of Italy, and conversed with men of the first distinction, he was preparing to pass over into Sicily and Greece, when the news from England, that a civil war was like to lay his country in blood, diverted his purpose; for as by his education and principles he was attached to the parliamentary interest, he thought it a mark of abject cowardice, for a lover of his country to take his pleasure abroad, while the friends of liberty were contending at home for the rights of human nature. He resolved therefore to return by way of Rome, tho' he was dissuaded from pursuing that resolution by the merchants, who were informed by their correspondents, that the English jesuits there were forming plots against his life, in case he should return thither, on account of the great freedom with which he had treated their religion, and the boldness he discovered in demonstrating the absurdity of the Popish tenets; for he by no means observed the rule recommended to him by Sir Henry Wotton, of keeping his thoughts close, and his countenance open. Milton was removed above dissimulation, he hated whatever had the appearance of disguise, and being naturally a man of undaunted courage, he was never afraid to assert his opinions, nor to vindicate truth tho' violated by the suffrage of the majority.

Stedfast in his resolutions, he went to Rome a second time, and stayed there two months more, neither concealing his name, nor declining any disputations to which his antagonists in religious opinions invited him; he escaped the secret machinations of the jesuits, and came safe to Florence, where he was received by his friends with as much tenderness as if he had returned to his own country. Here he remained two months, as he had done in his former visit, excepting only an excursion of a few days to Lucca, and then crossing the Appenine, and passing thro' Bologna, and Ferrara, he arrived at Venice, in which city he spent a month; and having shipped off the books he had collected in his travels, he took his course thro' Verona, Milan, and along the Lake Leman to Geneva. In this city he continued some time, meeting there with people of his own principles, and contracted an intimate friendship with Giovanni Deodati, the most learned professor of Divinity, whose annotations on the bible are published in English; and from thence returning to France the same way that he had gone before, he arrived safe in England after an absence of fifteen months, in which Milton had seen much of the world, read the characters of famous men, examined the policy of different countries, and made more extensive improvements than travellers of an inferior genius, and less penetration, can be supposed to do in double the time. Soon after his return he took a handsome house in Aldersgate-street, and undertook the education of his sister's two sons, upon a plan of his own. In this kind of scholastic solitude he continued some time, but he was not so much immersed in academical studies, as to stand an indifferent spectator of what was acted upon the public theatre of his country. The nation was in great ferment in 1641, and the clamour against episcopacy running very high, Milton who discovered how much inferior in eloquence and learning the puritan teachers were to the bishops, engaged warmly with the former in support of the common cause, and exercised all the power of which he was capable, in endeavouring to overthrow the prelatical establishment, and accordingly published five tracts relating to church government; they were all printed at London in 4to. The first was intitled, Reformation touching Church Discipline in England, and the Causes that have hitherto hindered it: two books written to a friend. The second was of Prelatical Episcopacy, and whether it may be deducted from Apostolical Times, by virtue of those Testimonies which are alledged to that purpose in some late treatises; one whereof goes under the name of James Usher archbishop of Armagh. The third was the Reason of Church Government urged against the Prelacy, by Mr. John Milton, in two books. The fourth was Animadversions upon the Remonstrants Defence against Smectymnuus; and the fifth an Apology for a Pamphlet called, a Modest Confutation of the Animadversions upon the Remonstrants against Smectymnuus; or as the title page is in some copies, an Apology for Smectymnuus, with the Reason of Church Government, by John Milton.

In the year 1643 Milton married the daughter of Richard Powel, Esq; of Forrest-hill in Oxfordshire; who not long after obtaining leave of her husband to pay a visit to her father in the country, but, upon repeated messages to her, refusing to return, Milton seemed disposed to marry another, and in 1644 published the Doctrine and Discipline of Divorce; the Judgment of Martin Bucer concerning Divorce, and the year following his Tetrachordon and Colasterion. Mr. Philips observes, and would have his readers believe, that the reason of his wife's aversion to return to him was the contrariety of their state principles. The lady being educated in loyal notions, possibly imagined, that if ever the regal power should flourish again, her being connected with a person so obnoxious to the King, would hurt her father's interest; this Mr. Philips alledges, but, with submission to his authority, I dissent from his opinion. Had she been afraid of marrying a man of Milton's principles, the reason was equally strong before as after marriage, and her father must have seen it in that light; but the true reason, or at least a more rational one, seems to be, that she had no great affection for Milton's person.

Milton was a stern man, and as he was so much devoted to study, he was perhaps too negligent in those endearments and tender intercourses of love which a wife has a right to expect. No lady ever yet was fond of a scholar, who could not join the lover with it; and he who expects to secure the affections of his wife by the force of his understanding only, will find himself miserably mistaken: indeed it is no wonder that women who are formed for tenderness, and whose highest excellence is delicacy, should pay no great reverence to a proud scholar, who considers the endearments of his wife, and the caresses of his children as pleasures unworthy of him. It is agreed by all the biographers of Milton, that he was not very tender in his disposition; he was rather boldly honourable, than delicately kind; and Mr. Dryden seems to insinuate, that he was not much subject to love. "His rhimes, says he, flow stiff from him, and that too at an age when love makes every man a rhymster, tho' not a poet. There are, methinks, in Milton's love-sonnets more of art than nature; he seems to have considered the passion philosophically, rather than felt it intimately."

In reading Milton's gallantry the breast will glow, but feel no palpitations; we admire the poetry, but do not melt with tenderness; and want of feeling in an author seldom fails to leave the reader cold; but from whatever cause his aversion proceeded, she was at last prevailed upon by her relations, who could foresee the dangers of a matrimonial quarrel, to make a submission, and she was again received with tenderness.

Mr. Philips has thus related the story.—'It was then generally thought, says he, that Milton had a design of marrying one of Dr. Davy's daughters, a very handsome and witty gentlewoman, but averse, as it is said, to this motion; however the intelligence of this caused justice Powel's family to let all engines at work to restore the married woman to the station in which they a little before had planted her. At last this device was pitched upon. There dwelt in the lane of St. Martin's Le Grand, which was hard by, a relation of our author's, one Blackborough, whom it was known he often visited, and upon this occasion the visits were more narrowly observed, and possibly there might be a combination between both parties, the friends on both sides consenting in the same action, tho' in different behalfs. One time above the rest, making his usual visits, his wife was ready in another room; on a sudden he was surprized to see one, whom he thought never to have seen more, making submission, and begging pardon on her knees before him. He might probably at first make some shew of aversion, and rejection, but partly his own generous nature, more inclinable to reconciliation than to perseverance in anger and revenge, and partly the strong intercession of friends on both sides, soon brought him to an act of oblivion and a firm league of peace for the future; and it was at length concluded that she should remain at a friend's house, till he was settled in his new house in Barbican, and all things prepared for her reception. The first fruits of her return to her husband was a brave girl, born within a year after, tho', whether by ill constitution, or want of care, she grew more and more decrepit.'

Mr. Fenton observes, that it is not to be doubted but the abovementioned interview between Milton and his wife must wonderfully affect him; and that perhaps the impressions it made on his imagination contributed much to the painting of that pathetic scene in Paradise Lost, b. 10. in which Eve addresses herself to Adam for pardon and peace, now at his feet submissive in distress.

About the year 1644 our author wrote a small piece in one sheet 4to, under this title, Education, to Mr. Samuel Hartly, reprinted at the end of his Poems on several occasions; and in the same year he published at London in 4to, his Areopagitica, or a speech of Mr. J. Milton for the liberty of unlicensed printing, to the Parliament of England.

In 1645 his Juvenile Poems were printed at London, and about this time his zeal for the republican party had so far recommended him, that a design was formed of making him adjutant-general in Sir William Waller's army; but the new modelling the army proved an obstruction to that advancement. Soon after the march of Fairfax and Cromwell with the whole army through the city, in order to suppress the insurrection which Brown and Massey were endeavouring to raise there, against the army's proceedings, he left his great house in Barbican, for a smaller in High Holborn, where he prosecuted his studies till after the King's trial and death, when he published his Tenure of Kings and Magistrates: His Observations on the Articles of peace between James Earl of Ormond for King Charles I. on the one hand, and the Irish Rebels and Papists on the other hand; and a letter sent by Ormond to colonel Jones governor of Dublin; and a representation of the Scotch Presbytery at Belfast in Ireland.

He was now admitted into the service of the Commonwealth, and was made Latin Secretary to the Council of State, who resolved neither to write nor receive letters but in the Latin tongue, which was common to all states.

'And it were to be wished,' says Dr. Newton, 'that succeeding Princes would follow their example, for in the opinion of very wise men, the universality of the French language will make way for the universality of the French Monarchy. Milton was perhaps the first instance of a blind man's possessing the place of a secretary; which no doubt was a great inconvenience to him in his business, tho' sometimes a political use might be made of it, as men's natural infirmities are often pleaded in excuse for their not doing what they have no great inclination to do. Dr. Newton relates an instance of this. When Cromwell, as we may collect from Whitlocke, for some reasons delayed artfully to sign the treaty concluded with Sweden, and the Swedish ambassador made frequent complaints of it, it was excused to him, because Milton on account of his blindness, proceeded slower in business, and had not yet put the articles of treaty into Latin. Upon which the ambassador was greatly surprized that things of such consequence should be entrusted to a blind man; for he must necessarily employ an amanuensis, and that amanuensis might divulge the articles; and said, it was very wonderful there should be only one man in England who could write Latin, and he a blind one.'

Thus we have seen Milton raised to the dignity of Latin Secretary. It is somewhat strange, that in times of general confusion, when a man of parts has the fairest opportunity to play off his abilities to advantage, that Milton did not rise sooner, nor to a greater elevation; he was employed by those in authority only as a writer, which conferred no power upon him, and kept him in a kind of obscurity, who had from nature all that was proper for the field as well as the cabinet; for we are assured that Milton was a man of confirmed courage.

In 1651 our author published his Pro Populo Anglicano Defensio, for which he was rewarded by the Commonwealth with a present of a thousand pounds, and had a considerable hand in correcting and polishing a piece written by his nephew Mr. John Philips, and printed at London 1652, under this title, Joannis Philippi Angli Responsio ad Apologiam Anonymi cujusdam Tenebrionis pro Rege & Populo Anglicano infantissimam. During the writing and publishing this book, he lodged at one Thomson's, next door to the Bull-head tavern Charing-Cross; but he soon removed to a Garden-house in Petty-France, next door to lord Scudamore's, where he remained from the year 1652 till within a few weeks of the Restoration. In this house, his first wife dying in child-bed, 1652, he married a second, Catherine, the daughter of Captain Woodcock of Hackney, who died of a consumption in three months after she had been brought to bed of a daughter. This second marriage was about two or three years after he had been wholly deprived of his sight; for by reason of his continual studies, and the head-ache, to which he was subject from his youth, and his perpetual tampering with physic, his eyes had been decaying for twelve years before.

In 1654 he published his Defensio Secunda; and the year following his Defensio pro Se. Being now at ease from his state adversaries, and political controversies, he had leisure again to prosecute his own studies, and private designs, particularly his History of Britain, and his new Thesaurus Linguæ Latinæ according to the method of Robert Stevens, the manuscript of which contained three large volumes in folio, and has been made use of by the editors of the Cambridge Dictionary, printed 4to, 1693.

In 1658 he published Sir Walter Raleigh's Cabinet Council; and in 1659 a Treatise of the Civil Power in Ecclesiastical Causes, Lond. 12mo. and Considerations touching the likeliest Means to remove Hirelings out of the Church; wherein are also Discourses of Tithes, Church-fees, Church-Revenues, and whether any Maintenance of Ministers can be settled in Law, Lond. 1659, 12mo.

Upon the dissolution of the Parliament by the army, after Richard Cromwell had been obliged to resign the Protectorship, Milton wrote a letter, in which he lays down the model of a commonwealth; not such as he judged the best, but what might be the readiest settled at that time, to prevent the restoration of kingly government and domestic disorders till a more favourable season, and better dispositions for erecting a perfect democracy. He drew up likewise another piece to the same purpose, which seems to have been addressed to general Monk; and he published in February 1659, his ready and easy way to establish a free Commonwealth. Soon after this he published his brief notes upon a late sermon, entitled, the Fear of God and the King, printed in 4to, Lond. 1660. Just before the restoration he was removed from his office of Latin secretary, and concealed himself till the act of oblivion was published; by the advice of his friends he absconded till the event of public affairs should direct him what course to take, for this purpose he retired to a friend's house in Bartholomew-Close, near West-Smithfield, till the general amnesty was declared.

The act of oblivion, says Mr. Phillips, proving as favourable to him, as could be hoped or expected, through the intercession of some that stood his friends both in Council and Parliament; particularly in the House of Commons, Mr. Andrew Marvel member for Hull, and who has prefixed a copy of verses before his Paradise Lost, acted vigorously in his behalf, and made a considerable party for him, so that together with John Goodwin of Coleman-Street, he was only so far excepted as not to bear any office in the Commonwealth; but as this is one of the most important circumstances in the life of our author, we shall give an account of it at large, from Mr. Richardson, in his life of Milton, prefixed to his Explanatory Notes, and Remarks on Paradise Lost.

His words are

'That Milton escaped is well known, but not how. By the accounts we have, he was by the Act of Indemnity only incapacitated for any public employment. This is a notorious mistake, though Toland, the bishop of Sarum, Fenton, &c, have gone into it, confounding him with Goodwin; their cases were very different, as I found upon enquiry. Not to take a matter of this importance upon trust, I had first recourse to the Act itself. Milton is not among the excepted. If he was so conditionally pardoned, it must then be, by a particular instrument. That could not be after he had been purified entirely by the general indemnity, nor was it likely the King, who had declared from Breda, he would pardon all but whom the Parliament should judge unworthy of it, and had thus lodged the matter with them, should, before they came to a determination, bestow a private act of indulgence to one so notorious as Milton. It is true, Rapin says, several principal republicans applied for mercy, while the Act was yet depending, but quotes no authority; and upon search, no such pardon appears on record, though many are two or three years after, but then they are without restrictions; some people were willing to have a particular, as well as a general pardon; but whatever was the case of others, there was a reason besides what has been already noted, that no such favour would be shewn to Milton. The House of Commons, June 16, 1660, vote the King to be moved to call in his two books, and that of John Goodwin, written in justification of the murder of the King, in order to be burnt, and that the Attorney General do proceed against them by indictment. June 27, an Order of Council reciting that Vote of the 16th, and that the persons were not to be found, directs a Proclamation for calling in Milton's two books, which are here explained, to be that against Salmasius, and the Eikon Basilike, as also Goodwin's book; and a Proclamation was issued accordingly, and another to the same purpose the 13th of August: as for Goodwin he narrowly escaped for his life, but he was voted to be excepted out of the Act of Indemnity, amongst the twenty designed to have penalties inflicted short of death, and August 27, these books of Milton and Goodwin were burnt by the hangman. The Act of Oblivion, according to Kennet's Register, was passed the 29th. It is seen by this account, that Milton's person and Goodwin's are separated, tho' their books are blended together. As the King's intention appeared to be a pardon to all but actual regicides, as Burnet says, it is odd, he should assert in the same breath, almost all people were surprized that Goodwin and Milton escaped censure. Why should it be so strange, they being not concerned in the King's blood? that he was forgot, as Toland says, some people imagined, is very unlikely. However, it is certain, from what has been shewn from bishop Kennet, he was not. That he should be distinguished from Goodwin, with advantage, will justly appear strange;

for his vast merit, as an honest man, a great scholar, and a most excellent writer, and his fame, on that account, will hardly be thought the causes, especially when it is remembered Paradise Lost was not produced, and the writings, on which his vast reputation stood, are now become criminal, and those most, which were the main pillars of his fame. Goodwin was an inconsiderable offender, compared with him; some secret cause must be recurred to in accounting for this indulgence. I have heard that secretary Morrice, and Sir Thomas Clarges were his friends, and managed matters artfully in his favour; doubtless they, or some body else did, and they very probably, as being powerful friends at that time. But still how came they to put their interest at such a stretch, in favour of a man so notoriously obnoxious? perplexed, and inquisitive as I was, I at length found the secret. It was Sir William Davenant obtained his remission, in return of his own life, procured by Milton's interest, when himself was under condemnation, Anno 1650. A life was owing to Milton (Davenant's) and it was paid nobly; Milton's for Davenant, at Davenant's intercession. The management of the affair in the house, whether by signifying the King's desire, or otherwise, was, perhaps by those gentlemen named.'

This account Mr. Richardson had from Mr. Pope, who was informed of it by Betterton, the celebrated actor, who was first brought upon the stage by Sir William Davenant, and honoured with an intimacy with him, so that no better authority need be produced to support any fact.

Milton being secured by his pardon, appeared again in public, and removed to Jewin street, where he married his third wife, Elizabeth, the daughter of Mr. Minshul of Cheshire, recommended to him by his friend Dr. Paget, to whom he was related, but he had no children by her: soon after the restoration he was offered the place of Latin secretary to the King, which, notwithstanding the importunities of his wife, he refused: we are informed, that when his wife pressed him to comply with the times, and accept the King's offer, he made answer, 'You are in the right, my dear, you, as other women, would ride in your coach; for me, my aim is to live and die an honest man.' Soon after his marriage with his third wife, he removed to a house in the Artillery Walk, leading to Bunhill-fields, where he continued till his death, except during the plague, in 1665, when he retired with his family to St. Giles's Chalfont Buckinghamshire, at which time his Paradise Lost was finished, tho' not published till 1667. Mr. Philips observes, that the subject of that poem was first designed for a tragedy, and in the fourth book of the poem, says he, there are ten verses, which, several years before the poem was begun, were shewn to me, and some others, as designed for the very beginning of the tragedy. The verses are,

O thou that with surpassing glory crown'd
Look'st from thy sole dominion like the god,
Of this new world; at whose sight all the stars
Hide their diminish'd heads; to thee I call,
But with no friendly voice, and add thy name,
O Sun, to tell thee how I hate thy beams,
Which brings to my remembrance, from what state
I fell; how glorious once above thy sphere,
'Till pride, and worse ambition, threw me down,
Warring in Heaven, 'gainst Heav'ns matchless King.

Mr. Philips further observes, that there was a very remarkable circumstance in the composure of Paradise Lost, which, says he, 'I have particular reason to remember, for whereas I had the perusal of it from the very beginning, for some years, as I went from time to time to visit him, in a parcel of ten, twenty, or thirty verses at a time, which being written by whatever hand came next, might possibly want correction, as to the orthography and pointing; having, as the summer came on, not been shewn any for a considerable while, and desiring the reason thereof, was answered, that his vein never happily flowed but from the autumnal equinox to the vernal, and that whatever he attempted at other times, was never to his satisfaction, though he courted his fancy never so much; so that in all the years he was about his poem, he may be said to have spent but half his time therein.'[3] Mr. Toland imagines that Mr. Philips must be mistaken in regard to the time, since Milton, in his Latin Elegy upon the Approach of the Spring, declares the contrary, and that his poetic talent returned with the spring. This is a point, as it is not worth contending, so it never can be settled; no poet ever yet could tell when the poetic vein would flow; and as no man can make verses, unless the inclination be present, so no man, can be certain how long it will continue, for if there is any inspiration now amongst men, it is that which the poet feels, at least the sudden starts, and flashes of fancy bear a strong resemblance to the idea we form of inspiration.

Mr. Richardson has informed us, 'that when Milton dictated, he used to sit leaning backwards obliquely in an easy chair, with his legs flung over the elbows of it; that he frequently composed lying a-bed in a morning, and that when he could not sleep, but lay awake whole nights, he tried, but not one verse could he make; at other times flowed easy his unpremeditated verse, with a certain Impetus as himself used to believe; then at what hour soever, he rung for his daughter to secure what came. I have been also told he would dictate many, perhaps 40 lines in a breath, and then reduce them to half the number.' I would not omit, says Mr. Richardson, the least circumstance; these indeed are trifles, but even such contract a sort of greatness, when related to what is great.

After the work was ready for the press, it was near being suppressed by the ignorance, or malice of the licenser, who, among other trivial objections, imagined there was treason in that noble simile, b. i. v. 594—

> —As when the sun new ris'n
> Looks thro' the horizontal misty air,
> Shorn of his beams; or from behind the moon,
> In dim eclipse, disastrous twilight sheds
> On half the nations, and with fear of change
> Perplexes monarchs.

The ignorance of this licenser, in objecting to this noble simile, has indeed perpetuated his name, but it is with no advantage; he, no doubt, imagined, that *Perplexes Monarchs* was levelled against the reigning Prince, which is, perhaps, the highest simile in our language; how ridiculously will people talk who are blinded by prejudice, or heated by party. But to return: After Milton had finished this noble work of genius, which does honour to human nature, he disposed of it to a Bookseller for the small price of fifteen pounds; under such prejudice did he then labour, and the payment of the fifteen pounds was to depend upon the sale of two numerous impressions. This engagement with his Bookseller proves him extremely ignorant of that sort of business, for he might be well assured, that if two impressions sold, a great deal of money must be returned, and how he could dispose of it thus conditionally for fifteen pounds, appears strange; but while it proves Milton's ignorance, or inattention about his interest in this affair, it, at the same time, demonstrates the Bookseller's honesty; for he could not be ignorant what money would be got by two numerous editions. After this great work was published, however, it lay some time in obscurity, and had the Bookseller advanced the sum stipulated, he would have had reason to repent of his bargain. It was generally reported, that the late lord Somers first gave Paradise Lost a reputation; but Mr. Richardson observes, that it was known and esteemed long before there was such a man as lord Somers, as appears by a pompous edition of it printed by subscription in 1688, where, amongst the list of Subscribers, are the names of lord Dorset, Waller, Dryden, Sir Robert Howard, Duke, Creech, Flatman, Dr. Aldrich, Mr. Atterbury, Sir Roger L'Estrange, lord Somers, then only John Somers, esq; Mr. Richardson further informs us, that he was told by Sir George Hungerford, an ancient Member of Parliament, that Sir John Denham came into the House one morning with a sheet of Paradise Lost, wet from the press, in his hand, and being asked what he was reading? he answered, part of the noblest poem that ever was written in any language, or in any age; however, it is certain that the book was unknown till about two years after, when the earl of Dorset recommended it, as appears from the following story related to Mr. Richardson, by Dr. Tancred Robinson, an eminent physician in London, who was informed by Sir Fleetwood Sheppard, 'that the earl, in company with that gentleman, looking over some books in Little Britain, met with Paradise Lost; and being surprized with some passages in turning it over, bought it. The Bookseller desired his lordship to speak in its favour, since he liked it, as the impression lay on his hands as waste paper. The earl having read the poem, sent it to Mr. Dryden, who, in a short time, returned it with this answer: This man cuts us all, and the ancients too.'

Critics have differed as to the source from which our author drew the first hint of writing Paradise Lost; Peck conjectures that it was from a celebrated Spanish Romance called Guzman, and Dr. Zachary Pearce, now bishop of Bangor, has alledged, that he took the first hint of it from an Italian Tragedy, called Il Paradiso Perso, still extant, and printed many years before he entered on his design. Mr. Lauder in his Essay on Milton's Use and Imitation of the Moderns, has insinuated that Milton's first hint of Paradise Lost, was taken from a Tragedy of the celebrated Grotius, called Adamus Exul, and that Milton has not thought it beneath him to transplant some of that author's beauties into his noble work, as well as some other flowers culled from the gardens of inferior genius's; but by an elegance of art, and force of nature, peculiar to him, he has drawn the admiration of the world upon passages, which in their original authors, stood neglected and undistinguished. If at any time he has adopted a sentiment of a cotemporary poet, it deserves another name than plagiary; for, as Garth expresses it, in the case of Dryden, who was charged with plagiary, that, like ladies of quality who borrow beggars children, it is only to cloath them the better, and we know no higher compliment could have been paid to these moderns, than that of Milton's doing them the honour to peruse them, for, like a Prince's accepting a present from a subject, the glory is reflected on him who offers the gift, not on the Monarch who accepts it. But as Mr. Lauder's book has lately made so great a noise in the world, we must beg leave to be a little more particular.

Had Mr. Lauder pursued his plan of disclosing Milton's resources, and tracing his steps through the vast tracts of erudition that our author travelled, with candour and dispassionateness, the design would have been noble and useful; he then would have produced authors into light who were before unknown; have recommended sacred poetry, and it would have been extreamly pleasing to have followed Milton over all his classic ground, and seen where the noblest genius of the world thought proper to pluck a flower, and by what art he was able to rear upon the foundation of nature so magnificent, so astonishing a fabric: but in place of that, Mr. Lauder suffers himself to be overcome by his passion, and instead of tracing him as a man of taste, and extensive reading, he hunts him like a malefactor, and seems to be determined on his execution.

Mr. Lauder could never separate the idea of the author of Paradise Lost, and the enemy of King Charles. Lauder has great reading, but greater ill nature; and Mr. Douglas has shewn how much his evidence is invalidated by some interpolations which Lauder has since owned. It is pity so much classical knowledge should have been thus prostituted by Lauder, which might have been of service to his country; but party-zeal seldom knows any bounds. The ingenious Moses Brown, speaking of this man's furious attack upon Milton, has the following pretty stanza.

> The Owl will hoot that cannot sing,
> Spite will displume the muse's wing,
> Tho' Phœbus self applaud her;
> Still Homer bleeds in Zoilus' page
> A Virgil 'scaped not the Mævius' rage,
> And Milton has his Lauder.[4]

But if Lauder is hot and furious, his passion soon subsides. Upon hearing that the grand-daughter of Milton was living, in an obscure situation in Shoreditch, he readily embraced the opportunity, in his postscript, of recommending her to the public favour; upon which, some gentlemen affected with the singularity of the circumstance, and ashamed that our country should suffer the grand-daughter of one from whom it derives its most lasting and brightest honour, to languish neglected, procured Milton's Comus to be performed for her benefit at Drury Lane, on the 5th of April, 1750: upon which, Mr. Garrick spoke a Prologue written by a gentleman, who zealously promoted the benefit, and who, at this time, holds the highest rank in literature.

This prologue will not, we are persuaded, be unacceptable to our readers.

A Prologue spoken by Mr. Garrick, Thursday, April 5, 1750. at the Representation of COMUS, for the Benefit of Mrs. Elizabeth Foster, MILTON's Grand-daughter, and only surviving descendant.

> Ye patriot crouds, who burn for England's fame,
> Ye nymphs, whose bosoms beat at Milton's name,
> Whose gen'rous zeal, unbought by flatt'ring rhimes,
> Shames the mean pensions of Augustan times;
> Immortal patrons of succeeding days,
> Attend this prelude of perpetual praise!

Let wit, condemn'd the feeble war to wage
With close malevolence, or public rage;
Let study, worn with virtue's fruitless lore,
Behold this theatre, and grieve no more.
This night, distinguish'd by your smile, shall tell,
That never Briton can in vain excel;
The slighted arts futurity shall trust,
And rising ages hasten to be just.

At length our mighty bard's victorious lays
Fill the loud voice of universal praise,
And baffled spite, with hopeless anguish dumb,
Yields to renown the centuries to come.
With ardent haste, each candidate of fame
Ambitious catches at his tow'ring name:
He sees, and pitying sees, vain wealth bestow:
Those pageant honours which he scorn'd below;
While crowds aloft the laureat dust behold,
Or trace his form on circulating gold.
Unknown, unheeded, long his offspring lay,
And want hung threat'ning o'er her slow decay.
What tho' she shine with no Miltonian fire,
No fav'ring muse her morning dreams inspire;
Yet softer claims the melting heart engage,
Her youth laborious, and her blameless age:
Hers the mild merits of domestic life,
The patient suff'rer, and the faithful wife.
Thus grac'd with humble virtue's native charms
Her grandsire leaves her in Britannia's arms,
Secure with peace, with competence, to dwell,
While tutelary nations guard her cell.
Yours is the charge, ye fair, ye wife, ye brave!
'Tis yours to crown desert—beyond the grave!

In the year 1670 our author published at London in 4to. his History of Britain, that part, especially, now called England, from the first traditional Beginning, continued to the Norman Conquest, collected out of the ancientest and best authors thereof. It is reprinted in the first volume of Dr. Kennet's compleat History of England. Mr. Toland in his Life of Milton, page 43, observes, that we have not this history as it came out of his hands, for the licensers, those sworn officers to destroy learning, liberty, and good sense, expunged several passages of it, wherein he exposed the superstition, pride, and cunning of the Popish monks in the Saxon times, but applied by the sagacious licensers to Charles IId's bishops. In 1681 a considerable passage which had been suppressed in the publication of this history, was printed at London in 4to under this title. Mr. John Milton's character of the Long Parliament and Assembly of Divines in 1651, omitted in his other works, and never before printed. It is reported, and from the foregoing character it appears probable, that Mr. Milton had lent most of his personal estate upon the public faith, which when he somewhat earnestly pressed to have restored, after a long, and chargeable attendance, met with very sharp rebbukes; upon which, at last despairing of any success in this affair, he was forced to return from them poor and friendless, having spent all his money, and wearied all those who espoused his cause, and he had not, probably, mended his circumstances in those days, but by performing such service for them, as afterwards he did, for which scarce any thing would appear too great. In 1671 he published at London in 8vo. Paradise Regained, a Poem in four Books, to which is added Sampson Agonistes: there is not a stronger proof of human weakness, than Milton's preferring this Poem of Paradise Regained, to Paradise Lost, and it is a natural and just observation, that the Messiah in Paradise Regained, with all his meekness, unaffected dignity, and clear reasoning, makes not so great a figure, as when in the Paradise Lost he appears cloathed in the Terrors of Almighty vengeance, wielding the thunder of Heaven, and riding along the sky in the chariot of power, drawn, as Milton greatly expresses it, 'with Four Cherubic Shapes; when he comes drest in awful Majesty, and hurls the apostate spirits headlong into the fiery gulph of bottomless perdition, there to dwell in adamantine chains and penal fire, who durst defy the Omnipotent to arms.'

Dr. Newton has dissented from the general opinion of mankind, concerning Paradise Regained: 'Certainly, says he, it is very worthy of the author, and contrary to what Mr. Toland relates, Milton may be seen in Paradise Regained as well as Paradise Lost; if it is inferior in poetry, I know not whether it is inferior in sentiment; if it is less descriptive, it is more argumentative; if it does not sometimes rise so high, neither doth it ever sink below; and it has not met with the approbation it deserves, only because it has not been more read and considered. His subject indeed is confined, and he has a narrow foundation to build upon, but he has raised as noble a superstructure, as such little room, and such scanty materials would allow. The great beauty of it is the contrast between the two characters of the tempter and Our Saviour, the artful sophistry, and specious insinuations of the one, refuted by the strong sense, and manly eloquence of the other.' The first thought of Paradise Regained was owing to Elwood the Quaker, as he himself relates the occasion, in the History of his own Life. When Milton had lent him the manuscript of Paradise Lost at St. Giles's Chalfont, and he returned it, Milton asked him how he liked it, and what he thought of it? 'which I modestly and freely told him (says Elwood) and after some further discourse about it, I pleasantly said to him, thou hast said much of Paradise Lost, but what hast thou to say of a Paradise Found? He made me no answer, but sat some time in a muse, then broke off that discourse, and fell upon another subject.' When Elwood afterwards waited upon him in London, Milton shewed him his Paradise Regained, and in a pleasant tone said to him, 'this is owing to you, for you put it into my head by the question you put me at Chalfont, which before I had not thought of.'

In the year 1672 he published his Artis Logicæ plenior Institutio ad Rami methodum concinnata, London, in 8vo. and in 1673, a Discourse intitled, Of True Religion, Heresy, Schism, Toleration, and what best Means may be used against the Growth of Popery, London, in 4to. He published likewise the same year, Poems, &c. on several Occasions, both English and Latin, composed at several times, with a small Tractate of Education to Mr. Hartlib, London, 8vo. In 1674 he published his Epistolarum familiarium, lib. i. & Prolusiones quædam Oratoriæ in Collegio Christi habitæ, London, in 8vo and in the same year in 4to. a Declaration of the Letters Patent of the King of Poland, John III. elected on the 22d of May, Anno Dom. 1674, now faithfully translated from the Latin copy. Mr. Wood tells us[5], that Milton was thought to be the author of a piece called the Grand Case of Conscience, concerning the Engagement Stated and Resolved; or a Strict Survey of the Solemn League and Covenant in reference to the present Engagement; but others are of opinion that the stile and manner of writing do not in the least favour that supposition. His State Letters were printed at London 1676 in 12mo. and translated into English, and printed 1694, as his Brief History of Muscovy, and of their less known Countries, lying Eastward of Russia, as far as Cathay, was in 1682 in 8vo. His Historical, Poetical, and Miscellaneous Works were printed in three volumes in folio 1698 at London, though Amsterdam is mentioned in the title page with the life of the author, by Mr. Toland; but the most compleat and elegant edition of his prose works was printed in two volumes in folio at London 1738, by the rev. Mr. Birch, now secretary to the Royal Society, with an Appendix concerning two Dissertations, the first concerning the Author of the ΕΙΚΩΝ ΒΑΣΙΛΙΚΗ, the Portraiture of his sacred Majesty in his solitude and sufferings; and the prayer of Pamela subjoined to several editions of that book; the second concerning the Commission said to be given by King Charles I. in 1641, to the Irish Papists, for taking up arms against the Protestants in Ireland. In this edition the several pieces are disposed according to the order in which they were printed, with the edition of a Latin Tract, omitted by Mr. Toland, concerning the Reasons of the War with Spain in 1655, and several pages in the History of Great Britain, expanged by the licensers of the press, and not to be met with in any former impressions. It perhaps is not my province to make any remarks upon the two grand disputations, that have subsisted between the friends and enemies of Charles I. about the author of the Basilike, and the Commission granted to the Irish Papists; as to the last, the reader, if he pleases, may consult at the Life of Lord Broghill, in which he will find the mystery of iniquity disclosed, and Charles entirely freed from the least appearance of being concerned in granting so execrable a commission; the forgery is there fully related, and there is all the evidence the nature of the thing will admit of, that the King's memory has been injured by so base an imputation. As to the first, it is somewhat difficult to determine, whether his Majesty was or was not the author of these pious Meditations; Mr. Birch has summed up the evidence on both sides; we shall not take upon us to determine on which it preponderates; it will be proper here to observe, the chief evidence against the King in this contention, is, Dr. Gauden, bishop of Exeter, who claimed that book as his, and who, in his letters to the earl of Clarendon, values himself upon it, and becomes troublesomely sollicitous for preferment on that account; he likewise told the two princes that the Basilike was not written by their father, but by him; now one thing is clear, that Gauden was altogether without parts; his Life of Hooker, which is the only genuine and indisputed work of his, shews him a man of no extent of thinking; his stile is loose, and negligently florid, which is diametrically opposite to that of these Meditations. Another circumstance much invalidates his evidence, and diminishes his reputation for honesty. After he had, for a considerable time, professed himself a Protestant, and been in possession of an English bishopric, and discovered an ardent desire of rising in the church, notwithstanding this, he declared himself at his death a Papist; and upon the evidence of such a man, none can determine a point in disputation; for he who durst thus violate his conscience, by the basest hypocrisy, will surely make no great scruple to traduce the memory of his sovereign.

In a work of Milton's called Icon Oclastes, or the Image broken, he takes occasion to charge the king with borrowing a prayer from Sir Philip Sidney's Arcadia, and placing it in his Meditations without acknowledging the favour. Soon after the sentence of the Regicides had been put in execution these Meditations were published, and as Anthony by shewing the body of murdered Cæsar, excited the compassion of multitudes, and raised their indignation against the enemies of that illustrious Roman; so these Meditations had much the same effect in England. The Presbyterians loudly exclaimed against the murder of the King; they asserted, that his person was sacred, and spilling his blood upon a scaffold was a stain upon the English annals, which the latest time could not obliterate. These tragical complaints gaining ground, and the fury which was lately exercised against his Majesty, subsiding into a tenderness for his memory, heightened by the consideration of his piety, which these Meditations served to revive, it was thought proper, in order to appease the minds of the people, that an answer should be wrote to them.

In this task Milton engaged, and prosecuted it with vigour; but the most enthusiastic admirer of that poet, upon reading it will not fail to discover a spirit of bitterness, an air of peevishness and resentment to run through the whole. Milton has been charged with interpolating the prayer of Pamela into the King's Meditations, by the assistance of Bradshaw, who laid his commands upon the printer so to do, to blast the reputation of the King's book. Dr. Newton is of opinion that this fact is not well supported, for it is related chiefly upon the authority of Henry Hills the printer, who had frequently affirmed it to Dr. Gill, and Dr. Bernard, his physicians, as they themselves have testified; but tho' Hills was Cromwell's printer, yet afterwards he turned Papist in the reign of King James II. in order to be that King's Printer; and it was at that time he used to relate this story; so that little credit is due to his testimony. It is almost impossible to believe Milton capable of such disingenuous meanness, to serve so bad a purpose, and there is as little reason for fixing it upon him, as he had to traduce the King for profaning the duty of prayer, with the polluted trash of romances; for in the best books of devotion, there are not many finer prayers, and the King might as lawfully borrow and apply it to his own purpose, as the apostle might make quotations from Heathen poems and plays; and it became Milton, the least of all men, to bring such an accusation against the King, as he was himself particularly fond of reading romances, and has made use of them in some of the best and latest of his writings.

There have been various conjectures concerning the cause that produced in Milton so great an aversion to Charles I. One is, that when Milton stood candidate for a professorship at Cambridge with his much esteemed friend Mr. King, their interest and qualifications were equal, upon which his Majesty was required by his nomination to fix the professor; his answer was, let the best-natured man have it; to which they who heard him, immediately replied; 'then we are certain it cannot be Milton's, who was ever remarkable for a stern ungovernable man.' — Whether this conjecture is absolutely true, we cannot determine; but as it is not without probability, it has a right to be believed, till a more satisfactory one can be given.

In whatever light Milton may be placed as a statesman, yet as a poet he stands in one point of view without a rival; the sublimity of his conceptions, the elevation of his stile, the fertility of his imagination, and the conduct of his design in Paradise Lost is inimitable, and cannot be enough admired.

Milton's character as a poet was never better pourtray'd than in the epigram under his picture written by Mr. Dryden.

> Three poets in three distant ages born,
> Greece, Italy, and England, did adorn.
> The first in loftiness of thought surpass'd;
> The next in majesty; in both the last:
> The force of nature could no further go,
> To make a third, she join'd the former two.—

This great man died at his house at Bunhill, Nov. 15, 1674, and was interred near the body of his father, in the chancel of the church of St. Giles, Cripplegate. By his first wife he had four children, a son and three daughters. The daughters survived their father. Anne married a master-builder, and died in child-bed of her first child, which died with her; Mary lived single; Deborah left her father when she was young, and went over to Ireland with a lady, and came to England again during the troubles of Ireland under King James II. She married Mr. Abraham Clark, a weaver in Spittal-fields, and died Aug. 24, 1727, in the 76th year of age. She had ten children, viz. seven sons, and three daughters, but none of them had any children except one of her sons named Caleb, and the youngest daughter, whose name is Elizabeth. Caleb went over to Fort St. George in the East-Indies, where he married and had two sons, Abraham and Isaac; of these Abraham the elder came to England with governor Harrison, but returned again upon advice of his father's death, and whether he or his brother be now living is uncertain. Elizabeth, the youngest child of Deborah, married Mr. Thomas Foster, a weaver, and lives now in Hog-lane, Shoreditch, for whom Comus, as we have already observed, was performed at Drury-Lane, and produced her a great benefit. She has had seven children, three sons and four daughters, who are all now dead. This Mrs. Foster is a plain decent looking Woman. Mr. John Ward, fellow of the Royal Society, and professor of rhetoric in Gresham-College, London, saw the above Mrs. Clark, Milton's daughter at the house of one of her relations not long before her death, when she informed me, says that gentleman, 'That she and her sisters used to read to their father in eight languages, which by practice they were capable of doing with great readiness, and accuracy, tho' they understood no language but English, and their father used often to say in their hearing, one tongue was enough for a woman. None of them were ever sent to school, but all taught at home by a mistress kept for that purpose. Isaiah, Homer, and Ovid's Metamorphoses were books which they were often called to read to their father; and at my desire she repeated a great number of verses from the beginning of both these poets with great readiness. I knew who she was upon the first sight of her, by the similitude of her countenance with her father's picture. And upon my telling her so, she informed me, that Mr. Addison told her the same thing, on her going to wait on him; for he, upon hearing she was living sent for her, and desired if she had any papers of her father's, she would bring them with her, as an evidence of her being Milton's daughter; but immediately on her being introduced to him, he said, Madam, you need no other voucher; your face is a sufficient testimonial whose daughter you are; and he then made her a handsome present of a purse of guineas, with a promise of procuring for her an annual provision for life; but he dying soon after, she lost the benefit of his generous design. She appeared to be a woman of good sense, and genteel behaviour, and to bear the inconveniencies of a low fortune with decency and prudence.'

Her late Majesty Queen Caroline sent her fifty pounds, and she received presents of money from several gentlemen not long before her death. Milton had a brother, Mr. Christopher Milton who was knighted and made one of the barons of the Exchequer in King James II's reign, but he does not appear to have been a man of any abilities, at least if he had any, they are lost to posterity in the lustre of his brother's.

There is now alive a grand-daughter of this Christopher Milton, who is married to one Mr. John Lookup, advocate at Edinburgh, remarkable for his knowledge of the Hebrew tongue. The lady, whom I have often seen, is extremely corpulent, has in her youth been very handsome, and is not destitute of a poetical genius. She has writ several copies of verses, published in the Edinburgh Magazines; and her face bears some resemblance to the picture of Milton.

Mr. Wood, and after him Mr. Fenton, has given us the following description of Milton's person.

"He was of a moderate size, well-proportioned, and of a ruddy complexion, light brown hair, and had handsome features, yet his eyes were none of the quickest. When he was a student in Cambridge, he was so fair and clear, that many called him the Lady of Christ's-College. His deportment was affable, and his gait erect and manly, bespeaking courage and undauntedness; while he had his sight he wore a sword, and was well skilled in using it. He had a delicate tuneable voice, an excellent ear, could play on the organ, and bear a part in vocal and instrumental music."[6]

The great learning and genius of Milton, have scarcely raised him more admirers, than the part he acted upon the political stage, has procured him enemies. He was in his inclination a thorough Republican, and in this he thought like a Greek or Roman, as he was very conversant with their writings.

And one day Sir Robert Howard, who was a friend of Milton's, and a well wisher to the liberty of his country, asked him, how he came to side with the Republicans? Milton answered, among other things, 'Because theirs was the most frugal government; for the trappings of a Monarchy might set up an ordinary Commonwealth.' But then his attachment to Cromwell must be condemned, as being neither consistent with his republican principles, nor with his love of liberty. It may be reasonably presumed, that he was far from entirely approving of Cromwell's proceeding; but considered him as the only person who could rescue the nation from the tyranny of the Presbyterians, who he saw, were about to erect a worse dominion of their own upon the ruins of prelatical episcopacy; for if experience may be allowed to teach us, the Presbyterian government carries in it more of ecclesiastical authority, and approaches more to the thunder of the Vatican, than any other government under the sun. Milton was an enemy to spiritual slavery, he thought the chains thrown upon the mind were the least tolerable; and in order to shake the pillars of mental usurpation, he closed with Cromwell and the independants, as he expected under them greater liberty of conscience. In matters of religion too, Milton has likewise given great offence, but infidels have no reason to glory. No such man was ever amongst them. He was persuaded of the truth of the christian religion; he studied and admired the holy scriptures, and in all his writings he plainly discovers a religious turn of mind.

When he wrote the Doctrine and Discipline of Divorce, he appears to have been a Calvinist; but afterwards he entertained a more favourable opinion of Arminius. Some have thought that he was an Arian, but there are more express passages in his works to overthrow this opinion, than any there are to confirm it. For in the conclusion of his Treatise on Reformation, he thus solemnly invokes the Trinity:

'Thou therefore that sittest in light and glory unapproachable, parent of angels and of men! next thee I implore omnipotent king, redeemer of that lost remnant, whose nature thou didst assume, ineffable and everlasting love! and thee the third subsistence of the divine infinitude, illuminating spirit, the joy and solace of created things! one tri-personal god-head.'

In the latter part of his life he was not a professed member of any particular sect of christians; he frequented no public worship, nor used any religious rite in his family; he was an enemy to all kinds of forms, and thought that all christians had in some things corrupted the simplicity and purity of the gospel. He believed that inward religion was the best, and that public communion had more of shew in it, than any tendency to promote genuine piety and unaffected goodness.

The circumstances of our author were never very mean, nor very affluent; he lived above want, and was content with competency. His father supported him during his travels. When he was appointed Latin secretary, his sallary amounted to 200 l. per ann. and tho' he was of the victorious party, yet he was far from sharing the spoils of his country. On the contrary, as we learn from his Second Defence, he sustained great losses during the civil war, and was not at all favoured in the imposition of taxes, but sometimes paid beyond his due proportion; and upon a turn of affairs, he was not only deprived of his place, but also lost 2000 l. which he had for security, put into the Excise office.

In the fire of London, his house in Bread-street was burnt, before which accident foreigners have gone out of devotion, says Wood, to see the house and chamber where he was born. Some time before he died, he sold the greatest part of his library, as his heirs were not qualified to make a proper use of it, and as he thought he could dispose of it to greater advantage, than they could after his death. He died (says Dr. Newton) by one means or other worth 1500 l. besides his houshold goods, which was no incompetent subsistence for him, who was as great a philosopher as a poet.

Milton seems not to have been very happy in his marriages. His first wife offended him by her elopement; the second, whose love, sweetness, and delicacy he celebrates, lived not a twelvemonth with him; and his third was said to be a woman of a most violent spirit, and a severe step-mother to his children.

'She died, says Dr. Newton, very old, about twenty years ago, at Nantwich in Cheshire, and from the accounts of those who had seen her, I have learned that she confirmed several things related before; and particularly that her husband used to compose his poetry chiefly in the winter, and on his waking on a morning would make her write down sometimes twenty or thirty verses: Being asked whether he did not often read Homer and Virgil, she understood it as an imputation upon him for stealing from these authors, and answered with eagerness, that he stole from no body but the muse that inspired him; and being asked by a lady present who the muse was, she answered, it was God's grace and holy spirit, that visited him nightly. She was likewise asked, whom he approved most of our English poets, and answered, Spenser, Shakespear, and Cowley; and being asked what he thought of Dryden, she said Dryden used sometimes to visit him, but he thought him no poet, but a good rhimist.'

The reader will be pleased to observe, that this censure of Milton's was before Dryden had made any great appearance in poetry, or composed those immortal works of genius, which have raised eternal monuments to him, and carried his name to every country where poetry and taste are known. Some have thought that Dryden's genius was even superior to Milton's: That the latter chiefly shines in but one kind of poetry; his thoughts are sublime, and his language noble; but in what kind of writing has not Dryden been distinguished? He is in every thing excellent, says Congreve, and he has attempted nothing in which he has not so succeeded as to be entitled to the first reputation from it.

It is not to be supposed, that Milton was governed by so mean a principle as envy, in his thus censuring Dryden. It is more natural to imagine, that as he was himself no friend to rhime, and finding Dryden in his early age peculiarly happy in the faculty of rhiming, without having thrown out any thoughts, which were in themselves distinguishedly great, Milton might, without the imputation of ill nature, characterise Dryden, as we have already seen.

These are the most material incidents in the life of this great man, who if he had less honour during the latter part of his life than he deserved, it was owing to the unfavourable circumstances under which he laboured. It is always unpleasing to a good man to find that they who have been distinguished for their parts, have not been equally so for their moral qualities; and in this case we may venture to assert, that Milton was good as well as great; and that if he was mistaken in his political principles, he was honestly mistaken, for he never deviated from his first resolution; no temptations could excite him to temporise, or to barter his honour for advantage; nor did he ever once presume to partake of the spoils of his ruined country. Such qualities as these are great in themselves, and whoever possesses them, has an unexceptionable claim to rank with the good.

We might have entered more minutely into the merit of Milton's poems, particularly the great work of Paradise Lost; but we should reckon it arrogant as well as superfluous in us, to criticise on a work whose beauties have been displayed by the hand of Mr. Addison. That critic has illustrated the most remarkable passages in Paradise Lost; such as are distinguished by their sublimity; and elevation; such whose excellence is propriety; others raised by the nobleness of the language; and those that are remarkable for energy and strong reasoning.

A later critic, the ingenious author of the Rambler, has animadverted upon Milton's versification with great judgment; and has discovered in some measure that happy art, by which Milton has conducted so great a design, with such astonishing success.

From these two writers may be drawn all the necessary assistances for reading the Paradise Lost with taste and discernment; and as their works are in almost in every body's hands, it would be needless to give any abstract of them here.

Footnotes:

1. Philips's Life of Milton, p. 4. Preface prefixed to the English Translation of his Letters of State.

2. Birch's Critical Account of Milton's Life and Writings.

3. Life of Milton, p. 40.

4. Gentleman's Magazine.

5. Fasti Oxon. col. 275.

6. Fasti Oxon. p. 266. Ed. 1721.

Mrs. Katherine Philips

The celebrated Orinda, was daughter of John Fowles of Bucklersbury, a merchant in London. She was born in the parish of St. Mary Wool Church, 1631. Mr. Aubrey tells us, (in a MS. of his in Mr. Ashmole's study, No. 18. Vol. 23.) that she had the early part of her education from her cousin Mrs. Blacker. At eight years old she was removed to a school at Hackney, and soon made great improvements under the care of Mrs. Salmon; so great that whoever reads the account that Mr. Aubrey gives of her at that time of her life, will consider her succeeding progress to be no more than what might be naturally expected from such indications of genius. He tells us, 'that she was very apt to learn, and made verses when she was at school; that she devoted herself to religious duties when she was very young; that she would then pray by herself an hour together; that she had read the bible through before she was full five years old; that she could say, by heart, many chapters and passages of scripture; was a frequent hearer of sermons, which she would bring away entire in her memory.'

The above is extracted from Mr. Ballard's account of the Ladies of Great Britain, who have been celebrated for their writings; and serves to shew the early piety of this amiable lady, who lived to be distinguished for her ripened understanding.—She became afterwards a perfect mistress of the French tongue, and learned the Italian under the tuition of her ingenious and worthy friend Sir Charles Cotterel. She was instructed in the Presbyterian principles, which it appears by her writings, she deserted, as soon as her reason was strong enough to exert itself in the examination of religious points. She warmly embraced the royal interest, and upon many occasions was a strenuous advocate for the authority of the established church.

She was married to James Philips of the Priory of Cardigan, Esq; about the year 1647. By this gentleman she had one son, who died in his infancy, and one daughter, married to a gentleman of Pembrokeshire. She proved an excellent wife, not only in the conjugal duties, and tender offices of love, but was highly serviceable to her husband in affairs, in which few wives are thought capable of being useful; for his fortune being much encumbered, she exerted her interest with Sir Charles Cotterel, and other persons of distinction, who admired her understanding (for she had few graces of person) in her husband's favour, who soon extricated him from the difficulties under which he laboured. It no where appears that the husband of Mrs. Philips was a man of any abilities, and if he met with respect in the world, it was probably reflected from his wife. This lady had too much piety and good sense to suffer her superior understanding to make her insolent; on the other hand, she always speaks of her husband with the utmost respect, under the name of Antenor. In a letter to Sir Charles Cotterel, after having mentioned her husband in the most respectful terms, and of his willingness to forward her journey to London, in order to settle his perplexed affairs, she adds

"And I hope God will enable me to answer his expectations, by making me an instrument of doing some handsome service, which is the only ambition I have in the world, and which I would purchase with the hazard of my life. I am extreamly obliged to my lady Cork for remembering me with so much indulgence; for her great desire to be troubled with my company; but above all for her readiness to assist my endeavours for Antenor, which is the most generous kindness can be done me."

As this lady was born with a genius for poetry, so she began early in life to improve it, and composed many poems on various occasions for her amusement, in her recess at Cardigan, and retirement elsewhere. These being dispersed among her friends and acquaintance, were by an unknown hand collected together, and published in 8vo. 1663, without her knowledge or consent. This accident is said to have proved so oppressive to our poetess, as to throw her into a fit of illness, and she pours out her complaints in a letter to Sir Charles Cotterel, in which she laments, in the most affecting manner, the misfortune and the injuries which had been done to her by this surreptitious edition of her Poems.

That Mrs. Philips might be displeased that her Poems were published without her consent, is extremely probable, as by these means they might appear without many graces, and ornaments which they otherwise would have possessed; but that it threw her into a fit of illness, no body who reads the human heart can believe. Surreptitious editions are a sort of compliment to the merit of an author; and we are not to suppose Mrs. Philips so much a saint, as to be stript of all vanity, or that natural delight, which arises from the good opinion of others, however aukwardly it may be discovered; and we may venture to affirm, that Mrs. Philips's illness proceeded from some other cause, than what is here assigned.

The reputation of her abilities procured her the esteem of many persons of distinction and fashion, and upon her going into Ireland with the viscountess of Duncannon, to transact her husband's affairs there, her great merit soon made her known to those illustrious peers, Ormond, Orrery, and Roscommon, and many other persons of the first fashion, who shewed her singular marks of their esteem. While Mrs. Philips remained in that kingdom, at the pressing importunity of the abovementioned noblemen, but particularly lord Roscommon, she translated, from the French of Corneille, the tragedy of Pompey, which was brought upon the Irish stage somewhat against her inclination; however it was several times acted in the new theatre there, with very great applause in the years 1663 and 1664, in which last year it was made public. It was afterwards acted with equal applause at the Duke of York's theatre, 1678. This play is dedicated to the Countess of Cork. Lord Roscommon wrote the Prologue, wherein he thus compliments the ladies and the translator.

> But you bright nymphs, give Cæsar leave to woo,
> The greatest wonder of the world, but you;
> And hear a muse, who has that hero taught
> To speak as gen'rously, as e'er he fought;
> Whose eloquence from such a theme deters
> All tongues but English, and all pens but hers.
> By the just fates your sex is doubly blest,
> You conquer'd Cæsar, and you praise him best.

She also translated from the French of Corneille, a Tragedy called Horace; Sir John Denham added a fifth Act to this Play, which was acted at Court by Persons of Quality. The Duke of Monmouth spoke the Prologue, in which are these lines.

> So soft that to our shame we understand
> They could not fall but from a lady's hand.
> Thus while a woman Horace did translate,
> Horace did rise above the name of fate.

While Mrs. Philips was in Ireland, she was happy in carrying on her former intimacy with the famous Jeremy Taylor, the bishop of Down and Connor, who had some time before done her much honour by writing, and publishing a Discourse on the Nature, Offices, and Measures of Friendship, with Rules for conducting it, in a letter addressed to her. It is probable that this prelate's acquaintance with so accomplished a lady as Mrs. Philips, might be one reason of his entertaining so high an opinion of the fair sex in general; it is certain he was a great admirer of them, by which the good sense, as well as piety, of that great man is demonstrated; for whoever has studied life, examined the various motives of human actions, compared characters, and, in a word, scrutinized the heart, will find that more real virtue, more genuine and unaffected goodness exist amongst the female sex, than the other, and were their minds cultivated with equal care, and did they move in the bustle of life, they would not fall short of the men in the acute excellences; but the softness of their natures exempts them from action, and the blushes of beauty are not to be effaced by the rough storms of adversity: that man is happy who enjoys in the conjugal state, the endearments of love and innocence, and if his wife is less acquainted with the world than he, she makes a large amends, by the artless blandishments of a delicate affection.

We are persuaded our fair readers will not be displeased if we insert a paragraph from the discourse already mentioned by this worthy churchman; it appearing to be so sincere a tribute to their merit. 'But by the way, madam, you may see how I differ from the majority of those cynics, who would not admit your sex into the community of a noble friendship. I believe some wives have been the best friends in the world; and few stories can outdo the nobleness and piety of that lady, that sucked the poisonous purulent matter from the wounds of the brave Prince in the holy land, when an assassin had pierced him with a venomed arrow: and if it be told that women cannot retain council, and therefore can be no brave friends, I can best confute them by the story of Porcia, who being fearful of the weakness of her sex, stabbed herself in the thigh to try how she could bear pain; and finding herself constant enough to that sufferance, gently chid her Brutus for not trusting her, since now she perceived, that no torment could wrest that secret from her, which she hoped might be entrusted to her. If there were no more things to be said for your satisfaction, I could have made it disputable, which have been more illustrious in their friendship, men or women. I cannot say that women are capable of all those excellencies by which men can oblige the world, and therefore a female friend, in some cases, is not so good a counsellor as a wise man, and cannot so well defend my honour, nor dispose of relief and assistances, if she be under the power of another; but a woman can love as passionately, and converse as pleasantly, and retain a secret as faithfully, and be useful in her proper ministries, and she can die for her friend, as well as the bravest Roman knight; a man is the best friend in trouble, but a woman may be equal to him in the days of joy: a woman can as well increase our comforts, but cannot so well lessen our sorrows, and therefore we do not carry women with us when we go to fight; but in peaceful cities and times, women are the beauties of society, and the prettinesses of friendship, and when we consider that few persons in the world have all those excellences by which friendship can be useful, and illustrious, we may as well allow women as men to be friends; since they have all that can be necessary and essential to friendships, and those cannot have all by which friendships can be accidentally improved.'

Thus far this learned prelate, whose testimony in favour of women is the more considerable, as he cannot be supposed to have been influenced by any particular passion, at least for Mrs. Philips, who was ordinary in her person and was besides a married lady. In the year 1663 Mrs. Philips quitted Ireland, and went to Cardigan, where she spent the remaining part of that, and the beginning of the next year, in a sort of melancholy retirement; as appears by her letters, occasioned, perhaps, by the bad success of her husband's affairs. Going to London, in order to relieve her oppressed spirits with the conversation of her friends there, she was seized by the smallpox, and died of it (in Fleet street,) to the great grief of her acquaintance, in the 32d year of her age, and was buried June 22, 1664, in the church of St. Bennet Sherehog[1], under a large monumental stone, where several of her ancestors were before buried. Mr. Aubrey in his manuscript abovementioned, observes, that her person was of a middle stature, pretty fat, and ruddy complexioned.

Soon after her death, her Poems and Translations were collected and published in a volume in folio, to which was added Monsieur Corneille's Pompey and Horace, Tragedies; with several other Translations out of French, London 1667, with her picture, a good busto, before them, standing on a pedestal, on which is inscribed Orinda; it was printed again at London 1678. In a collection of Letters published by Mr. Thomas Brown, in 1697, are printed four Letters from Mrs. Philips to the Honourable Berenice. Many years after her death, were published a volume of excellent Letters from Mrs. Philips to Sir Charles Cotterel with the ensuing title, Letters from Orinda to Polliarchus, 8vo. London 1705. Major Pack, in his Essay on Study, inserted in his Miscellanies, gives the following character of these Letters; 'The best Letters I have met with in our English tongue, are those of the celebrated Mrs. Philips to Sir Charles Cotterel; as they are directed all to the same person, so they run all in the same strain, and seem to have been employed in the service of a refined and generous friendship. In a word, they are such as a woman of spirit and virtue, should write to a courtier of honour, and true gallantry.' The memory of this ingenious lady has been honoured with many encomiums. Mr. Thomas Rowe in his epistle to Daphne, pays the following tribute to her fame.

> At last ('twas long indeed!) Orinda came,
> To ages yet to come an ever glorious name;
> To virtuous themes, her well tun'd lyre she strung;　}
> Of virtuous themes in easy numbers sung.　}
> Horace and Pompey in her line appear,　}

With all the worth that Rome did once revere:
Much to Corneille they owe, and much to her.
Her thoughts, her numbers, and her fire the same,
She soar'd as high, and equal'd all his fame.
Tho' France adores the bard, nor envies Greece
The costly buskins of her Sophocles.
More we expected, but untimely death,
Soon stopt her rising glories with her breath.

More testimonies might be produced in favour of Mrs. Philips, but as her works are generally known, and are an indelible testimony of her merit, we reckon it superfluous. Besides the poetical abilities of the amiable Orinda, she is said to have been of a generous, charitable disposition, and a friend to all in distress.

As few ladies ever lived more happy in her friends than our poetess, so those friends have done justice to her memory, and celebrated her, when dead, for those virtues they admired, when living. Mr. Dryden more than once mentions her with honour, and Mr Cowley has written an excellent Ode upon her death. As this Ode will better shew the high opinion once entertained of Mrs. Philips, than any thing we can say, after giving a specimen of her poetry, we shall conclude with this performance of Cowley's, which breathes friendship in every line, and speaks an honest mind: so true is the observation of Pope, upon the supposition that Cowley's works are falling into oblivion,

Lost is his epic, nay, pindaric art,
But still I love the language of his heart.

Mrs. Philips's poetry has not harmony of versification, or amorous tenderness to recommend it, but it has a force of thinking, which few poets of the other sex can exceed, and if it is without graces, it has yet a great deal of strength. As she has been celebrated for her friendship, we shall present the reader with an Ode upon that subject, addressed to her dearest Lucasia.

I.

Come my Lucasia, since we see
That miracles men's faith do move
By wonder, and by prodigy;
To the dull angry world lets prove
There's a religion in our love.

II.

For tho' we were designed t'agree,
That fate no liberty destroys,
But our election is as free
As angels, who with greedy choice
Are yet determined to their joys.

III.

Our hearts are doubled by the loss,
Here mixture is addition grown;
We both diffuse, and both engross:
And we whose minds are so much one,
Never, yet ever are alone.

IV.

We court our own captivity,
Than thrones more great and innocent:
'Twere banishment to be set free,
Since we wear fetters whose intent
Not bondage is, but ornament.

V.

Divided joys are tedious found,
And griefs united easier grow:
We are ourselves, but by rebound,
And all our titles shuffled so,
Both princes, and both subjects too.

VI.

Our hearts are mutual victims laid,
While they (such power in friendship lies)
Are altars, priests, and offerings made:
And each heart which thus kindly dies,
Grows deathless by the sacrifice.

On the Death of Mrs. PHILIPS.

I.

Cruel disease! ah, could it not suffice,
Thy old and constant spite to exercise
Against the gentlest and the fairest sex,
Which still thy depredations most do vex?
Where still thy malice, most of all
(Thy malice or thy lust) does on the fairest fall,
And in them most assault the fairest place,
The throne of empress beauty, ev'n the face.
There was enough of that here to assuage,
(One would have thought) either thy lust or rage;
Was't not enough, when thou, profane disease,
Didst on this glorious temple seize:
Was't not enough, like a wild zealot, there,
All the rich outward ornaments to tear,
Deface the innocent pride of beauteous images?
Was't not enough thus rudely to defile,
But thou must quite destroy the goodly pile?
And thy unbounded sacrilege commit
On th'inward holiest holy of her wit?
Cruel disease! there thou mistook'st thy power;
No mine of death can that devour,
On her embalmed name it will abide
An everlasting pyramide,
As high as heav'n the top, as earth, the basis wide.

II.

All ages past record, all countries now,
In various kinds such equal beauties show,
That ev'n judge Paris would not know
On whom the golden apple to bestow,
Though goddesses to his sentence did submit,
Women and lovers would appeal from it:
Nor durst he say, of all the female race,
This is the sovereign face.
And some (tho' these be of a kind that's rare,
That's much, oh! much less frequent than the fair)
So equally renown'd for virtue are,
That is the mother of the gods might pose,

When the best woman for her guide she chose.
But if Apollo should design
A woman Laureat to make,
Without dispute he would Orinda take,
Though Sappho and the famous nine
Stood by, and did repine.
To be a Princess or a Queen
Is great; but 'tis a greatness always seen;
The world did never but two women know,
Who, one by fraud, th'other by wit did rise
To the two tops of spiritual dignities,
One female pope of old, one female poet now.

III.

Of female poets, who had names of old,
Nothing is shown, but only told,
And all we hear of them perhaps may be
Male-flatt'ry only, and male-poetry.
Few minutes did their beauties light'ning waste,
The thunder of their voice did longer last,
But that too soon was past.
The certain proofs of our Orinda's wit,
In her own lasting characters are writ,
And they will long my praise of them survive,
Though long perhaps too that may live,
The trade of glory manag'd by the pen
Though great it be, and every where is found.
Does bring in but small profit to us men;
'Tis by the number of the sharers drown'd.
Orinda on the female coasts of fame,
Ingrosses all the goods of a poetic name.
She does no partner with her see,
Does all the business there alone, which we
Are forc'd to carry on by a whole company.

IV.

But wit's like a luxuriant vine;
Unless to virtue's prop it join,
Firm and erect towards Heav'n bound;
Tho' it with beauteous leaves and pleasant fruit be crown'd,
It lyes deform'd, and rotting on the ground.

Now shame and blushes on us all,
Who our own sex superior call!
Orinda does our boasting sex out do,
Not in wit only, but in virtue too.
She does above our best examples rise,
In hate of vice, and scorn of vanities.
Never did spirit of the manly make,
And dipp'd all o'er in learning's sacred lake,
A temper more invulnerable take.
No violent passion could an entrance find,
Into the tender goodness of her mind;
Through walls of stone those furious bullets may
Force their impetuous way,
When her soft breast they hit, damped and dead they lay.

V.

The fame of friendship which so long had told
Of three or four illustrious names of old,
'Till hoarse and weary with the tale she grew,
Rejoices now t'have got a new,
A new, and more surprizing story,
Of fair Leucasia's and Orinda's glory.
As when a prudent man does once perceive
That in some foreign country he must live,
The language and the manners he does strive
To understand and practise here,
That he may come no stranger there;
So well Orinda did her self prepare,
In this much different clime for her remove,
To the glad world of poetry and love.

Footnote:

1. Ballard's Memoirs.

Margaret, Duchess of Newcastle

The second wife of William Cavendish, duke of Newcastle, was born at St. John's near Colchester in Essex, about the latter end of the reign of King James I. and was the youngest daughter of Sir Charles Lucas, a gentleman of great spirit and fortune, who died when she was very young. The duchess herself in a book intitled Nature's Pictures, drawn by Fancy's pencil to the life, has celebrated both the exquisite beauty of her person, and the rare endowments of her mind. This lady's mother was remarkably assiduous in the education of her children, and bestowed upon this, all the instructions necessary for forming the minds of young ladies, and introducing them into life with advantage. She found her trouble in cultivating this daughter's mind not in vain, for she discovered early an inclination to learning, and spent so much of her time in study and writing, that some of her Biographers have lamented her not being acquainted with the learned languages, which would have extended her knowledge, corrected the exuberances of genius, and have been of infinite service to her, in her numerous compositions.

In the year 1643 she obtained leave of her mother to go to Oxford, where the court then resided, and was made one of the Maids of Honour to Henrietta Maria, the Royal Consort of King Charles I. and when the Queen was forced to leave the arms of her Husband, and fly into France, by the violence of the prevailing power, this lady attended her there. At Paris she met with the marquis of Newcastle, whose loyalty had likewise produced his exile; who, admiring her person and genius, married her in the year 1645. The marquis had before heard of this lady, for he was a patron and friend of her gallant brother, lord Lucas, who commanded under him in the civil wars. He took occasion one day to ask his lordship what he could do for him, as he had his interest much at heart? to which he answered, that he was not sollicitous about his own affairs, for he knew the worst could be but suffering either death, or exile in the Royal cause, but his chief sollicitude was for his sister, on whom he could bestow no fortune, and whose beauty exposed her to danger: he represented her amiable qualities, and raised the marquis's curiosity to see her, and from that circumstance arose the marquis's affection to this lady. From Paris they went to Rotterdam, where they resided six months: from thence they returned to Antwerp, where they settled, and continued during the time of their exile, as it was the most quiet place, and where they could in the greatest peace enjoy their ruined fortune. She proved a most agreeable companion to the marquis, during the gloomy period of exile, and enlivened their recess, both by her writing and conversation, as appears by the many compliments and addresses he made her on that occasion.

The lady undertook a voyage into England, in order to obtain some of the marquis's rents, to supply their pressing necessities, and pay the debts they had been there obliged to contract; and accordingly went with her brother to Goldsmith's Hall, where, it seems, the committee of sequestration sat, but could not obtain the smallest sum out of the marquis's vast inheritance, which, amounted to 20,000 l. per annum; and had it not been for the generosity and tenderness of Sir Charles Cavendish (who greatly reduced his own fortune, to support his brother in distress) they must have been exposed to extreme poverty.

Having raised a considerable sum, by the generosity of her own, and the marquis's, relations, she returned to Antwerp, where she continued with her lord, till the restoration of Charles II, upon which, the marquis, after six years banishment, made immediate preparation for his return to his native country, leaving his lady behind him to dispatch his affairs there, who, having conducted them to his lordship's satisfaction, she soon followed her consort into England. Being now restored to the sunshine of prosperity, she dedicated her time to writing poems, philosophical discourses, orations and plays. She was of a generous turn of mind, and kept a great many young ladies about her person, who occasionally wrote what she dictated. Some of them slept in a room, contiguous to that in which her Grace lay, and were ready, at the call of her bell, to rise any hour of the night, to write down her conceptions, lest they should escape her memory.

The young ladies, no doubt, often dreaded her Grace's conceptions, which were frequent, but all of the poetical or philosophical kind, for though she was very beautiful, she died without issue: she is said to have been very reserved and peevish, perhaps owing to the circumstance just mentioned, of having never been honoured with the name of mother.

Mr. Jacob says, that she was the most voluminous writer of all the female poets; that she had a great deal of wit, and a more than ordinary propensity to dramatic poetry; and Mr. Langbaine tells us, that all the language and plots of her plays were her own, which, says he, is a commendation preferable to fame built on other people's foundation, and will very well atone for some faults in her numerous productions. As the Duchess is said to be negligent, in regard to chronology in her historical writings, so others have been equally remiss, in this respect, with regard to her Grace, for, among the many authors who have taken notice of her, not one has mentioned the year in which she died, and even her monumental inscription, where one might reasonably expect it, is silent, both in respect to her age, and the time of her death. But Mr. Fulman, in the 15th volume of his MS. collections in the Corpus Christi College Archives, observes, that she died in London Anno 1673, and was buried at Westminster, January 7, 1673-4, where an elegant monument is erected to her memory, of which, take the following account given by Dr. Crul in the Antiquities of that Church. 'Against the skreen of the chapel of St. Michael, is a most noble spacious tomb of white marble, adorned with two pillars of black marble, with entablatures of the Corinthian order, embellished with arms, and most curious trophy works; on the pedestal lye two images, in full proportion, of white marble in a cumbent posture, in their robes, representing William Cavendish, duke of Newcastle, and Margaret his duchess, his second and last wife, being the daughter of Sir Charles, and the sister of lord Lucas of Colchester; who as she had deservedly acquired the reputation of a lady of uncommon wit, learning, and liberality; so the duke her husband had rendered himself famous for his loyalty, and constant fidelity to the royal family, during the civil wars in this kingdom and in Scotland. The duke having caused this stately monument to be erected here to the memory of his lady, died soon after in the year 1676, aged 84, and was interred here.'

The Epitaph for the Duchess.

"Here lies the loyal Duke of Newcastle and his Duchess, his second wife, by whom he had no issue. Her name was Margaret Lucas, youngest sister to the Lord Lucas of Colchester, a noble family, for all the brothers were valiant, and all the sisters virtuous. This Duchess was a wise, witty, and learned Lady, which her many books do well testify: She was a most virtuous, and loving, and careful wife, and was with her Lord all the time of his banishment and miseries; and when they came home never parted with him in his solitary retirements."

The following is a catalogue of her works, in which we have taken pains to be as accurate as possible, in order to do justice to the poetical character of this lady.

1.   The World's Olio.

2.   Nature's Picture drawn by Fancy's Pencil to the Life.

> In this volume there are several feigned stories of natural descriptions, as comical, tragical, and tragi-comical, poetical, romancical, philosophical, and historical, both in prose and verse, some all verse, some all prose, some mixt; partly prose, and partly verse; also some morals, and some dialogues, Lond. 1656. folio.

3. Orations of different sorts, on different occasions, Lond. 1662.

4. Philosophical and Physical Opinions, 1633, folio.

5. Observations on Experimental Philosophy; to which is added, the Description of a New World. Mr. James Bristow began to translate some of these Philosophical Discourses into Latin.

6. Philosophical Letters; or modest Reflections on some Opinions in Natural Philosophy, maintained by several famous and learned authors of this age, expressed by way of letters, Lond. 1664, fol.

7. Poems and Fancies, Lond. 1664, folio.

8. Sociable Letters, 1664, folio.

9. The Life of the Duke of Newcastle her husband, which was translated into Latin, and is thought to be the best performance of this lady.

10. Observations of the Duke's, with Remarks of her own,

In the Library of the late Mr. Thomas Richardson was the Duchess of Newcastle's poems, 2 Vol. fol. MS. and in the library of the late bishop Willis was another MS. of her poems in folio.

Her Dramatic Works are,

1. Apocryphal Ladies, a Comedy; it is not divided into acts.

2. Bell in Campo, a Tragedy, in two parts.

3. Blazing World, a Comedy.

4. Bridals, a Comedy.

5. Comical Hash, a Comedy.

6. Convent of Pleasure, a Comedy.

7. Female Academy, a Comedy.

8. Lady Contemplation, a Comedy, in two parts.

9. Love's Adventure, in two parts, a Comedy.

10. Matrimonial Troubles, in two parts; the second being a Tragedy, or as the authoress stiles it, a Tragi-comedy.

11. Nature's three Daughters, Beauty, Love, and Wit, a Comedy, in two parts.

12. Presence, a Comedy.

13. Public Wooing, a Comedy, in which the Duke wrote several of the suitors speeches.

14. Religious, a Tragi-Comedy.

15. Several Wits, a Comedy.

16. Sociable Companions, or the Female Wits, a Comedy.

17. Unnatural Tragedy. Act II. Scene III. the Duchess inveighs against Mr. Camden's Britannia.

18. Wit's Cabal, a Comedy, in two parts.

19. Youth's Glory, and Death's Banquet, a Tragedy in two parts.

Mr. Langbaine has preserved part of the general prologue to her plays, which we shall insert as a specimen of her versification:

> But noble readers, do not think my plays
> Are such as have been writ in former days;
> As Johnson, Shakespear, Beaumont, Fletcher writ,
> Mine want their learning, reading, language, wit.
> The Latin phrases, I could never tell,
> But Johnson could, which made him write so well.
> Greek, Latin poets, I could never read,
> Nor their historians, but our English Speed:
> I could not steal their wit, nor plots out-take;
> All my plays plots, my own poor brain did make.
> From Plutarch's story, I ne'er took a plot,
> Nor from romances, nor from Don Quixote.

William Cavendish

Baron Ogle, viscount Mansfield, earl, marquis, and duke of Newcastle, justly reckoned one of the most finished gentlemen, as well as the most distinguished patriot, general, and statesman of his age. He was son of Sir Charles Cavendish, youngest son of Sir William Cavendish, and younger brother of the first earl of Devonshire, by Katherine daughter of Cuthbert lord Ogle[1].

He was born in the year 1592, and discovered in his infancy a promptness of genius, and a love of literature. His father took care to have him instructed by the best masters in every science. He no sooner appeared at the court of King James I. than the reputation of his abilities drew the attention of that monarch upon him, who made him a knight of the Bath 1610, at the creation of Henry Prince of Wales[2].

In 1617 his father died, who left him a great estate; and having interest at court, he was by letters patent, dated Nov. 3, 1620, raised to the dignity of a peer of the realm, by the stile and title of baron Ogle, and viscount Mansfield; and having no less credit with King Charles I. than he had with his father, in the third year of the reign of that prince, he was advanced to the higher title of earl of Newcastle upon Tyne, and at the same time he was created baron Cavendish of Balsovor. Our author's attendance upon court, tho' it procured him honour, yet introduced him very early into difficulties; and it appears by Strafford's letters, that he did not stand well with the favourite duke of Buckingham, who was jealous of his growing interest, and was too penetrating not to discover, that the quickness of his lordship's parts would soon suggest some methods of rising, independent of the favourite, and perhaps shaking his influence. "But these difficulties, says Clarendon, (for he was deeply plunged in debt) tho' they put him on the thoughts of retirement, never in the least prevented him from demonstrating his loyalty when the King's cause demanded it."

Notwithstanding the earl's interest was not high with the ministers, yet he found means so to gain and to preserve the affection of his Majesty, that in the year 1638, when it was thought necessary to take the Prince of Wales out of the hands of a woman, his Majesty appointed the earl his governor, and by entrusting to his tuition the heir apparent of his kingdoms, demonstrated the highest confidence in his abilities and honour[3].

In the spring of the year 1639, the troubles of Scotland breaking out, induced the King to assemble an army in the North, soon after which he went to put himself at the head of it, and in his way was splendidly entertained by the earl at his seat at Welbeck, as he had been some years before when he went into Scotland to be crowned, which in itself, tho' a trivial circumstance, yet such was the magnificence of this noble peer, that both these entertainments found a place in general histories, and are computed by the duchess of Newcastle, who wrote the life of her lord, to have amounted to upwards of ten thousand pounds. He invited all the neighbouring gentry to pay their compliments to his Majesty, and partake of the feast, and Ben Johnson was employed in fitting such scenes and speeches as he could best devise; and Clarendon after mentioning the sumptuousness of those entertainments, observes, that they had a tendency to corrupt the people, and inspire a wantonness, which never fails to prove detrimental to morals.

As such an expedition as the King's against the Scots required immense sums, and the King's treasury being very empty, his lordship contributed ten thousand pounds, and raised a troop of horse, consisting of about 200 knights and gentlemen, who served at their own charge, and was honoured with the title of the Prince's troop[4].

Tho' these instances of loyalty advanced him in the esteem of the King, yet they rather heightened than diminished the resentment of the ministers, of which the earl of Holland having given a stronger instance, than his lordship's patience could bear, he took notice of it in such a way, as contributed equally to sink his rival's reputation, and raise his own; and as there is something curious in the particular manner in which the earl of Holland's character suffered in this quarrel, we shall upon the authority of the duchess of Newcastle present it to the reader.

The troop which the earl of Newcastle raised was stiled the Prince's, but his lordship commanded it as captain. When the army drew near Berwick, he sent Sir William Carnaby to the earl of Holland, then general of the horse, to know where his troop should march; his answer was, next after the troops of the general officers. The earl of Newcastle sent again to represent, that having the honour to march with the Prince's colours, he thought it not fit to march under any of the officers of the field; upon which the general of the horse repeated his orders, and the earl of Newcastle ordered the Prince's colours to be taken off the staff, and marched without any. When the service was over, his lordship sent Mr. Francis Palmer, with a challenge to the earl of Holland, who consented to a place, and hour of meeting; but when the earl of Newcastle came thither, he found not his antagonist, but his second. The business had been disclosed to the King, by whose authority (says Clarendon) the matter was composed; but before that time, the earl of Holland was never suspected to want courage; and indeed he was rather a cunning, penetrating, than a brave honest man, and was remarkably selfish in his temper.

The earl of Newcastle however found himself hard pressed by the ministerial faction, and being unwilling to give his Majesty any trouble about himself, he was generous enough to resign his place as governor to the Prince, and the marquis of Hertford was appointed in his room.

His lordship having no more business at court, and being unwilling to expose himself further to the machinations of his enemies, thought proper to retire to the country, where he remained quiet till he received his Majesty's orders to revisit Hull: Tho' this order came at twelve o'clock at night, yet such was his unshaken loyalty and affection, that he went directly, and tho' forty miles distant, he entered the place with only three or four servants early the next morning. He offered to his Majesty, says Clarendon, to have secured for him that important fortress, and all the magazines that were in it; but instead of receiving such a command, he had instructions sent him to obey the orders of the Parliament, who suspecting his principles not to be favourable to the schemes of opposition then engaged in, called him to attend the service of the house; and some disaffected members formed a design to have attacked him, but his character being unexceptionable, their scheme proved abortive, and he had leave to retire again into the country. This he willingly did, as he saw the affairs of state hastening to confusion and his country ready to be steeped in blood, and sacrificed to the fury of party. But when the opposition rose high, and it would have been cowardice to have remained unactive, he embraced the royal cause, accepted a commission for raising men, to take care of the town of Newcastle, and the four adjoining counties, in which he was so expeditious and successful, that his Majesty constituted him general of all the forces raised North of Trent; and likewise general and commander in chief of such as might be raised in the counties of Lincoln, Nottingham, Chester, Leicester, Rutland, Cambridge, Huntingdon, Norfolk, Suffolk, and Essex, with power to confer the honour of knighthood, coin money, print, and set forth such declarations as should seem to him expedient: of all which extensive powers, tho freely conferred, and without reserve, his lordship made a very sparing use; but with respect to the more material point of raising men, his lordship prosecuted it with such diligence, that in three months he had an army of eight thousand horse, foot, and dragoons, with which he marched directly into Yorkshire; and his forces having defeated the enemy at Pierce Bridge, his lordship advanced to York, where Sir Thomas Glenham, the governor, presented him with the keys, and the earl of Cumberland and many of the nobility resorted thither to compliment, and assist his lordship[5].

In the course of this civil war, we find the earl of Newcastle very successful in his master's service; he more than once defeated Sir Thomas Fairfax the general of the Parliament, and won several important forts and battles; for which his Majesty in gratitude for his services, by letters patent, dated the 27th of Oct. 1643, advanced him to the dignity of marquiss of Newcastle; and in the preamble of his patent, all his services (says Dugdale) are mentioned with suitable encomiums.

In the year 1644, after Prince Rupert had been successful in raising the siege of York, and flushed with the prosperity of his arms, against the consent of the marquis, he risked the battle of Marston Moor, in which the marquis's infantry were cut to pieces. Seeing the King's affairs in these counties totally undone, he made the best of his way to Scarborough, and from thence with a few of the principal officers of his army took shipping for Hamburgh, and left his estates, which were valued at upwards of twenty thousand pounds per ann. to be plundered by the Parliament's forces. After staying six months at Hamburgh, he went by sea to Amsterdam, and from thence made a journey to Paris, where he continued for some time, and where, notwithstanding the vast estate he had when the civil war broke out, his circumstances were now so bad, that himself and his young wife, were reduced to pawn their cloaths for sustenance[6]. He removed afterwards to Antwerp, that he might be nearer his own country; and there, tho' under very great difficulties, he resided for several years, while the Parliament in the mean time levied vast sums upon his estate, insomuch that the computation of what he lost by the disorders of those times, tho' none of the particulars can be disproved, amount to an incredible sum; but notwithstanding all these severities of fortune, he never lost his spirit, and was often heard to say, that if he was not much mistaken, the clouds of adversity which then hung over his country, would be dispersed at last by the King's restoration; that rebellion would entangle itself in its own toils, and after an interval of havock and confusion, order would return once more by the restoration of an exiled Prince. Notwithstanding the hardships of an eighteen years banishment, in which he experienced variety of wretchedness, he retained his vigour to the last. He was honoured by persons of the highest distinction abroad, and Don John of Austria and several princes of Germany visited him[7]. But what comforted him most, was the company frequently of his young King, who in the midst of his sufferings bestowed upon him the most noble Order of the Garter. The gloomy period at last came to an end, and the marquis returned to his country with his sovereign; and by letters patent dated the 16th of March 1664, he was advanced to the dignity of earl of Ogle, and duke of Newcastle. He spent the evening of his days in a country retirement, and indulged himself in those studies, with which he was most affected.

This noble person from his earliest youth was celebrated for his love of the muses, and was the great patron of the poets, in the reign of King Charles I. This propension has drawn on him, tho' very unjustly, the censure of some grave men. Lord Clarendon mentions it, with decency; but Sir Philip Warwick, in his history of the rebellion, loses all patience, and thinks it sufficient to ruin this great general's character, that he appointed Sir William Davenant, a poet, his lieutenant general of the ordnance, insinuating that it was impossible a man could have a turn for poetry, and a capacity for any thing else at the same time; in which observation, Sir Philip has given a convincing proof of his ignorance of poetry, and want of taste. The example of the glorious Sidney is sufficient to confute this historian; and did not Mr. Chillingworth combat with great success, though in other branches of literature, against the Papal church, by the dint of reason and argument, and at the same time served as engineer in the royal army with great ability[8]? The truth is, this worthy nobleman having himself a taste for the liberal arts, was always pleased to have men of genius about him, and had the pleasure to rescue necessitous merit from obscurity. Ben Johnson was one of his favourites, and he addressed to him some of his verses, which may be seen in his works.

In the busy scenes of life it does not appear that this nobleman suffered his thoughts to stray so far from his employment, as to turn author; but in his exile, resuming his old taste of breaking and managing horses, (than which there cannot be a more manly exercise) he thought fit to publish his sentiments upon a subject of which he was perfectly master. The title is, The New Method for managing Horses, with cuts, Antwerp 1658. This book was first written in English, and afterwards translated into French, by his lordship's directions.

This great man died in the possession of the highest honours and fairest reputation the 25th of December 1676, in the 84th year of his age. His grace was twice married, but had issue only by his first lady. His titles descended to his son, Henry earl of Ogle, who was the last heir male of his family, and died 1691, with whom the title of Newcastle in the line of Cavendish became extinct.

In his exile he wrote two comedies, viz.

The Country Captain, a Comedy, printed at Antwerp 1649, afterwards presented by his Majesty's servants at Black-Fryars, and very much commended by Mr. Leigh.

Variety, a Comedy, presented by his Majesty's Servants at Black-Fryars, and first printed in 1649, and generally bound with the Country Captain; it was also highly commended in a copy of verses by Mr. Alexander Brome.

He likewise has written

The Humourous Lovers, a Comedy, acted by his royal highness's servants, Lond. 1677, 4to. This was received with great applause, and esteemed one of the best plays of that time.

The Triumphant Widow; or, the Medley of Humours, a Comedy, acted by his royal highness's servants, Lond. 1677, 4to. which pleased Mr. Shadwell so well, that he transcribed a part of it into his Bury Fair, one of the most taking plays of that poet.

Shadwell says of his grace, that he was the greatest master of wit, the most exact observer of mankind, and the most accurate judge of humour, that ever he knew.

Footnotes:

1. Dugdale's Baron. vol. 2.

2. Dugdale vol. 2. p. 421.

3. Dugdale, ubi supra.

4. Rushworth's collection, vol. 1. p. 929.

5. Clarendon, p. 283.

6. Life of the D. of Newcastle, p. 56.

7. Ashmole's order of the garter.

8. See his life by Mr. des Maizeaux.

Sir John Birkenhead

Winstanley, in his short account of this gentleman, says, that they who are ignorant of his works, must plead ignorance of all wit and learning; but the truth is, though he made some figure in his time, yet it was not so considerable as to transmit his name with any lustre to posterity, and Winstanley has been too peremptory, in secluding those from wit, who should be ignorant of the fame of Birkenhead. This observation, however, excited us to a search after some particulars concerning him; for Winstanley himself has given very few, and closes his life in his usual way, with only informing the readers that he lived in such a reign. The best account we could find of him, is in the Athenæ Oxon. of Wood. Our author was son of Randal Birkenhead of Northwich in Cheshire, Sadler, and was born there; he became a servitor of Oriel College, under the tuition of Humphrey Lloyd, afterwards lord bishop of Bangor. He continued in the college till he was made bachelor of arts, and then becoming Amanuensis to Dr. Laud, afterwards archbishop of Canterbury, who, taking a liking to him for his ingenuity, did, by his diploma make him master of arts, An. 1639, and by his letters commendatory thereupon, he was elected probationer fellow of All-Souls College, in the year following. After the rebellion broke out, and the King set up his court at Oxford, our author was appointed to write the Mercurii Aulici, which being very pleasing to the loyal party, his Majesty recommended him to the electors, that they would chuse him moral philosophy reader; which being accordingly done, he continued in that office, with little profit from it, till 1648, at which time he was not only turned out thence, but from his fellowship, by the Presbyterian visitors. Afterwards, in this destitute situation, Wood observes, that he retired to London, and made shift to live upon his wits; having some reputation in poetry, he was often applied to by young people in love, to write epistles for them, and songs, and sonnets on their mistresses: he was also employed in translating and writing other little things, so as to procure a tolerable livelihood.

Having, in this manner, supported the gloomy period of confusion, he was, at his Majesty's restoration, by virtue of his letters, sent to the university, created doctor of the civil law, and in 1661 he was elected a Burgess for Wilton, to serve in that Parliament which began at Westminster the 8th of May, the same year. In 1662, November 14, he received the honour of knighthood, and January 1663 he was constituted one of the masters of requests, in the room of Sir Richard Fanshaw, when he went ambassador into Spain, he being then also master of the faculties, and a member of the Royal Society. An anonymous writer tells us, that Sir John Berkenhead was a poor alehouse-keeper's son, and that he rose by lying, or buffooning at court, to be one of the masters of requests, and faculty office, and also got by gifts at court 3000 l. This is a poor reflexion upon him, and indeed rather raises, than detracts from his reputation, for a man certainly must have merit, who can rise without the advantage of fortune or birth, whereas these often procure a fool preferment, and make him eminent, who might otherwise have lived and died in obscurity. It is said of Birkenhead, that when an unmannerly Member of Parliament, in opposing him, took occasion to say, that he was surprized to hear an alehouse-keeper's son talk so confidently in the House, he coolly replied, I am an alehouse-keeper's son, I own it, and am not ashamed of it, but had the gentleman, who upbraided me with my birth, been thus descended, in all probability he would have been of the same profession himself; a reply at once, sensible and witty. Mr. Wood, however, seems to be of opinion, that he was too much given to bantering, and that if he had thrown less of the buffoon or mimic into his conversation, his wit would have been very agreeable. He is charged by Wood with a higher failing, which ought indeed rather to be construed one of the blackest crimes, that is, ingratitude to those who assisted him in distress, whom, says he, he afterwards slighted. This is a heavy charge, and, if true, not a little diminishes his reputation, but methinks some apology may even be made for his slighting those who assisted him in distress; we find they were such persons as could never challenge esteem, young men in love, for whom he wrote sonnets, and for whom he might have no friendship; it often happens, that men of parts are so unhappy as to be obliged to such people, with whom, were their situation otherwise, it would be beneath them to associate; and it is no wonder when prosperity returns, that they, in some measure, forget obligations they owed to those of a rank so much inferior: and something must be allowed to that pride, which a superior understanding naturally inspires.

Our author's works are

Mercurius Aulicus. Communicating the Intelligence, and the Affairs of the Court at Oxford to the rest of the Kingdom, the first of these was published on the 1st of January, 1642, and were carried on till about the end of 1645, after which time they were published but now and then. They were printed weekly in one sheet, and sometimes in more, in 4to, and contain, says Wood, a great deal of wit and buffoonery.

News from Pembroke and Montgomery, or Oxford Manchestered, &c. printed in 1648 in one sheet 4to. It is a feigned speech, as spoken by Philip, earl of Pembroke, in the Convocation House at Oxford, April 12, 1648, when he came to visit, and undo the University, as Edward, Earl of Manchester had done that of Cambridge, while he was Chancellor thereof. It is exceeding waggish, and much imitating his Lordship's way of speaking.

Paul's Church-yard; Libri Theologici, Politici, Historici, mundinis Paulinis (una cum Templo) prostant venales, &c. printed in three several sheets in 4to. Anno 1649. These Pamphlets contain feigned Titles of Books, and Acts of Parliaments, and several Questions, all reflecting on the Reformers, and Men in those times.

The Four Legg'd Quaker, a Ballad, to the Tune of the Dog and Elders Maid, London 1659, in three columns in one side of a sheet of paper.

A New Ballad of a famous German Prince, without date.

The Assembly Man, written 1647, London 1663, in three sheets in 4to. The copy of it was taken from the author by those that said they could not rob, because all was theirs; at length after it had slept several years, the author published it to avoid false copies; it is also printed in a Book entitled Wit and Loyalty Revived, in a Collection of some smart Satires in Verse and Prose, on the late times, London 1682, said to be written by Cowley, our Author, and the famous Butler; he hath also scattered Copies of Verses and Translations extant, to which are vocal Compositions, set by Henry Lawes, such as Anacreon's Ode, called The Lute.

An Anniversary on the Nuptial of John, Earl of Bridgwater. He has also wrote a Poem on his staying in London, after the Act of Banishment for Cavaliers, and another called the Jolt, made upon Cromwel's being thrown off the Coach-box of his own Coach, which he would drive through Hyde Park, drawn by six German Horses, sent him as a present by the Count of Oldenburgh, while his Secretary John Thurloe sat in the Coach, July 1654. Our author died within the Precincts of Whitehall, in the year 1679, and was buried in the Church-yard of St. Martin's in the Fields, leaving behind him a collection of Pamphlets, which came into the hands of his executors, Sir Richard Mason, and Sir Muddeford Bramston.

Roger Boyle, Earl of Orrery

Was younger brother of Richard earl of Burlington and Cork, and fifth son of Richard, stiled the great earl of Cork. He was born April 25, 1621, and independent of the advantage of his birth and titles, was certainly one of the ablest politicians, as well as most accomplished noblemen of his age. By the influence of his father with lord deputy Faulkland, he was raised to the dignity of baron Broghill, in the kingdom of Ireland in 1628, when only seven years old[1]. He received his education at the college of Dublin, where he studied with so much diligence as gave great hopes of his future atchievements, and the rapid progress he made in erudition, induced his father to send him about 1636 to make the tour of France and Italy, under the care of one Mr. Marcomes, and in the company of lord Kynalmeaky, his elder brother; and this method the earl took to perfect all his sons, after they had gone through the course of a domestic education; and it is remarkable, that all his children travelled under the same gentleman's protection, who has no small honour reflected on him from his illustrious pupils. Upon his return from his travels, he found a war ready to break out against the Scots, and was pressed by the earl of Northumberland, the commander in chief of the expedition, to share in reducing them; but this commotion subsiding, his lordship employed himself another way. By his father's desire, who loved to settle his children early in the world, he married lady Margaret Howard, daughter to the earl of Suffolk, and setting out for Ireland, landed there the very day the rebellion broke out, viz. Oct. 23, 1641. The post assigned him in this time of danger, was the defence of his father's castle of Lismore; in which he gave proofs of the most gallant spirit, as well as political conduct: The first of which he shewed in the vigorous sally he made to the relief of Sir Richard Osborn, who was besieged in his own house by the rebels, till relieved by lord Broghill, who raised the siege, and saved him and all his family[2]; and a strong proof of the latter, by advising Sir William St. Leger, then president of Munster, to act vigorously against the Irish, notwithstanding they produced the King's commission, which he was penetrating enough to discern to be a forgery.

After the cessation in Ireland, lord Broghill came to Oxford, then the residence of King Charles I. and paid his duty to that monarch, and was honoured with many private audiences, when he represented to his

Majesty, the temper and disposition of the Irish Papists, and the falshood of the pretended Committee they had sent over to mislead his Majesty, that the King was convinced the Irish never meant to keep the cessation, and that therefore it was not the interest of the English subjects to depend upon it.

Now that we have mentioned the Irish Papists, one thing must not be omitted, as it is both curious in itself, and reflects honour on lord Broghill. Many years after the reduction of these rebels, his lordship, who was then earl of Orrery, happened to pay a visit to the duke of Ormond at Kilkenny, where he met with lord Muskerry, who headed the insurrection, and produced a false commission for what he did. Finding Muskerry in an open good humour, he took occasion to retire with him, and to ask him in a pleasant manner, how he came by that commission which had so much the appearance of being genuine: 'Lord Muskerry answered, I'll be free, and unreserved with you, my lord; it was a forged commission drawn up by one Walsh, a lawyer, and others; who having a writing to which the Great Seal was affixed, one of the company very dextrously took off the sealed wax from the label of that writing, and fixed it to the label of the forged commission. Whilst this was doing another accident happened, which startled all present; and almost disconcerted the scheme. The forged commision being finished, while the parchment was handling and turning, in order to put on the seal, a tame wolf which lay asleep by the fire, awakened at the crackling of the parchment, and running to it, seized it, and tore it to pieces, notwithstanding their haste and struggle to prevent him; so that after all their pains, they were obliged to begin a new, and write it all over again.'[3] Lord Orrery struck with the daring wickedness of this action, could not help expressing himself to that effect, while Muskerry replied merrily, it would have been impossible to have kept the people together without this device.

'Till the death of King Charles I. we find lord Broghill warm in the royal interest, and that he abhorred those measures which he foresaw would distract his country; and as soon as that melancholy event happened, he quitted his estate[4] as ruined past all hopes, and hid himself in the privacy of a close retirement. How he came, afterwards to alter his conduct, and join with a party he before so much abhorred, we shall endeavour to shew.

Upon his lordship's coming from Ireland, he withdrew to Marston in Somersetshire, where he had leisure to reflect on the ruined state of the Kingdom[5]; and when he revolved in his mind its altered and desperate situation, he was ashamed to think that he should remain an idle spectator of his country's miseries, being of a different opinion from Mr. Addison: 'That when vice prevails, and wicked men bear sway, the post of honour is a private station.' These reflexions roused him to action, and produced a scheme worthy of himself. He resolved to attempt something in favour of the King; and accordingly under the pretence of going to the Spa for his health, he determined to cross the seas, and apply to Charles II. for a commission to raise forces in Ireland, in order to restore his Majesty, and recover his own estate. Having formed this resolution, he desired the earl of Warwick, who had an interest with the prevailing party, to procure a licence for him to go to the Spa. He communicated his scheme to some confirmed royalists, in whom he thought he could confide, and having rais'd a considerable sum of money, he came up to London to prosecute his voyage. Lord Broghill, however, was betrayed, and the committee, who then took upon them the government of the realm, threatened him with destruction. Cromwell interceeded, and being sensible of his lordship's great abilities, obtained a permission to talk privately with him before they proceeded to extremities. Cromwell waited upon Broghill, and reproached him gently for his intention, which his lordship denied; but Cromwell producing letters of his writing to several Royalists, in whom he confided, he found it was in vain to dissemble any longer. The General then told him, that he was no stranger to his merit, tho' he had never before seen him; and that as the reduction of Ireland was intrusted to him, he had authority from the Committee to offer his lordship a command in that war, and insisted upon his answer immediately, as the Committee were then sitting, and waiting his return. Lord Broghill was infinitely surprized at so generous and unexpected an offer from Cromwell: He thought himself at liberty, by all the rules of honour to serve against the Irish, whose cruelty and rebellion were equally detested by the royal party, as by the Parliament; and his life and freedom being in danger if he refused, he accepted the commission, and immediately repaired to Bristol to wait there till forces should be sent him. This story we have from Mr. Morrice, who heard it from lord Orrery himself; and he adds, that it is very probable his lordship's design was betrayed out of pure love and affection by his sister Ranelagh, but how this love and affection enabled her to foresee that Cromwell would interpose to remove the danger which she exposed him to, is left by the reverend author unaccounted for. Ever after this interposition and friendly offer of Cromwell, we find gratitude binding lord Broghill to a faithfull service in his interest; and in the course of his ministry to Cromwell, he prevented many shameful acts of cruelty, which would have been otherwise perpetrated.

No sooner had Broghill arrived in Ireland, but his old friends flocked round him, and demonstrated the great heighth of popularity to which he had risen in that kingdom; nor did his accepting this new commission make him negligent of their interest, for he did all he could for the safety of their persons and estates. An opportunity soon presented in which he very remarkably distinguished himself. He engaged at Macroom (with two thousand horse and dragoons) a party of Irish, consisting of upwards of five thousand, whom he totally defeated, and took their general the titular bishop of Ross prisoner[6]. This battle was fought May 10, 1650. Lord Broghill offered the bishop his life, if he would order those who were in the castle of Carigdrog-hid to surrender, which he promised; but when he was conducted to the place, he persuaded the garrison to defend it to the last extremity. Upon this lord Broghill caused him to be hanged; (tho' Mr. Morrice says, the soldiers hanged him without orders) and then commanded his heavy artillery to be brought up, which astonished his own army exceedingly, they knowing he had not so much as a single piece of battering cannon. He caused, however, several large trees to be cut, and drawn at a distance by his baggage horses; the besieged judging by the slowness of their motion, they were a vast size, capitulated before they came up, as his lordship advised, threatening otherwise to give them no quarter. He relieved Cromwell at Clonmell, and assisted both him and his father-in-law Ireton in their expedition; but because he could not moderate the fury of one, and mitigate the cruelty of the other, he incurred the displeasure of both; and Ireton was heard to say, that neither he nor Cromwell could be safe while Broghill had any command. Notwithstanding the aversion of Ireton to his lordship, yet he took care not to remit any of his diligence in prosecuting the war, he marched to that general's assistance at the siege of Limerick, and by his conduct and courage was the means of that town's falling into the hands of the Commonwealth; and till Ireland was entirely reduced, he continued active in his commission.

When Oliver rose to the dignity of Lord Protector, he sent for lord Broghill, merely to have his advice; and we are told by Oldmixon in his history of the Stewarts, that he then proposed to Cromwell to marry his daughter to King Charles II. and that as the Prince was then in distress abroad, he doubted not but his necessity would make him comply with the offer; he represented to the Protector the great danger to which he was exposed by the fickle humour of the English, who never doat long upon a favourite, but pull that man from eminence to day, whom they had but yesterday raised out of the dust; that this match would rivet his interest, by having the lawful prince so nearly allied to him; and perhaps his grandchild the indisputed heir of the crown. That he might then rule with more safety, nor dread either the violence of the Royalists, or the insidious enemies of his own government. Upon hearing this, Cromwell made a pause, and looking stedfastly in my lord's face, he asked him if he was of opinion, that the exiled prince could ever forgive his father's murderer; he answered as before, that his necessity was great, and in order to be restored to his crown, would even sacrifice his natural resentment to his own ease and grandeur; but Cromwell could not be induced to believe that ever Charles could pardon him.

Whether lord Broghill was serious in this proposal cannot be determined; but if he was, it is certain, he had a mean opinion of Charles; to have capitulated upon any terms with Cromwell, would have been betraying the dignity of his birth, and his right to reign; but to have stooped so low, as to take to his arms a child of his, who had murdered his father, and driven him to his exile, would have been an instance of the most infamous meanness that ever was recorded in history; and all the blemishes of that luxurious Prince's character, and the errors of his reign collected, do not amount to any thing so base, as would have been those nuptials.

In the year 1656 it was proposed to his lordship by the Protector to go down to Scotland, with an absolute authority, either because he suspected Monk, or was willing to give the people of that country some satisfaction, who complained of his severity; but he was very unwilling to receive the charge, and took it at last upon these conditions[7]: The first was: that he should be left to himself, and receive no orders; and the second, that no complaints should find credit, or procure directions in his absence; and the third, that he should be recalled in a year. He was very acceptable to the Scotch, and gained a great influence over them by speaking and acting with moderation. After his return, he was with Whitlock and Thurloe admitted into all the confidence that could be expected from a person in the Protector's circumstances; who if he had any chearful moments, spent them in their company, where he appeared quite another person than in the ordinary course of his conduct, which was built on a policy suited to his condition, the people he had to deal with, and the critical juncture of the times. Our author stood high in Cromwell's favour to the last; and it was, no doubt, in some measure owing to his gratitude, that he attached himself so firmly to his son and successor Richard. It perhaps will appear strange, but it is supported by evidence, that Cromwell did not love his own family so well as lord Broghill did. Being asked upon his death-bed whom he appointed his successor, he answered, "That in such a closet his will would be found," in which he named Fleetwood, but one of the Protector's daughters getting first to the drawer, she took the will and destroyed it[8].

Thus Richard against his father's intention obtained the government, which, however, it is very plain he was not fit to hold; for all the art and industry of Broghill could never so govern his proceedings, but that some steps either too violent or too remiss were taken, by which his administration fell into contempt; and doubtless the reason why Cromwell excluded his son, was, that he discovered his weakness, and found him without a capacity of reigning. When the oppression of committees, the general distraction amongst the people, and the anarchy into which the English affairs had fallen, began to point towards a restoration, we find lord Broghill declaring early for the King, going over into Ireland, there sounding the minds of the officers, and preparing that kingdom for the reception of his Majesty with open arms.

Thus we have seen him discharge with honour the debt of gratitude he owed to Cromwell; but notwithstanding the figure he made in the service, it is by no means clear that ever he was warmly attached to the republic; he was detected in having drank the King's health in company with the Protector's children, which Oliver very prudently thought proper to pass over. After the restoration, Broghill wanted not enemies, who insinuated things against him to King Charles, and blamed his tardiness in procuring his Majesty's return; but his lordship made it clear, that he was the first who declared for him in Ireland, and the most zealous, as well as the most powerful promoter of his interest. His Majesty was so well satisfied with his lordship's proceedings, that he wrote to him with his own hand, and thanked him for his loyalty[9]. On September 5, 1660, as an incontested proof of his Majesty's affection for his lordship, he by letters patent advanced him to the honour of earl of Orrery in the county of Cork[10]; and Sir Maurice Eustace, a friend of the duke of Ormond's, being appointed chancellor, Roger earl of Orrery, and Charles Coote, earl of Montrath, were with him made lords justices, about the close of that memorable year.

From that time till his death we find lord Orrery in the highest esteem in the three nations: He was employed by his Majesty to confer with the earl of Clarendon, whose imperious steps, it seems, had highly disobliged his master, and when that great man fell, the King made an offer of the seals to the earl of Orrery, who on account of his want of bodily vigour, declined it. At the same time he accepted a most arduous and unpleasing office from the King, and that was, to expostulate with the duke of York, and bring him to ask pardon for the haughty and insolent measures he took in supporting the chancellor.

His Majesty warmly pressed him to become a favourer of the French alliance, and for the reduction of the Dutch; neither of which were at all agreeable to his notions, and therefore that he might more concisely express the mischievous consequences he apprehended from these measures, he reduced his thoughts into a poem; and this was very well received by the King, who thought to have made some impression on him, in his turn, in a long audience he gave him for that purpose; but the earl's duty would not permit him to coincide in his opinion with the King, when he was sensible that the King's scheme was contrary to the interest of the nation; and this led him in plain terms to declare, that he never would concur in counsels to aggrandize France, which was already too great; or to break the power of the Dutch, which was barely sufficient for their own defence[11].

There is a particular circumstance in relation to this affair, which must not be omitted. When lord Orrery came from the audience of his Majesty, he was met by the earl of Danby, who asked him, whether he had closed with the King's proposals; to which lord Orrery answered, no. Then replied the other statesman, "Your lordship may be the honester man, but you will never be worth a groat." This passage is the more remarkable, because Danby was of the same opinion with Orrery, and temporized purely for the sake of power, which cost him afterwards a long imprisonment, and had very near lost him his life: So dear do such men often pay for sacrificing honour to interest. In the year 1679, Oct. 16, this great statesman died in the full possession of honours and fame: he had lived in the most tumultuous times; he had embarked in a dangerous ocean, and he had the address to steer at last to a safe haven. As a man, his character was very amiable; he was patient, compassionate, and generous; as a soldier, he was of undaunted courage; as a statesman, of deep penetration, and invincible industry; and as a poet, of no mean rank.

Before we give an account of his works, it will not be amiss, in order to illustrate the amiable character of lord Orrery, to shew, that tho' he espoused the Protector's interest, yet he was of singular service to the nation, in restraining the violence of his cruelty, and checking the domineering spirit of those slaves in authority, who then called themselves the legislature.

The authors of the Biographia Britannica, say, 'that our author opposed in Parliament, and defeated, the blackest measure Cromwell ever entered into, which was the passing a law for decimating the royal party, and his lordship's conduct in this, was by far the greatest action of his whole life. He made a long and an elaborate speech, in which he shewed the injustice, cruelty, and folly, of that truly infamous and Nero-like proposition. Finding that he was likely to lose the question upon the division, which probably would have issued in losing his life also; he stood up and boldly observed, "That he did not think so many Englishmen could be fond of slavery." 'Upon which so many members rose and followed him, that the Speaker without telling, declared from the chair the Noes have it, and the bill was accordingly thrown out. Upon this, he went immediately up to Cromwell, and said, "I have done you this day as great a service as ever I did in my life. How? returned Cromwell; by hindring your government, replied my lord, from becoming hateful, which already begins to be disliked; for if this bill had passed, three kingdoms would have risen up against you; and they were your enemies, and not your friends who brought it in." 'This Cromwell so firmly believed, that he never forgave nor trusted them afterwards.'

King Charles II. put my lord upon writing plays, which he did, upon the occasion of a dispute that arose in the Royal presence, about writing plays in rhime. Some affirmed, that it was to be done, others that it would spoil the fancy to be so confined; but lord Orrery was of another opinion, and his Majesty being willing, that a trial should be made, laid his commands on his lordship, to employ some of his leisure time that way, which his lordship readily complied with, and soon after composed the Black Prince.

It is difficult to give a full and accurate account of this nobleman's compositions; for it must be owned, he was a better statesman than a poet, and fitter to act upon the wide theatre of life, than to write representations for the circumscribed theatre of the stage. In the light of an author he is less eminent, and lived a life of too much hurry to become proficient in poetry, a grace which not only demands the most extensive abilities, but much leisure and contemplation. But if he was not extremely eminent as a poet, he was far removed above contempt, and deserves to have full mention made of all his writings; and we can easily forgive want of elegance and correctness in one who was of so much service to his country, and who was born rather to live than to write a great part.

According to the least exceptionable account, his works are as follow:

1. The Irish Colours displayed, in a reply of an English Protestant, to an Irish Roman Catholic, Lond. 1662, 4to.

2. An Answer to a scandalous Letter lately printed and subscribed be a Peter Walsh, procurator for the Secular and Romish priests of Ireland: This was the same infamous Walsh who forged the commisssion to act against the Protestants. In this letter his lordship makes a full discovery of the treachery of the Irish rebels, Dublin 1662, 4to. Lond. 1662, 4to.

3. A Poem on his Majesty's Restoration, presented by the earl himself to the King.

4. A Poem on the Death of the celebrated Mr. Abraham Cowley, Lond. 1667, fol. reprinted by Dr. Sprat, before his edition of Cowley's works; also reprinted and much commended by Mr. Budgel.

5. History of Henry V. a tragedy. Lond. 1668, fol. In this play Mr. Harris who played Henry, wore the Duke of York's coronation suit; and Betterton, who played Owen Tudor, by which he got reputation, wore the King's; and Mr. Liliston, to whom the part of the Duke of Burgundy was given, wore the Earl of Oxford's.

6. Mustapha the Son of Solyman the Magnificent, a Tragedy, Lond. 1667, fol. This play succeeded tollerably well.

7. The Black Prince, a Tragedy, Lond. 1672, fol. When this play was begun his lordship lay ill of the gout, and after he had finished two acts of it, he sent it to the King for his perusal, and at the same time told his Majesty,

that while he laboured under that disorder, he had done these two acts; and perhaps would do no more till he was taken ill again; upon which his Majesty pleasantly said, that if it was not to be compleated till the return of the gout, he wished him a lusty fit of it[12].

8. Tryphon, a Tragedy, Lond. 1672, fol. These four plays were collected, and printed in fol. 1690, and make the entire first volume of the new edition of the earl's Dramatic Works.

9. Parthenissa, a Romance, in three volumes, Lond. 1665, 4to. 1677, fol. This romance is divided into six parts, the last written at the desire of, and therefore dedicated to, her royal highness the Princess Henrietta Maria, Duchess of Orleans, sister to King Charles II.

10. A Dream. This poem has been before mentioned. In it, the genius of France is introduced, saying every thing the French ministers could insinuate to inveigle King Charles II. to endeavour at making himself arbitrary, or to deceive him into a mean and scandalous dependence on Lewis XIV. to all which the ghost of Charles I. is next brought in, giving reasons why the sole foundation of a Monarch's power, is the love and confidence of his people.

11. The Art of War, Lond. 1677, fol. This work he addresses to the King, in a large dedication, which was but the first part of what he intended upon the subject; and was so strangely received, that the second never appeared.

12. Poems on most of the festivals of the church. This work, tho' printed and published, was never finished by our author. It was written in the last year of his life, under much weakness of body; and Budgel observes, very justly, that his poetry in this composition runs low; and indeed his characteristical fault as a poet, is want of elevation.

His posthumous works are these;

1. Mr. Anthony, a Comedy, 4to. Lond. 1692.

2. Guzman, a Comedy. 1693, 4to. upon a Spanish plot, and written in the Spanish manner.

3. Herod the Great, a Tragedy, Lond. 1694, 4to.

4. Altemira a Tragedy, brought upon the stage by Mr. Francis Manning 1702, dedicated to Lionel earl of Orrery, grandson to the author, with a prologue by lord viscount Bolingbroke. We may add to them his state letters, which have been lately published in one volume fol. The rest of his lordship's political papers perished in the flames, when his house at Charleville was burnt in the year 1690, by a party of King James's soldiers, with the duke of Berwick at their head.

We shall give a specimen of his lordship's poetry from a speech in Altemira, in a scene between Altemira and her lover.

> ALTEM. I can forgive you all my Lycidor,
> But leaving me, and leaving me for war,
> For that, so little argument I find,
> My reason makes the fault look more unkind.

> LYCIDOR. You see my griefs such deep impressions give,
> I'd better die than thus afflicted live.
> Yet to those sorrows under which I groan,
> Can you still think it fit to add your own?

> ALTEM. 'Tis only you, have your own troubles wrought,
> For they alas! are not impos'd but sought;
> Did you but credit what you still profess,
> That I alone can make your happiness:
> You would not your obedience now decline,
> But end by paying it, your griefs and mine.

Footnotes:

1. Earl of Cork's True Remembrance.

2. Morrice's Memoirs of E. Orrery, chap. 6.

3. Memoirs of the Earl of Orrery, p. 36.

4. Carte's Life of the Duke of Ormond.

5. Memoirs of the Interregnum, p. 133.

6. Cox's History of Ireland, vol. 2. part 2d. p. 16.

7. Thurloe's State Papers.

8. Morrice's Memoirs chap. 5.

9. Budgel's Memoirs of the family of the Boyles.

10. Collin's peerage, vol. iv. p. 26.

11. Love's Memoirs of the Earl of Orrery.

12. Memoirs of the Earl of Orrery.

Richard Head

Was the son of a minister in Ireland, who being killed in the rebellion there in 1641, amongst the many thousands who suffered in that deplorable massacre, our author's mother came with her son into England, and he having, says Winstanley, been trained up in learning, was by the help of some friends educated at Oxford, in the same college where his father formerly had been a student; but as his circumstances were mean, he was taken away from thence, and bound apprentice to a bookseller in London, but his genius being addicted to poetry, before his time was expired, he wrote a piece called Venus Cabinet unlocked; and afterwards he married and set up for himself, in which condition, he did not long continue, for being addicted to gaming, he ruined his affairs. In this distress he went over to Ireland, and composed his Hic & Ubique, a noted comedy; and which gained him some reputation. He then returned to England, reprinted his comedy, and dedicated it to the duke of Monmouth, from whom he received no great encouragement. This circumstance induced him to reflect, that the life of an author was at once the most dissipated and unpleasing in the world; that it is in every man's power to injure him, and that few are disposed to promote him. Animated by these reflexions, he again took a house, and from author resumed his old trade of a bookseller, in which, no doubt he judged right; for while an author (be his genius and parts ever so bright) is employed in the composition of one book, a bookseller may publish twenty; so that in the very nature of things, a bookseller without oppression, a crime which by unsuccessful writers is generally imputed to them, may grow rich, while the most industrious and able author can arrive at no more than a decent competence: and even to that, many a great genius has never attained.

No sooner had Mr. Head a little recovered himself, than we find him cheated again by the syren alurements of pleasure and poetry, in the latter of which, however, it does not appear he made any proficiency. He failed a second time, in the world, and having recourse to his pen, wrote the first part of the English Rogue, which being too libertine, could not be licensed till he had expunged some of the most luscious descriptions out of it.

Mr. Winstanley, p. 208, has informed us, that at the coming out of this first part, he was with him at the Three Cup tavern in Holborn drinking a glass of Rhenish, and made these verses upon him,

> What Gusman, Buscan, Francion, Rablais writ,
> I once applauded for most excellent wit;
> But reading thee, and thy rich fancy's store,
> I now condemn what I admir'd before.
> Henceforth translations pack away, be gone,
> No Rogue so well writ, as the English one.

We cannot help observing, that Winstanley has a little ridiculously shewn his vanity, by informing the world, that he could afford to drink a glass of Rhenish; and has added nothing to his reputation by the verses, which have neither poetry nor wit in them.

This English Rogue, described in the life of Meriton Latroon, a witty extravagant, was published anno 1666, in a very large 8vo. There were three more parts added to it by Francis Kirkman and Mr. Head in conjunction.

He also wrote

Jackson's Recantation; or the Life and Death of a notorious highwayman, then hanging in chains at Hamstead, 1674.

Proteus Redivivus; or, the Art of wheedling, Lond. 1675.

The Floating Island; or a voyage from Lambethanio to Ramalia.

A Discovery of Old Brazil.

The Red Sea.

He wrote a Pamphlet against Dr. Wild, in answer to Wild's letter directed to his friend, upon occasion of his Majesty's declaration for liberty of conscience: This he concludes in the following manner, by which it will be seen that he was but a poor versifier.

> Thus, Sir, you have my story, but am sorry
> (Taunton excuse) it is no better for ye,
> However read it, as your pease are shelling;
> For you will find, it is not worth the telling.
> Excuse this boldness, for I can't avoid
> Thinking sometimes you are but ill employ'd.
> Fishing for souls more fit, than frying fish;
> That makes me throw pease-shellings in your dish.

You have a study, books wherein to look,
How comes it then the Doctor turn'd a cook?
Well Doctor Cook, pray be advised hereafter,
Don't make your wife the subject of our laughter.
I find she's careless, and your maid a slut,
To let you grease your Cassock for your gut.
You are all three in fault, by all that's blest;
Mend you your manners first, then teach the rest.

Mr. Winstanley says, that our author met with a great many afflictions and crosses in his time, and was cast away at sea, as he was going to the Isle of Wight 1678.

Thomas Hobbs

This celebrated philosopher was son of Thomas Hobbs, vicar of Westport, within the Liberty of Malmesbury, and of Charlton in Wilts, and was born at Westport on the 5th of April 1588[1]. It is related by Bayle, that his mother being frighted at the rumours of the report of the Spanish Armada, was brought to bed of him before her time, which makes it somewhat surprizing that he should live to so great an age. He had made an extraordinary progress in the languages before he arrived at his 14th year, when he was sent to Oxford, where he studied for five years Aristotle's philosophy. In the year 1607 he took the degree of batchelor of arts, and upon the recommendation of the principal of the college, he entered into the service of William Cavendish, baron Hardwicke, soon afterwards earl of Devonshire[2], by whom being much esteemed for his pleasantry and humour, he was appointed tutor to his son lord William Cavendish, several years younger than Hobbs. Soon after our author travelled with this young nobleman thro' France and Italy, where he made himself master of the different languages of the countries thro' which he travelled; but finding that he had in a great measure forgot his Greek and Latin, he dedicated his leisure hours to the revival of them, and in order to fix the Greek language more firmly in his mind, upon his return to England, he set about and accomplished a translation of Thucydides, who appeared to him preferable to all other Greek historians, and by rendering him into English he meant to shew his countrymen from the Athenian history, the disorders and confusions of a democratical government.

In the year 1628, the earl of Devonshire dying, after our author had served him 20 years, he travelled again into France with a son of Sir Gervas Clifton; at which time, and during which preregrination (says Wood) 'he began to make an inspection into the elements of Euclid, and be delighted with his method, not only for the theorems contained in it, but for his art of reasoning. In these studies he continued till 1631, when his late pupil the earl of Devonshire called him home in order to undertake the education of his son, then only thirteen years of age, in all the parts of juvenile literature; and as soon as it was proper for him to see the world, Hobbs again set out for France and Italy, and directed his young pupil to the necessary steps for accomplishing his education.

When our author was at Paris, he began to search into the fundamentals of natural science, and contracted an intimacy with Marius Marsennus a Minim, conversant in that kind of philosophy, and a man of excellent moral qualities.

In 1637 he was recalled to England, but finding the civil war ready to break out, and the Scots in arms against the King, instigated by a mean cowardice, he deferred his country in distress, and returned to Paris, that he might without interruption pursue his studies there, and converse with men of eminence in the sciences. The Parliament prevailing, several of the Royalists were driven from their own country, and were obliged to take shelter in France. The Prince of Wales was reduced likewise to quit the kingdom and live at Paris: Hobbs was employed to teach the young Prince mathematics, in which he made great proficiency; and our author used to observe, that if the Prince's application was equal to the quickness of his parts, he would be the foremost man in his time in every species of science. All the leisure hours that Hobbs enjoyed in Paris, he dedicated to the composition of a book called, The Leviathan, a work by which he acquired a great name in Europe; and which was printed at London while he remained at Paris. Under this strange name he means the body politic. The divines of the church of England who attended King Charles II. in France, exclaimed vehemently against this performance, and said that it contained a great many impious assertions, and that the author was not of the royal party. Their complaints were regarded, and Hobbs was discharged the court; and as he had extremely provoked the Papists, he thought it not safe for him to continue longer in France, especially as he was deprived of the protection of the King of England. He translated his Leviathan into Latin, and printed it with an appendix in 1668.

About ten years afterwards, the Leviathan was printed in Low Dutch. The character of this work is drawn as under, by bishop Burnet.

'His [Hobbs's] main principles were, that all men acted under an absolute necessity, in which he seemed protected by the then received doctrine of absolute decrees. He seemed to think that the universe was god, and that souls were material, Thought being only subtle and imperceptible motion. He thought interest and fear were the chief principles of society; and he put all morality in the following that which was our own private will or advantage. He thought religion had no other foundation than the laws of the land; and he put all the law in the will of the Prince, or of the people: For he writ his book at first in favour of absolute monarchy, but turned it afterwards to gratify the Republican party.'

Upon his return to England, he lived retired at the seat of the earl of Devonshire, and applied himself to the study of philosophy; and as almost all men who have written any thing successfully would be thought poets, so Hobbs laid claim to that character, tho' his poetry is too contemptible for criticism. Dr. White Kennet in his memoirs of the family of Cavendish informs us, 'That while Mr. Hobbs lived in the earl of Devonshire's family, his professed rule was to dedicate the morning to his health, and the afternoon to his studies; and therefore at his first rising he walked out, and climbed any hill within his reach; or if the weather was not dry, he fatigued himself within doors, by some exercise or other till he was in a sweat, recommending that practice upon his opinion, that an old man had more moisture than heat; and therefore by such motion heat was to be acquired, and moisture expelled; after this he took a breakfast, and then went round the lodgings to wait upon the earl, the countess, and the children, and any considerable strangers, paying some short addresses to them all. He kept these rounds till about 12 o'clock, when he had a little dinner provided for him, which he eat always by himself without ceremony. Soon after dinner he retired into his study, and had his candle, with ten or twelve pipes of tobacco laid by him, then shutting the door he fell to smoking and thinking, and writing for several hours.'

He retained a friend or two at court to protect him if occasion should require; and used to say, it was lawful to make use of evil instruments to do ourselves good. 'If I were cast (said he) into a deep pit, and the Devil should put down his cloven foot, I should take hold of it to be drawn out by it.'

Towards the end of his life he read very few books, and the earl of Clarendon says, that he had never read much but thought a great deal; and Hobbs himself used to observe, that if he had read as much as other philosophers, he should have been as ignorant as they. If any company came to visit him, he would be free of his discourse, and behave with pleasantry, till he was pressed, or contradicted, and then he had the infirmities of being short and peevish, and referring them to his writings, for better satisfaction. His friends who had the liberty of introducing strangers to him, made these terms with them before admission, that they should not dispute with the old man, or contradict him.

In October 1666, when proceedings against him were depending, with a bill against atheism and profaneness, he was at Chatsworth, and appeared extremely disturbed at the news of it, fearing the messengers would come for him, and the earl of Devonshire would deliver him up, the two houses of Parliament commit him to the bishops, and they decree him a heretic. This terror upon his spirits greatly disturbed him. He often confessed to those about him, that he meant no harm, was no obstinate man, and was ready to make any satisfaction; for his prevailing principle and resolution was, to suffer for no cause whatever.

Under these apprehensions of danger, he drew up, in 1680, an historical naration of heresy, and the punishments thereof, endeavouring to prove that there was no authority to determine heresy, or to punish it, when he wrote the Leviathan.

Under the same fears he framed an apology for himself and his writings; observing, that the exceptionable things in his Leviathan were not his opinions, so much as his suppositions, humbly submited to those who had the ecclesiastical power, and never since dogmatically maintained by him either in writing or discourse; and it is much to be suspected, as Dr. Kennet observes, that upon this occasion, he began to make a more open shew of religion and church communion. He now frequented the chapel, joined in the service, and was generally a partaker of the sacrament; and when any strangers used to call in question his belief, he always appealed to his conformity in divine service, and referred them to the chaplain for a testimony of it. Others thought it a meer compliance with the orders of the family; and observed, he never went to any parish church, and even in the chapel upon Sundays he went out after prayers, and would not condescend to hear the sermon, and when any friend asked the reason of it, he gave no other answer but this, that preachers could tell him nothing but what he knew. He did not conceal his hatred to the clergy; but it was visible his aversion proceeded from the dread of their civil power and interest. He had often a jealousy that the bishops would burn him; and of all the bench he was most afraid of Dr. Seth Ward, bishop of Sarum, because he had most offended him. Dr. Kennet further observes, that his whole life was governed by his fears.

In the first Parliament of 1640, while it seemed to favour the measures of the court, he wrote a little tract in English wherein he demonstrated as himself tells us, that all the power and rights necessary for the peace of the kingdom, were inseparably annexed to the sovereignty of the King's person. But in the second parliament of that year, when they proceeded fiercely against those who had written or preached in defence of the regal power; he was the first that fled, went over into France, and there continued eleven years. Whether from the dread of assassination, or as some have thought from the notion of ghosts and spirits, is uncertain, but he could not endure to be left in an empty house; whenever the earl of Devonshire removed, he would accompany him; even in his last stage from Chatsworth to Hardwick, when in a weak condition, he dared not be left behind, but made his way upon a feather bed in a coach, tho' he survived the journey but a few days. He could not bear any discourse of death, and seemed to cast off all thoughts of it; he delighted to reckon upon longer life. The winter before he died he had a warm coat made him, which he said must last him three years, and then he would have such another. A few days after his removal to Hardwick, Wood says that he was struck with a dead palsy, which stupified his right side from head to foot, depriving him of his speech and reason at the same time; but this circumstance is not so probable, since Dr. Kennet has told us, that in his last sickness he frequently enquired, whether his disease was curable; and when it was told him that he might have ease but no remedy, he used these expressions. 'I shall be glad then to find a hole to creep out of the world at;' which are reported to be his last sensible words, and his lying some days following in a state of stupefaction, seemed to be owing to his mind, more than to his body. The only thought of death which he appeared to entertain in time of health, was to take care of some inscription on his grave; he would suffer some friends to dictate an epitaph, amongst which he was best pleased with these words:

"This is the true Philosopher's Stone."

He died at Hardwick, as above-mentioned, on the 4th of Dec. 1679. Notwithstanding his great age, for he exceeded 90 at his death, he retained his judgment in great vigour till his last sickness.

Some writers of his life maintain, that he had very orthodox notions concerning the nature of God and of all the moral virtues; notwithstanding the general notion of his being a downright atheist; that he was affable, kind, communicative of what he knew, a good friend, a good relation, charitable to the poor, a lover of justice, and a despiser of money. This last quality is a favourable circumstance in his life, for there is no vice at once more despicable and the source of more base designs than avarice. His warmest votaries allow, that when he was young he was addicted to the fashionable libertinism of wine and women, and that he kept himself unmarried lest wedlock should interrupt him in the study of philosophy.

In the catalogue of his faults, meanness of spirit and cowardice may be justly imputed to him. Whether he was convinced of the truth of his philosophy, no man can determine; but it is certain, that he had no resolution to support and maintain his notions: had his doctrines been of ever so much consequence to the world, Hobbs would have abjured them all, rather than have suffered a moment's pain on their account. Such a man may be admired for his invention, and the planning of new systems, but the world would never have been much illuminated, if all the discoverers of truth, like the philosopher of Malmsbury, had had no spirit to assert it against opposition. In a piece called the Creed of Mr. Hobbs examined, in a feigned Conference between him and a Student of Divinity, London 1670, written by Dr. Tenison, afterwards archbishop of Canterbury, the Dr. charges Mr. Hobbs with affirming, 'that God is a bodily substance, though most refined, and forceth evil upon the very wills of men; framed a model of government pernicious in its consequences to all nations; subjected the canon of scripture to the civil powers, and taught them the way of turning the Alcoran into the Gospel; declared it lawful, not only to dissemble, but firmly to renounce faith in Christ, in order to avoid persecution, and even managed a quarrel against the very elements of Euclid.' Hobbs's Leviathan met with many answers, immediately after the restoration, especially one by the earl of Clarendon, in a piece called a Brief View and Survey of the dangerous and pernicious Errors to Church and State, in Mr. Hobbs's Book entitled Leviathan, Oxon. 1676. The university of Oxford condemned his Leviathan, and his Book de Cive, by a decree passed on the 21st of July 1638, and ordered them to be publickly burnt, with several other treatises excepted against.

The following is a catalogue of his works, with as full an account of them as consists with our plan.

He translated into English the History of the Grecian War by Thucydides, London 1628, and 1676 in fol. and since reprinted in two volumes in octavo.

De Mirabilibus Pecci, a Latin Poem, printed at London 1636; it was translated into English by a person of quality, and the translation was published with the original at London 1678.

Elementa Philosophica, seu Politica de Cive, id est, de Vita civili & politicâ prudenter instituendâ, Paris 1642 in 4to. Mr. Hobbs printed but a few copies of this book, and revised it afterwards, and made several additions to it, with which improvements it was printed at Amsterdam, under the direction of Monsieur Forbier, who published a French translation of it. Dr. John Bramhall, bishop of Derry in Ireland, in the Preface to his Book entitled a Defence of true Liberty, from an antecedent and extrinsical Necessity, tells us, 'that ten years before he had given Mr. Hobbs about sixty exceptions, one half political, and the other half theological to that book, and every exception justified by a number of reasons, to which he never yet vouchsafed any answer.' Gassendus, in a letter to Sorbiere, tells us, that our author's Book de Cive, deserves to be read by all who would have a deep insight into the subject. Puffendorf observes, that he had been much obliged to Mr. Hobbs, whose hypothesis in this book, though it favours a little of irreligion, is in other respects sufficiently ingenious and sound.

An Answer to Sir William Davenant's Epistle or Preface to Gondibert, Paris 1650, 12mo. and afterwards printed with Gondibert. See Davenant.

Human Nature, or the Fundamental Elements of Policy, being a Discovery of the Faculties, Acts, and Passions of the Soul of Man, from their original Causes, according to such philosophical Principles as are not commonly known or asserted.

De Corpore Politico, or the Elements of Law, London 1650.

Leviathan, or the Matter, Power, and Form of a Commonwealth, London 1651 in fol. reprinted again in fol. 1680; a Latin Version was published at Amsterdam 1666 in 4to; it was likewise translated into Low Dutch, and printed at Amsterdam 1678 in 4to. To the English editions is subjoined a Review of the Leviathan.

A Compendium of Aristotle's Rhetoric and Rhamus's Logic.

A Letter about Liberty and Necessity, London 1654 in 12mo. to this piece several answers were given, especially by Dr. Bernard Laney, and Dr. Bramhall, bishop of Derry, London 1656 in 4to.

Elementorum Philosophiæ sectio prima de Corpore, London 1655 in 8vo; in English, London 1656 in 4to. sectio secunda, London 1657 in 4to. Amsterdam 1680 in 4to.

Six Lessons to the Professors of Mathematics of the Institution of Sir Henry Saville, London 1656 in 4to; this is written against Dr. Seth Ward, and Dr. John Wallis.

The Remarks of the Absurd Geometry, Rural Language, &c. of Dr. John Wallis, London 1657 in 8vo. Dr. Wallis having published in 1655 his Elenchus Geometriæ Hobbianæ. It occasioned a notable controversy between these two great men.

Examinatio et Emendatio Mathematicæ hodiernæ, &c. in sex Dialogis, London 1660, in 4to. Amsterdam 1668 in 4to.

Dialogus Physicus, sive de Natura Aeris, London 1661 in 4to.

De Duplicatione Cubi, London 1661, 4to. Amsterdam 1668 in 4to.

Problemata Physica, una cum magnitudine Circuli, London 1662, 4to.

De Principiis et Ratiocinatione Geometrarum, contra sastuosum Professorem Geometræ, Amsterdam 1668 in 4to.

Quadratura Circuli, Cubatio sphæræ, Duplicatio Cubi; una cum Responsione ad Objectiones Geometriæ Professoris Saviliani Oxoniæ editas Anno 1669, London in 4to. 1669.

Rosetum Geometricum, sive Propositiones aliquot frustra antehac tentatæ, cum censura brevi Doctrinæ Wallisianæ de Motu, London 1671 in 4to. There is an account of this book in the Philosophical Transactions, Numb. 72, for the year 1671.

Three Papers presented to the Royal Society against Dr. Wallis, with Considerations on Dr. Wallis's Answer to them, London 1671, 4to.

Lux Mathematica &c.

Censura Doctrinæ Wallisianæ de Libra.

Rosetura Hobbesii, London 1672 in quarto.

Principia et Problemata aliquot Geometrica ante desperata, nunc breviter explicata & demonstrata, London 1674, 4to.

Epistola ad Dom. Ant. Wood Authorem Historiæ & Antiquitat Universit. Oxon. dated April 20, 1674; the substance of this letter is to complain of the figure which Mr. Wood makes him appear in, in that work; Hobbs, who had an infinite deal of vanity, thought he was entitled to higher encomiums, and more a minute relation of his life than that gentleman gave. An Answer was written to it by Dr. Fell, in which Hobbs is treated with no great ceremony.

A Letter to William, Duke of Newcastle, concerning the Controversy he had with Dr. Laney, Bishop of Ely, about Liberty and Necessity, London 1670 in 12mo.

Decameron Phisiologicum, or Ten Dialogues on Natural Philosophy, London 1678, 8vo. To this is added the Proportion of a Straight Line to hold the Arch of a Quadrant; an account of this book is published in the Philosophical Transactions, Numb. 138.

His Last Words, and Dying Legacy, printed December 1679, and published by Charles Blunt, Esq; from the Leviathan, in order to expose Mr. Hobbs's Doctrine.

His Memorable Sayings in his Books, and at the Table, printed with his picture before it.

Behemoth, the History of the Civil Wars of England, from 1640 to 1660, printed London, 1679.

Vita Thomæ Hobbs; this is a Latin Poem, written by himself, and printed in 4to, 1679.

Historical Narration of Heresy, and the Punishment thereof, London 1680, in four sheets and a half in folio, and in 1682 in 8vo. of this we have already made some mention.

Vita Thomæ Hobbs, written by himself in prose, and printed at Caropolis, i.e. London, and prefixed to Vitæ Hobbianæ Auctarium 1681 in 8vo. and 1682 in 4to.

A Brief of the Art of Rhetoric, containing the Substance of all that Aristotle hath written in his three Books on that Subject, printed in 12mo. but without a date.

A Dialogue between a Philosopher and a Student of the Common Law of England.

An Answer to Archbishop Bramhall's Book called the Catching of the Leviathan, London 1682 in 8vo.

Seven Philosophical Problems, and two Positions of Geometry, London 1682 in 8vo. dedicated to the King 1662.

An Apology for himself and his Writings, of which we have already taken notice.

Historia Ecclesiastica carmine elegiaco concinnata, London 1688 in 8vo.

Tractatus Opticus, inserted in Mersennus's Cogitata Physico-Mathematica, Paris 1644 in 4to.

He translated into English Verse the Voyages of Ulysses, or Homer's Odysseys. B. ix, x, xi, xii. London 1674 in 8vo.

Homer's Iliads and Odysseys, London 1675, and 1677 in 12mo; to which is prefixed a Preface concerning Heroic Poetry. Mr. Pope in his Preface to his Translation of Homer's Iliad, says, 'that Mr. Hobbs, in his Version, has given a correct explanation of the sense in general, but for particulars and circumstances, lops them, and often omits the most beautiful. As for its being a close translation, I doubt not, many have been led into that error by the shortness of it, which proceeds not from the following the original line by line, but from the contractions above mentioned. He sometimes omits whole similes and sentences, and is now and then guilty of mistakes, into which no writer of his learning could have fallen but through carelessness. His poetry, like Ogilby's, is too mean for criticism.' He left behind likewise several MSS. Mr. Francis Peck has published two original Letters of our author; the first is dated at Paris October 21, 1634, in which he resolves the following question. Why a man remembers less his own face, which he sees often in a glass, than the face of a friend he has not seen a great time? The other Letter is dated at Florence, addressed to his friend Mr. Glen 1636, and relates to Dr. Heylin's History of the Sabbath.

Thus have we given some account of the life and writings of the famous Philosopher of Malmsbury, who made so great a figure in the age in which he lived, but who, in the opinion of some of the best writers of that time, was more distinguished for his knowledge than his morals, and there have not been wanting those who have declared, that the lessons of voluptuousness and libertinism, with which he poisoned the mind of the young King Charles II. had so great an effect upon the morals of that Prince, that our nation dearly suffered by this tutorage, in having its wealth and treasure squandered by that luxurious Monarch. Hobbs seems not to have been very amiable in his life; he was certainly incapable of true friendship, for the same cowardice, or false principle, which could instigate him to abandon truth, would likewise teach him to sacrifice his friend to his own safety. When young, he was voluptuous, when old, peevish, destitute alike of resolution and honour. However high his powers, his character is mean, he flattered the prevailing follies, he gave up virtue to fashion, and if he can be produced as a miracle of learning, he can never be ranked with those venerable names, who have added virtue to erudition, and honour to genius; who have illuminated the world by their knowledge, and reformed it by example.

Footnotes:

1. Wood, ubi supra.

2. Athen. Oxon. p. 251.

Sir Aston Cokaine

A gentleman who lived in the reign of Charles I. He was son of Thomas Cokaine, esq; and descended from a very ancient family at Ambourne in the Peak of Derbyshire; born in the year 1608, and educated at both the universities[1]. Mr. Langbaine observes, that Sir Aston's predecessors had some evidence to prove themselves allied to William the Conqueror, and in those days lived at Hemmingham Castle in Essex. He was a fellow-commoner at Trinity College in Cambridge, as he himself confesseth in one of his books. After he had left the university, he went to the Inns of Court, where continuing awhile for fashion's sake, he travelled afterwards with Sir Kenelm Digby into France, Italy, Germany, &c. and was absent the space of twelve years, an account of which he has written to his son[2], but it does not appear to have been printed. He lived the greatest part of his time in a lordship belonging to him called Pooley, in the parish of Polesworth in Warwickshire, and addicted himself much to books and the study of poetry. During the civil wars he suffered much for his religion, which was that of Rome, and the King's cause; he pretended then to be a baronet, created by King Charles I. after by violence he had been drawn from the Parliament, about June 10, 1641; yet he was not deemed so by the officers of the army, because no patent was enrolled to justify it, nor any mention of it made in the docquet books belonging to the clerk of the crown in Chancery, where all Patents are taken notice of which pass the Great Seal. Sir Aston was esteemed by some a good poet, and was acknowledged by all a great lover of the polite arts; he was addicted to extravagance; for he wasted all he had, which, though he suffered in the civil wars, he was under no necessity of doing from any other motive but profusion.

Amongst our author's other poetical productions, he has written three plays and a masque, which are in print, which we shall give in the same order with Mr. Langbaine.

1. A Masque, presented at Bretbie in Derbyshire, on Twelfth-Night 1639. This Entertainment was presented before the Right Honourable Philip, first Earl of Chesterfield, and his Countess, two of their sons acting in it.

2.   The Obstinate Lady, a Comedy, printed in 8vo. London 1650. Langbaine observes, that Sir Aston's Obstinate Lady, seems to be a cousin Jerman to Massinger's Very Woman, as appears by comparing the characters.

3.   The Tragedy of Ovid, printed in 8vo. 1669. 'I know not (says Mr. Langbaine) why the author calls this Ovid's Tragedy, except that he lays the scene in Tomos, and makes him fall down dead with grief, at the news he received from Rome, in sight of the audience, otherwise he has not much business on the stage, and the play ought rather to have taken the name of Bassane's Jealousy, and the dismal Effects thereof, the Murder of his new Bride Clorina, and his Friend Pyrontus.'

4.   Trapolin creduto Principe, or Trapolin supposed a Prince, an Italian Tragi-Comedy, printed in 8vo. London 1658. The design of this play is taken from one he saw acted at Venice, during his abode in that city; it has been since altered by Mr. Tate, and acted at the Theatre in Dorset-Garden; it is now acted under the title of Duke and No Duke.

He has written besides his plays,

What he calls a Chain of Golden Poems, embellished with Mirth, Wit, and Eloquence. Another title put to these runs thus: Choice Poems of several sorts; Epigrams in three Books. He translated into English an Italian Romance, called Dianea, printed at London 1654.

Sir Aston died at Derby, upon the breaking of the great Frost in February 1683, and his body being conveyed to Polesworth in Warwickshire beforementioned, was privately buried there in the chancel of the church. His lordship of Pooley, which had belonged to the name of Cokaine from the time of King Richard II. was sold several years before he died, to one Humphrey Jennings, esq; at which time our author reserved an annuity from it during life. The lordship of Ambourne also was sold to Sir William Boothby, baronet. There is an epigram of his, directed to his honoured friend Major William Warner, which we shall here transcribe as a specimen of his poetry, which the reader will perceive is not very admirable.

> Plays, eclogues, songs, a satyr I have writ,
> A remedy for those i' th' amorous fit:
> Love elegies, and funeral elegies,
> Letters of things of diverse qualities,
> Encomiastic lines to works of some,
> A masque, and an epithalamium,

Two books of epigrams; all which I mean
Shall in this volume come upon the scene;
Some divine poems, which when first I came
To Cambridge, I writ there, I need not name.
Of Dianea, neither my translation,
Omitted here, as of another fashion.
For Heaven's sake name no more, you say I cloy you;
I do obey you; therefore friend God b'wy you.

Footnotes:

1. Athen. Oxon. p. 756, vol. ii.

2. Wood, ubi supra.

Sir George Wharton

Was descended of an ancient family in Westmoreland, and born at Kirby-Kendal in that county, the 4th of April 1617, spent some time at Oxford, and had so strong a propensity to the study of astronomy and mathematics, that little or no knowledge of logic and philosophy was acquired by him[1]. After this, being possesed of some patrimony, he retired from the university, and indulged his genius, till the breaking out of the civil wars, when he grew impatient of sollitude, and being of very loyal principles turned all his inheritance into money, and raised for his Majesty a gallant troop of horse, of which he himself was captain.

After several generous hazards of his person, he was routed, about the 21st of March 1645, near Stow on the Would in Gloucestershire, where Sir Jacob Astley was taken prisoner, and Sir George himself received several scars of honour, which he carried to his grave[2]. After this he retired to Oxford the then residence of the King, and had in recompence of his losses an employment conferred upon him, under Sir John Heydon, then lieutenant-general of the ordnance, which was to receive and pay off money, for the service of the magazine, and artillery; at which time Sir Edward Sherborne was commissary-general of it. It was then, that at leisure hours he followed his studies, was deemed a member of Queen's-College, being entered among the students there, and might with other officers have had the degree of master of arts conferred on him by the members of the venerable convocation, but neglected it. After the surrender of the garrison of Oxford, from which time, the royal cause daily declined, our author was reduced to live upon expedients; he came to London, and in order to gain a livelihood, he wrote several little things, which giving offence to those in power, he was seized on, and imprisoned, first in the Gatehouse, then in Newgate, and at length in Windsor Castle, at which time, when he expected the fevered stroke of an incensed party to fall upon him, he found William Lilly, who had formerly been his antagonist, now his friend, whose humanity and tenderness, he amply repaid after the restoration, when he was made treasurer and paymaster of his Majesty's ordnance, and Lilly stood proscribed as a rebel. Sir George who had formerly experienced the calamity of want, and having now an opportunity of retrieving his fortune, did not let it slip, but so improved it, that he was able to purchase an estate, and in recompence of his stedfast suffering and firm adherence to the cause of Charles I. and the services he rendered Charles II. he was created a baronet by patent, dated 31st of December 1677.

Sir George was esteemed, what in those days was called, a good astrologer, and Wood calls him, in his usual quaint manner, a thorough paced loyalist, a boon companion, and a waggish poet. He died in the year 1681, at his house at Enfield in Middlesex, and left behind him the name of a loyal subject, and an honest man, a generous friend, and a lively wit.

We shall now enumerate his works, and are sorry we have not been able to recover any of his poems in order to present the reader with a specimen. Such is commonly the fate of temporary wit, levelled at some prevailing enormity, which is not of a general nature, but only subsists for a while. The curiosity of posterity is not excited, and there is little pains taken in the preservation of what could only please at the time it was written.

His works are

Hemeroscopions; or Almanacks from 1640 to 1666, printed all in octavo, in which, besides the Gesta Britannorum of that period, there is a great deal of satirical poetry, reflecting on the times.

Mercurio-cælico Mastix; or an Anti caveat to all such as have had the misfortune to be cheated and deluded by that great and traiterous impostor, John Booker, in answer to his frivolous pamphlet, entitled, Mercurius Cælicus; or, a Caveat to the People of England, Oxon. 1644, in twelve sheets in 4to.

England's Iliads in a Nutshell; or a Brief Chronology of the Battles, Sieges, Conflicts, &c. from December 1641, to the 25th of March 1645, printed Oxon. 1645.

An Astrological Judgment upon his Majesty's present March, begun from Oxon. 7th of May 1645 printed in 4to.

Bellum Hybernicale; or Ireland's War, Astrologically demonstrated from the late Celestial Congress of two Malevolent Planets, Saturn and Mars, in Taurus, the ascendant of that kingdom, &c. printed 1647, 40.

Merlini Anglici Errata; or the Errors, Mistakes, &c. of Mr. William Lilly's new Ephemeris for 1647, printed 1647.

Mercurius Elenictus; communicating the unparallelled Proceedings at Westminster, the head quarters, and other places, printed by stealth in London.

This Mercury which began the 29th of October came out sheet by sheet every week in 4to. and continuing interruptedly till the 4th of April 1649, it came out again with No. 1, and continued till towards the end of that year. Mr. Wood says, he has seen several things that were published under the name of Mercurius Elenictus; particularly the Anatomy of Westminster Juncto; or a summary of their Designs against the King and City, printed 1648 in one sheet and a half, 4to. and also the first and second part of the Last Will and Testament of Philip Earl of Pembroke, &c. printed 1649; but Mr. Wood is not quite positive whether Wharton is the author of them or no.

A Short Account of the Fasts and Festivals, as well of the Jews as Christians, &c.

The Cabal of the Twelve Houses astrological, from Morinus, written 1659; and approved by William Oughtred.

A learned and useful Discourse teaching the right observation, and keeping of the holy feast of Easter, &c. written 1665.

Apotelesma; or the Nativity of the World, and revolution thereof.

A Short Discourse of Years, Months, and Days of Years.

Something touching the Nature of Eclipses, and also of their Effects.

Of the Crises in Diseases, &c.

Of the Mutations, Inclinations, and Eversions, &c.

Discourse of the Names, Genius, Species, &c. of all Comets.

Tracts teaching how Astrology may be restored from Marinus.

Secret Multiplication of the Effects of the Stars, from Cardan.

Sundry Rules, shewing by what laws the Weather is governed, and how to discover the Various Alterations of the same.

He also translated from Latin into English the Art of divining by Lines and Signatures, engraven in the Hand of Man, written by John Rockman, M.D. Lond. 1652, 8vo.

This is sometimes called Wharton's Chiromancy.

Most of these foregoing treatises were collected and published together, anno 1683, in 8vo, by John Gadbury; together with select poems, written and published during the civil wars.

Footnotes:

1. Wood Athen Oxon. v. ii.

2. Wood, ubi supra.

Anne Killegrew

This amiable young lady, who has been happy in the praises of Dryden, was daughter of Dr. Henry Killegrew, master of the Savoy, and one of the prebendaries of Westminster. She was born in St. Martin's-Lane in London, a little before the restoration of King Charles II. and was christened in a private chamber, the offices of the Common prayer not being then publickly allowed. She gave the earliest discoveries of a great genius, which being improved by the advantage of a polite education, she became eminent in the arts of poetry and painting, and had her life been prolonged, she might probably have excelled most of the prosession in both[1]. Mr. Dryden is quite lavish in her praise; and we are assured by other cotemporary writers of good probity, that he has done no violence to truth in the most heightened strains of his panegyric: let him be voucher for her skill in poetry.

> Art she had none, yet wanted none,
> For nature did that art supply,
> So rich in treasures of her own,
> She might our boasted stores defy;
> Such noble vigour did her verse adorn,
> That it seem'd borrow'd, where 'twas only born.

That great poet is pleased to attribute to her every poetical excellence. Speaking of the purity and chastity of her compositions, he bestows on them this commendation,

> Her Arethusian stream remains unsoil'd,   }
> Unmix'd with foreign filth and undefil'd;   }
> Her wit was more than man, her innocence a child.   }

She was a great proficient in the art of painting, and drew King James II, and his Queen; which pieces are also highly applauded by Mr. Dryden. She drew several history pieces, also some portraits for her diversion, exceeding well, and likewise some pieces of still life.

Those engaging and polite accomplishments were the least of her perfections; for she crowned all with an exemplary piety, and unblemished virtue. She was one of the maids of honour to the Duchess of York, and died of the small-pox in the very flower of her age, to the unspeakable grief of her relations and acquaintance, on the 16th day of June 1685, in her 25th year.

On this occasion, Mr. Dryden's muse put on a mournful habit, and in one of the most melting elegiac odes that ever was written, has consigned her to immortality.

In the eighth stanza he does honour to another female character, whom he joins with this sweet poetess.

> Now all those charms, that blooming grace,
> The well-proportion'd shape, and beauteous face,
> Shall never more be seen by mortal eyes;
> In earth, the much lamented virgin lies!
> Not wit, nor piety could fate prevent;
> Nor was the cruel destiny content
> To finish all the murder at a blow,
> To sweep at once her life, and beauty too;
> But like a hardened felon took a pride
> To work more mischievously flow,
> And plundered first, and then destroy'd.
> O! double sacrilege, on things divine,
> To rob the relique, and deface the shrine!

> But thus Orinda died;

> Heav'n by the same disease did both translate,
> As equal was their souls, so equal was their fate.

Miss Killegrew was buried in the chancel of St. Baptist's chapel in the Savoy hospital, on the North side of which is a very neat monument of marble and free-stone fixed in the wall, with a Latin inscription, a translation of which into English is printed before her poems.

The following verses of Miss Killegrew's were addressed to Mrs. Philips.

> Orinda (Albion, and her sex's grace)
> Ow'd not her glory to a beauteous face.
> It was her radiant soul that shone within,
> Which struck a lustre thro' her outward skin;

That did her lips and cheeks with roses dye,
Advanc'd her heighth, and sparkled in her eye.
Nor did her sex at all obstruct her fame.
But high'r 'mongst the stars it fixt her name;
What she did write, not only all allow'd,
But evr'y laurel, to her laurel bow'd!

Soon after her death, her Poems were published in a large thin quarto, to which Dryden's ode in praise of the author is prefixed.

Footnote:

1.Ballard's Memoirs of Learned Ladies.

Nat. Lee

This eminent dramatic poet was the son of a clergyman of the church of England, and was educated at Westminster school under Dr. Busby. After he left this school, he was some time at Trinity College, Cambridge; whence returning to London, he went upon the stage as an actor.

Very few particulars are preserved concerning Mr. Lee. He died before he was 34 years of age, and wrote eleven tragedies, all of which contain the divine enthusiasm of a poet, a noble fire and elevation, and the tender breathings of love, beyond many of his cotemporaries. He seems to have been born to write for the Ladies; none ever felt the passion of love more intimately, none ever knew to describe it more gracefully, and no poet ever moved the breasts of his audience with stronger palpitations, than Lee. The excellent Mr. Addison, whose opinion in a matter of this sort, is of the greatest weight, speaking of the genius of Lee, thus proceeds[1]. "Among our modern English poets, there is none who was better turned for tragedy than our author; if instead of favouring the impetuosity of his genius, he had restrained it, and kept it within proper bounds. His thoughts are wonderfully suited for tragedy; but frequently lost in such a cloud of words, that it is hard to see the beauty of them. There is an infinite fire in his works, but so involved in smoke, that it does not appear in half its lustre. He frequently succeeds in the passionate part of the tragedy; but more particularly where he slackens his efforts, and eases the stile of those epithets and metaphors in which he so much abounds."

It is certain that our author for some time was deprived of his senses, and was confined in Bedlam; and as Langbaine observes, it is to be regretted, that his madness exceeded that divine fury which Ovid mentions, and which usually accompany the best poets.

Est Deus in nobus agitante calescimus illo.

His condition in Bedlam was far worse; in a Satire on the Poets it is thus described,

There in a den remov'd from human eyes,

Possest with muse, the brain-sick poet lies,

Too miserably wretched to be nam'd;

For plays, for heroes, and for passion fam'd:

Thoughtless he raves his sleepless hours away   }

In chains all night, in darkness all the day.   }

And if he gets some intervals from pain,   }

The fit returns; he foams and bites his chain,

His eye-balls roll, and he grows mad again.

The reader may please to observe, the two last lines are taken from Lee himself in his description of madness in Cæsar Borgia, which is inimitable. Dryden has observed, that there is a pleasure in being mad, which madmen only know, and indeed Lee has described the condition in such lively terms, that a man can almost imagine himself in the situation,

To my charm'd ears no more of woman tell,
Name not a woman, and I shall be well:
Like a poor lunatic that makes his moan,
And for a while beguiles his lookers on;
He reasons well.—His eyes their wildness lose   }
He vows the keepers his wrong'd sense abuse.   }
But if you hit the cause that hurt his brain,   }
Then his teeth gnash, he foams, he shakes his chain,
His eye-balls roll, and he is mad again.

If we may credit the earl of Rochester, Mr. Lee was addicted to drinking; for in a satire of his, in imitation of Sir John Suckling's Session of the Poets, which, like the original, is destitute of wit, poetry, and good manners, he charges him with it.

The lines, miserable as they are, we shall insert;

Nat. Lee stept in next, in hopes of a prize;
Apollo remembring he had hit once in thrice:
By the rubies in's face, he could not deny,
But he had as much wit as wine could supply;
Confess'd that indeed he had a musical note,
But sometimes strain'd so hard that it rattled in the throat;

Yet own'd he had sense, and t' encourage him for't
He made him his Ovid in Augustus's court.

The testimony of Rochester indeed is of no great value, for he was governed by no principles of honour, and as his ruling passion was malice, he was ready on all occasions to indulge it, at the expence of truth and sincerity. We cannot ascertain whether our author wrote any of his plays in Bedlam, tho' it is not improbable he might have attempted something that way in his intervals.

Mad people have often been observed to do very ingenious things. I have seen a ship of straw, finely fabricated by a mad ship-builder; and the most lovely attitudes have been represented by a mad statuary in his cell.

Lee, for aught we know, might have some noble flights of fancy, even in Bedlam; and it is reported of him, that while he was writing one of his scenes by moon-light, a cloud intervening, he cried out in ecstasy, "Jove snuff the Moon;" but as this is only related upon common report, we desire no more credit may be given to it, than its own nature demands. We do not pretend notwithstanding our high opinion of Lee, to defend all his rants and extravagancies; some of them are ridiculous, some bombast, and others unintelligible; but this observation by no means holds true in general; for tho' some passages are too extravagant, yet others are nobly sublime, we had almost said, unequalled by any other poet.

As there are not many particulars preserved of Lee's life, we think ourselves warranted to enlarge a little upon his works; and therefore we beg leave to introduce to our reader's acquaintance a tragedy which perhaps he has not for some time heard of, written by this great man, viz. Lucius Junius Brutus, the Father of his country.

We mention this tragedy because it is certainly the finest of Lee's, and perhaps one of the most moving plays in our language. Junius Brutus engages in the just defence of the injured rights of his country, against Tarquin the Proud; he succeeds in driving him out of Rome. His son Titus falls in love, and interchanges vows with the tyrant's daughter; his father commands him not to touch her, nor to correspond with her; he faithfully promises; but his resolutions are baffled by the insinuating and irresistible charms of Teraminta; he is won by her beauties; he joins in the attempt to restore Tarquin; the enterprize miscarries, and his own father sits in judgment upon him, and condemns him to suffer.

The interview between the father and son is inexpressibly moving, and is only exceeded by that between the son and his Teraminta. Titus is a young hero, struggling between love and duty. Teraminta an amiable Roman lady, fond of her husband, and dutiful to her father.

There are throughout this play, we dare be bold to affirm, as affecting scenes as ever melted the hearts of an audience. Why it is not revived, may be difficult to account for. Shall we charge it to want of taste in the town, or want of discernment in the managers? or are our present actors conscious that they may be unequal to some of the parts in it? yet were Mr. Quin engaged, at either theatre, to do the author justice in the character of Brutus, we are not wanting in a Garrick or a Barry, to perform the part of Titus; nor is either stage destitute of a Teraminta. This is one of those plays that Mr. Booth proposed to revive (with some few alterations) had he lived to return to the stage: And the part of Brutus was what he purposed to have appeared in.

As to Lee's works, they are in every body's hands, so that we need not trouble the reader with a list of them.

In his tragedy of the Rival Queens, our author has shewn what he could do on the subject of Love; he has there almost exhausted the passion, painted it in its various forms, and delineated the workings of the human soul, when influenced by it.

He makes Statira thus speak of Alexander.

> Not the spring's mouth, nor breath of Jessamin,
> Nor Vi'lets infant sweets, nor op'ning buds
> Are half so sweet as Alexander's breast!
> From every pore of him a perfume falls,
> He kisses softer than a Southern wind
> Curls like a Vine, and touches like a God!
> Then he will talk! good Gods! how he will talk!
> Even when the joy he sigh'd for is possess'd,
> He speaks the kindest words, and looks such things,
> Vows with such passion, swears with so much grace
> That 'tis a kind of Heaven to be deluded by him.
> If I but mention him the tears will fall,
> Sure there is not a letter in his name,
> But is a charm to melt a woman's eyes.

His Tragedy of Theodosius, or the Force of Love, is the only play of Lee's that at present keeps possession of the stage, an argument, in my opinion, not much in favour of our taste, that a Genius should be so neglected.

It is said, that Lee died in the night, in the streets, upon a frolic, and that his father never assisted him in his frequent and pressing necessity, which he was able to do. It appears that tho' Lee was a player, yet, for want of execution, he did not much succeed, though Mr. Cibber says, that he read excellently, and that the players used to tell him, unless they could act the part as he read it, they could not hope success, which, it seems, was not the case with Dryden, who could hardly read to be understood. Lee was certainly a man of great genius; when it is considered how young he died, he performed miracles, and had he lived 'till his fervour cooled, and his judgment strengthened, which might have been the consequence of years, he would have made a greater figure in poetry than some of his contemporaries, who are now placed in superior rank.

Footnote:

1. Spectator. No. 39, vol. 1st.

Samuel Butler

The celebrated author of Hudibras, was born at Strensham in Worcestershire, 1612; His father, a reputable country farmer, perceiving in his son an early inclination to learning, sent him for education to the free-school of Worcester, under the care of Mr. Henry Bright, where having laid the foundation of grammar learning, he was sent for some time to Cambridge, but was never matriculated in that university[1]. After he had resided there six or seven years, he returned to his native county, and became clerk to Mr. Jefferys of Earl's-Croom, an eminent justice of the peace for that county, with whom he lived for some years, in an easy, though, for such a genius, no very reputable service; during which time, through the indulgence of a kind master, he had sufficient leisure to apply himself to his favourite studies, history and poetry, to which, for his diversion, he added music and painting.

The anonymous author of Butler's Life tells us, that he had seen some pictures of his drawing, which were preserved in Mr. Jefferys's family, which I mention not (says he) 'for the excellency of them, but to satisfy the reader of his early inclination to that noble art; for which also he was afterwards entirely loved by Mr. Samuel Cooper, one of the most eminent Painters of his time.' Wood places our poet's improvement in music and painting, to the time of his service under the countess of Kent, by whose patronage he had not only the opportunity of consulting all kinds of books, but conversing also with the great Mr. Selden, who has justly gained the epithet of a living library of learning, and was then conversant in that lady's family, and who often employed our poet to write letters beyond sea, and translate for him. He lived some time also with Sir Samuel Luke, a gentleman of a good family in Bedfordshire, and a famous commander under Oliver Cromwel.

Much about this time he wrote (says the author of his Life) 'the renowned Hudibras; as he then had opportunities of conversing with the leaders of that party, whose religion he calls hypocrisy, whose politics rebellion, and whose speeches nonsense;' he was of an unshaken loyalty, though he was placed in the house of a rebel, and it is generally thought, that under the character of Hudibras, he intended to ridicule Sir Samuel Luke. After the restoration of Charles II. he was made secretary to the earl of Carbury, lord president of the principality of Wales, who appointed him steward of

Ludlow Castle, when the court was revived there; and about this time he married one Mrs. Herbert, a gentlewoman of very good family. Anthony Wood says, she was a widow, and that Butler supported himself by her jointure; for though in his early years he had studied the common law, yet he had made no advantage by the practice of it; but others assert, that she was not a widow, and that though she had a competent fortune, it proved of little or no advantage to Butler, as most of it was unfortunately lost by being put out on bad security. Mr. Wood likewise says, that he was secretary to the duke of Buckingham, when that lord was chancellor of the university of Cambridge, and the life writer assures us he had a great kindness for him: but the late ingenious major Richardson Pack tells a story, which, if true, overthrows both their assertions, and as it is somewhat particular, we shall give it a place here. Mr. Wycherley had taken every opportunity to represent to his grace the duke of Buckingham, how well Mr. Butler had deserved of the Royal Family, by writing his inimitable Hudibras, and that it was a reproach to the court, that a person of his loyalty and wit should languish in obscurity, under so many wants. The duke seemed always to hearken to him with attention, and, after some time, undertook to recommend his pretentions to his Majesty. Mr. Wycherly, in hopes to keep him steady to his word, obtained of his Grace to name a day, when he might introduce that modest, unfortunate poet to his new patron; at last an appointment was made, Mr. Butler and his friend attended accordingly, the duke joined them. But, as the devil would have it (says the major) 'the door of the room, where he sat, was open, and his Grace, who had seated himself near it, observing a pimp of his acquaintance (the creature too was a knight) trip by with a brace of ladies, immediately quitted his engagement to follow another kind of business, at which he was more ready, than at doing good offices to men of desert, though no one was better qualified than he, both in regard to his fortune, and understanding to protect them, and from that hour to the day of his death, poor Butler never found the least effect of his promise, and descended to the grave oppressed with want and poverty.'

The excellent lord Buckhurst, the late earl of Dorset and Middlesex, was a friend to our poet, who, as he was a man of wit and parts himself, knew how to set a just value on those who excelled. He had also promises of places and employment from lord chancellor Clarendon, but, as if poor Butler had been doomed to misfortunes, these proved[2] meer court promises. Mr. Butler in short, affords a remarkable instance of that coldness and neglect, which great genius's often experience from the court and age in which they live; we are told indeed by a gentleman, whose father was intimate with Butler, Charles Longueville, Esq; that Charles II. once gave him a gratuity of three hundred pounds, which had this compliment attending it, that it passed all the offices without any fee, lord Danby being at that time high treasurer, which seems to be the only court favour he ever received; a strange instance of neglect! when we consider King Charles was so excessive fond of this poem of Hudibras; that he carried it always in his pocket, he quoted it almost on every occasion, and never mentioned it, but with raptures.

This is movingly represented in a poem of our author's, published in his remains called Hudibras at Court. He takes occasion to justify his poem, by hinting its excellences in general, and paying a few modest compliments to himself, of which we shall transcribe the following lines.

> Now you must know, sir Hudibras,
> With such perfections gifted was,
> And so peculiar in his manner,
> That all that saw him did him honour;
> Amongst the rest, this prince was one,
> Admired his conversation:
> This prince, whose ready wit, and parts
> Conquer'd both men and women's hearts;
> Was so o'ercome with knight and Ralph,
> That he could never claw it off.
> He never eat, nor drank, nor slept,
> But Hudibras still near him kept;
> Nor would he go to church or so,
> But Hudibras must with him go;
> Nor yet to visit concubine,
> Or at a city feast to dine,
> But Hudibras must still be there,
> Or all the fat was in the fire.
> Now after all was it not hard,
> That he should meet with no reward,
> That fitted out the knight and squire,
> This monarch did so much admire?
> That he should never reimburse
> The man for th' equipage and horse,
> Is sure a strange ungrateful thing
> In any body, but a King.
> But, this good King, it seems was told
> By some, that were with him too bold,
> If e'er you hope to gain your ends,
> Caress your foes, and trust your friends.
> Such were the doctrines that were taught,

'Till this unthinking King was brought
To leave his friends to starve and die;
A poor reward for loyalty.

After having lived to a good old age, admired by all, though personally known but to few, he died September 25, 1680, and was buried at the expence of his good friend Mr. Longueville of the Temple, in the church-yard of St. Paul's Covent-Garden. Mr. Longueville had a strong inclination to have him buried in Westminster Abbey, and spoke with that view to several persons who had been his admirers, offering to pay his part, but none of them would contribute; upon which he was interred privately, Mr. Longueville, and seven or eight more, following him to the grave. Mr. Alderman Barber erected a monument to Butler in Westminster-Abbey.

The poem entitled Hudibras, by which he acquired so high a reputation, was published at three different times; the first part came out in 1668 in 8vo. afterwards came out the second part, and both were printed together, with several additions, and annotations; at last, the third and last part was published, but without any annotations, as appears by the printed copy 1678. The great success and peculiarity of manner of this poem has produced many unsuccessful imitations of it, and some vain attempts have been made to translate some parts of it into Latin. Monsieur Voltaire gives it a very good character, and justly observes, that though there are as many thoughts as words in it, yet it cannot be successfully translated, on account of every line's having some allusion to English affairs, which no foreigner can be supposed to understand, or enter into. The Oxford antiquary ascribes to our author two pamphlets, supposed falsely, he says, to be William Prynne's; the one entitled Mola Asinaria, or the Unreasonable and Insupportable Burthen pressed upon the Shoulders of this Groaning Nation, London 1659, in one sheet 4to. the other, Two Letters: One from John Audland, a Quaker, to William Prynne; the other, Prynne's Answer, in three sheets fol. 1672. The life writer mentions a small poem in one sheet in 4to. on Du Val, a notorious highwayman, said to be written by Butler. These pieces, with a great many others, are published together, under the title of his Posthumous Works. The life writer abovementioned has preserved a fragment of Mr. Butler's, given by one whom he calls the ingenious Mr. Aubrey, who assured him he had it from the poet himself; it is indeed admirable, and the satire sufficiently pungent against the priests.

No jesuit e'er took in hand
To plant a church in barren land;
Nor ever thought it worth the while
A Swede or Russ to reconcile.
For where there is no store of wealth,

Souls are not worth the charge of health.
Spain in America had two designs:
To sell their gospel for their mines:
For had the Mexicans been poor,
No Spaniard twice had landed on their shore.
'Twas gold the Catholic religion planted,
Which, had they wanted gold, they still had wanted.

Mr. Dryden[3] and Mr. Addison[4] have joined in giving testimony against our author, as to the choice of his verse, which they condemn as boyish and being apt to degenerate into the doggrel; but while they censure his verse, they applaud his matter, and Dryden observes, that had he chose any other verse, he would even then have excelled; as we say of a court favourite, that whatever his office be, he still makes it uppermost, and most beneficial to him.

We cannot close the life of this great man, without a reflection on the degeneracy of those times, which suffered him to languish in obscurity; and though he had done more against the Puritan interest, by exposing it to ridicule, than thousands who were rioting at court with no pretensions to favour, yet he was never taken notice of, nor had any calamity redressed, which leaves a stain on those who then ruled, that never can be obliterated. A minister of state seldom fails to reward a court tool, and a man of pleasure pays his instruments for their infamy, and what character must that ministration bear, who allow wit, loyalty and virtue to pass neglected, and, as Cowley pathetically expresses it,

'In that year when manna rained on all, why
should the muses fleece be only dry.'

The following epigram is not unworthy of a place here.

Whilst Butler, needy wretch, was yet alive,
No gen'rous patron would a dinner give;
But lo behold! when dead, the mould'ring dust,
Rewarded with a monumental bust!
A poet's fate, in emblem here is shewn,
He ask'd for bread, and he received —a stone.

Footnotes:

1. Life of Butler, p 6.

2. Posthumous Works of Wycherly, published by Mr. Theobald.

3. Juv. Ded.

4. Spect. No. 6. Vol. i.

Edmund Waller Esq;

Was descended of a family of his name in Buckinghamshire, a younger branch of the Wallers of Kent. He was born March 3, 1605 at Coleshill, which gives Warwickshire the honour of his birth. His father dying when he was very young, the care of his education fell to his mother, who sent him to Eton School, according to the author of his life, but Mr. Wood says, 'that he was mostly educated in grammaticals under one Dobson, minister of Great Wycombe in Bucks, who had been educated in Eton school,' without mentioning that Mr. Waller had been at all at Eton school: after he had acquired grammar learning, he was removed to King's college in Cambridge, and it is manifest that he must have been extremely assiduous in his studies, since he acquired so fine a taste of the ancients, in so short a time, for at sixteen or seventeen years of age, he was chosen into the last Parliament of King James I. and served as Burgess for Agmondesham.

In the year 1623, when Prince Charles nearly escaped being cast away in the road of St. Andre, coming from Spain, Mr. Waller wrote a Poem on that occasion, at an age when, generally speaking, persons of the acutest parts just begin to shew themselves, and at a time when the English poetry had scarce any grace in it. In the year 1628 he addressed a Poem to his Majesty, on his hearing the news of the duke of Buckingham's death, which, with the former, procured him general admiration: harmony of numbers being at that time so great a novelty, and Mr. Waller having, at once, so polished and refined versification, it is no wonder that he enjoyed the felicity of an universal applause. These poems recommended him to court-favour, and rendered him dear to persons of the best taste and distinction that then flourished. A Writer of his life observes, as a proof of his being much caressed by people of the first reputation, that he was one of the famous club, of which the great lord Falkland, Sir Francis Wainman, Mr. Chillingworth, Mr. Godolphin, and other eminent men were members. These were the immortals of that age, and to be associated with them, is one of the highest encomiums which can possibly be bestowed, and exceeds the most laboured strain of a panegyrist.

A circumstance related of this club, is pretty remarkable: One evening, when they were convened, a great noise was heard in the street, which not a little alarmed them, and upon enquiring the cause, they were told, that a son of Ben Johnson's was arrested. This club was too generous to suffer the child of one, who was the genuine son of Apollo, to be carried to a Jail, perhaps for a trifle: they sent for him, but in place of being Ben Johnson's son, he proved to be Mr. George Morley, afterwards bishop of Winchester. Mr. Waller liked him so well, that he paid the debt, which was no less than one hundred pounds, on condition that he would live with him at Beconsfield, which he did eight or ten years together, and from him Mr. Waller used to say, that he learned a taste of the ancient poets, and got what he had of their manner. But it is evident from his poems, written before this incident of Mr. Morley's arrest, that he had early acquired that exquisite Spirit; however, he might have improved it afterwards, by the conversation and assistance of Mr. Morley, to whom this adventure proved very advantageous.

It is uncertain, at what time our author was married, but, it is supposed, that his first wife Anne, daughter and heir of Edward Banks, esq; was dead before he fell in love with lady Dorothy Sidney, daughter to the earl of Leicester, whom he celebrates under the name of Sacharissa. Mr. Waller's passion for this lady, has been the subject of much conversation; his verses, addressed to her, have been renowned for their delicacy, and Sacharissa has been proposed, as a model to succeeding poets, in the celebration of their mistresses. One cannot help wishing, that the poet had been as successful in his Addresses to her, as he has been in his love-strains, which are certainly the sweetest in the world. The difference of station, and the pride of blood, perhaps, was the occasion, that Sacharissa never became the wife of Waller; though in reality, as Mr. Waller was a gentleman, a member of parliament, and a person of high reputation, we cannot, at present, see so great a disproportion: and, as Mr. Waller had fortune, as well as wit and poetry, lord Leicester's daughter could not have been disgraced by such an alliance. At least we are sure of one thing, that she lives for ever in Waller's strains, a circumstance, which even her beauty could not have otherwise procured, nor the lustre of the earl of Sunderland, whom she afterwards married: the countess of Sunderland, like the radiant circles of that age, long before this time would have slept in oblivion, but the Sacharissa of Waller is consigned to immortality, and can never die but with poetry, taste, and politeness.

Upon the marriage of that lady to lord Spenser, afterwards earl of Sunderland, which was solemnized July 11, 1639, Mr. Waller wrote the following letter to lady Lucy Sidney, her sister, which is so full of gallantry, and so elegantly turned, that it will doubtedly give pleasure to our readers to peruse it.

MADAM,

'In this common joy at Penshurst[1], I know, none to whom complaints may come less unseasonable than to your ladyship, the loss of a bedfellow, being almost equal to that of a mistress, and therefore you ought, at least, to pardon, if you consent not to the imprecations of the deserted, which just Heaven no doubt will hear. May my lady Dorothy, if we may yet call her so, suffer as much, and have the like passion for this young lord, whom she has preferred to the rest of mankind, as others have had for her; and may his love, before the year go about, make her taste of the first curse imposed upon womankind, the pains of becoming a mother. May her first born be none of her own sex, nor so like her, but that he may resemble her lord, as much as herself. May she, that always affected silence and retirement, have the house filled with the noise and number of her children, and hereafter of her grand-children; and then may she arrive at that great curse, so much declined by fair ladies, old age; may she live to be very old, and yet seem young; be told so by her glass, and have no aches to inform her of the truth; and when she shall appear to be mortal, may her lord not mourn for her, but go hand in hand with her to that place, where we are told there is neither marrying, nor giving in marriage, that being there divorced, we may all have an equal interest in her again! my revenge being immortal, I wish all this may befall her posterity to the world's end, and afterwards! To you, madam, I wish all good things, and that this loss may, in good time, be happily supplied, with a more constant bedfellow of the other sex. Madam, I humbly kiss your hands, and beg pardon for this trouble, from

'Your ladyship's

'most humble servant,

'E. WALLER.'

He lived to converse with lady Sunderland when she was very old, but his imprecations relating to her glass did not succeed, for my lady knew she had the disease which nothing but death could cure; and in a conversation with Mr. Waller, and some other company at lady Wharton's, she asked him in raillery, 'When, Mr. Waller, will you write such fine verses upon me again?' 'Oh Madam,' said he, 'when your ladyship is as young again.'

In the year 1640, Mr. Waller was returned Burgess for Agmondesham, in which Parliament he opposed the court measures. The writer of his life observes[2], 'that an intermission of Parliaments for 12 years disgusted the nation, and the House met in no good humour to give money. It must be confessed, some late proceedings had raised such jealousies as would be sure to discover themselves, whenever the King should come to ask for a supply;

and Mr. Waller was one of the first to condemn those measures. A speech he made in the House upon this occasion, printed at the end of his poems, gives us some notion of his principles as to government.' Indeed we cannot but confess he was a little too inconstant in them, and was not naturally so steady, as he was judicious; which variable temper was the cause of his losing his reputation, in a great measure, with both parties, when the nation became unhappily divided. His love to poetry, and his indolence, laid him open to the insinuations of others, and perhaps prevented his fixing so resolutely to any one party, as to make him a favourite with either. As Mr. Waller did not come up to the heighths of those who were for unlimited monarchy, so he did not go the lengths of such as would have sunk the kingdom into a commonwealth, but had so much credit at court, that in this parliament the King particularly sent to him, to second his demands of some subsidies to pay the army; and Sir Henry Vane objecting against first voting a supply, because the King would not accept it, unless it came up to his proportion; Mr. Waller spoke earnestly to Sir Thomas Jermyn, comptroller of the houshold, to save his master from the effects of so bold a falsity; for, says he, I am but a country gentleman, and cannot pretend to know the King's mind: but Sir Thomas durst not contradict the secretary; and his son the earl of St. Alban's, afterwards told Mr. Waller, that his father's cowardice ruined the King.

In the latter end of the year 1642, he was one of the commissioners appointed by the Parliament, to present their propositions for peace to his Majesty at Oxford. Mr. Whitelocke, in his Memorials, tells us, that when Mr. Waller kissed the King's hand in the garden at Christ's Church, his Majesty said to him, 'though you are last, yet you are not the worst, nor the least in our favour.' The discovery of a plot, continues Mr. Whitelocke, 'then in hand in London to betray the Parliament, wherein Mr. Waller was engaged, with Chaloner, Tomkins, and others, which was then in agitation, did manifest the King's courtship of Mr. Waller to be for that service.'

In the beginning of the year 1643, our poet was deeply engaged in the design for the reducing the city of London, and the Tower, for the service of his Majesty, which being discovered, he was imprisoned, and fined ten thousand pounds. As this is one of the most memorable circumstances in the life of Waller, we shall not pass it slightly over, but give a short detail of the rise, progress, and discovery of this plot, which issued not much in favour of Mr. Waller's reputation.

Lord Clarendon observes[3], 'that Mr. Waller was a gentleman of very good fortune and estate, and of admirable parts, and faculties of wit and eloquence, and of an intimate conversation and familiarity with those who had that reputation. He had, from the beginning of the Parliament, been looked upon by all men, as a person of very entire affections to the King's service, and to the established government of church and state; and by having no manner of relation to the court, had the more credit and interest to promote the service of it. When the ruptures grew so great between the King, and the two houses, that many of the Members withdrew from those councils, he, among the rest, absented himself, but at the time the standard was set up, having intimacy and friendship with some persons now of nearness about the King, with his Majesty's leave he returned again to London, where he spoke, upon all occasions, with great sharpness and freedom, which was not restrained, and therefore used as an argument against those who were gone upon pretence, that they were not suffered to declare their opinion freely in the House; which could not be believed, when all men knew what liberty Mr. Waller took, and spoke every day with impunity, against the proceedings of the House; this won him a great reputation with all people who wished well to the King; and he was looked upon as the boldest champion the crown had in either House, so that such Lords and Commons who were willing to prevent the ruin of the kingdom, complied in a great familiarity with him, at a man resolute in their ends, and best able to promote them; and it may be, they believed his reputation at court so good, that he would be no ill evidence there of other men's zeal and affection; so all men spoke their minds freely to him, both of the general distemper, and of the passions and ambition of particular persons, all men knowing him to be of too good a fortune, and too wary a nature, to engage himself in designs of hazard.'

Mr. Tomkins already mentioned, had married Waller's sister, and was clerk of the Queen' council, and of very good fame for honesty and ability; great interest and reputation in the city, and conversed much with those who disliked the proceedings of the Parliament, from whom he learned the dispositions of the citizens on all accidents, which he freely communicated to his brother Waller, as the latter imparted to him whatever observations he made from those with whom he conversed. Mr. Waller told him, that many lords and commons were for a peace. Mr. Tomkins made the same relation with respect to the most substantial men of London, which Mr. Waller reported to the well affected members of both houses; and Mr. Tomkins to the well affected citizens; whence they came to a conclusion, that if they heartily united in the mutual assistance of one another, they should be able to prevent those tumults which seemed to countenance the distractions, and both parties would be excited to moderation. The lord Conway at that time coming from Ireland incensed against the Scotch, discontented with the Parliament here, and finding Waller in good esteem with the earl of Northumberland, and in great friendship with the earl of Portland, entered into the same familiarity; and being a soldier, in the discourses they had, he insinuated, it was convenient to enquire into the numbers of the well affected in the city, that they might know whom they had to trust to. Mr. Waller telling Mr. Tomkins this, the latter imparted it to his confidents there; and it was agreed, that some trusty persons in every ward and parish about London should make a list of all the inhabitants, and by guessing at their several affections, compute the strength of that party which opposed an accommodation, and that which was for it.

Lord Clarendon declares, that he believes this design, was to beget such a combination among the well affected parties, that they would refuse to conform to those ordinances of the twentieth part, and other taxes for the support of the war; and thereby or by joint petitioning for peace, and discountenancing the other who petitioned against it, to prevail with the Parliament to incline to a determination of the war, 'but that there ever was, says the earl, 'any formed design either of letting the King's army into London, which was impossible to be effected, or raising an army there, and surprizing the Parliament, or any person of it, or of using any violence in, or upon the city, I could never yet see cause to believe.' But it unluckily happened, that while this combination was on foot, Sir Nicholas Crisp procured a commission of array to be sent from Oxford to London, which was carried by the lady Aubigny, and delivered to a gentleman employed by Sir Nicholas to take it of her; and this being discovered at the same time Mr. Waller's plot was, the two conspiracies were blended into one; tho' the earl of Clarendon is satisfied that they were two distinct designs. His lordship relates the discovery of Mr. Waller's plot in this manner: 'A servant of Mr. Tomkins, who had often cursorily overheard his master and Mr. Waller discourse of the subject which we are upon, placed himself behind the hangings, at a time when they were together; and there whilst either of them discovered the language and opinion of the company which they kept, overheard enough to make him believe, that his information and discovery could make him welcome to those whom he thought concerned, and so went to Mr. Pym, and acquainted him with all he had heard, or probably imagined. The time when Mr. Pym was made acquainted with it, is not known; but the circumstance of publishing it was such as filled all men with apprehensions.'

'It was on Wednesday the 31st of May, their solemn fast day, when being all at their sermon in St. Margaret's church, Westminster, according to their custom, a letter or message was brought privately to Mr. Pym; who thereupon with some of the most active members rose from their seats, and after a little whispering together, removed out of the church. This could not but exceedingly affect those who stayed behind. Immediately they sent guards to all the prisons, at Lambeth-house, Ely-house, and such places where malignants were in custody, with directions to search the prisoners, and some other places which they thought fit should be suspected. After the sermon was ended, the houses met, and were only then told, that letters were intercepted going to the King and the court at Oxford, which expressed some notable conspiracy in hand, to deliver up the Parliament and the city into the hands of the Cavaliers; and that the time for the execution of it drew near. Hereupon a committee was appointed to examine all persons they thought fit, and to apprehend some nominated at that time; and the same night this committee apprehended Mr. Waller and Mr. Tomkins, and the next day such as they suspected.'

The Houses were, or seemed to be, so alarmed with the discovery of the plot, that six days after they took a sacred vow and covenant, which was also taken by the city and army, denouncing war against the King more directly than they had done before. The earl of Portland and lord Conway were imprisoned on Mr. Waller's accusation, and often confronted with him before the committee, where they as peremptorily denying, as he charging them, and there being no other witness but him against them, they were kept a while in restraint, and then bailed. Mr. Waller, after he had had 'says the earl of Clarendon, with incredible dissimulation, acted such a remorse of conscience, that his trial was put off out of christian compassion, till he should recover his understanding (and that was not till the heat and fury of the prosecutors was abated by the sacrifices they had made) and by drawing visitants to himself of the most powerful ministers of all factions, had by his liberality and penitence, his receiving vulgar and vile sayings from them with humility and reverence, as clearer convictions, and informations than in his life he had ever had; and distributing great sums to them for their prayers and ghostly council, so satisfied them, that they satisfied others; was brought at his suit to the bar of the House of Commons on on the 4th of July 1643, where being a man in truth very powerful in language, and who, by what he spoke, and the manner of speaking it, exceedingly captivated the good will, and benevolence of his hearers, with such flattery, as was most exactly calculated to that meridian, with such a submission as their pride took delight in, and such a dejection of mind and spirit, as was like to couzen the major part. He laid before them, their own danger and concernment if they should suffer one of their body, how unworthy and monstrous soever, to be tried by the soldiers, who might thereby grow to such power hereafter, that they would both try those they would not be willing should be tried, and for things which they would account no crime, the inconvenience and insupportable mischief whereof wise commonwealths had foreseen and prevented, by exempting their own members from all judgments but their own. He prevailed, not to be tried by a Council of War, and thereby preserved his dear-bought life; so that in truth he did as much owe the keeping his head to that oration, as Cataline did the loss of his to those of Tully; and having done ill, very well, he by degrees drew that respect to his parts, which always carries some companion to the person, that he got leave to compound for his transgression and them to accept of ten thousand pounds for his liberty; whereupon he had leave to recollect himself in another country (for his liberty was to be banishment) how miserable he had made himself in obtaining that leave to live out of his own. And there cannot be a greater evidence of the inestimable value of his parts, than that he lived in the good affection and esteem of many, the pity of most, and the reproach and scorn of few, or none.'

After this storm had subsided, Mr. Waller travelled into France, where he continued several years. He took over his lady's jewels to support him, and lived very hospitably at Paris, and except that of lord Jermyn, afterwards earl of St. Alban's, who was the Queen of England's prime minister when she kept her court there, there was no English table but Mr. Waller's; which was so costly to him, that he used to say, 'he was at last come to the Rump Jewel.' Upon his return to England, such was the unsteadiness of his temper, he sided with those in power, particularly the Lord Protector, with whom he lived in great intimacy as a companion, tho' he seems not to have acted for him. He often declared that he found Cromwell very well acquainted with the Greek and Roman story; and he frequently took notice, that in the midst of their discourse, a servant has come to tell him, that such and such attended; upon which Cromwell would rise and stop them; talking at the door, where Mr. Waller could over-hear him say, 'The lord will reveal, the lord will help,' and several such expressions; which when he returned to Mr. Waller, he excused, saying, 'Cousin Waller, I must talk to these men after their own way.'

In 1654 he wrote a panegyric on Oliver Cromwell, as he did a poem on his death in 1658. At the restoration he was treated with great civility by King Charles II, who always made him one of his party in his diversions at the duke of Buckingham's, and other places, and gave him a grant of the provostship of Eaton-College; tho' that grant proved of no effect. He sat in several Parliaments after the restoration, and wrote a panegyric upon his Majesty's return, which however, was thought to fall much short of that which he before had wrote on Cromwell. The King one day asked him in raillery, 'How is it Waller, that you wrote a better encomium on Cromwell than on me.' May it please your Majesty, answered the bard, with the most admirable fineness, 'Poets generally succeed best in fiction.' Mr. Waller continued in the full vigour of his genius to the end of his life; his natural vivacity bore up against his years, and made his company agreeable to the last; which appears from the following little story.

King James II having ordered the earl of Sunderland to desire Mr. Waller to attend him one afternoon; when he came, the King carried him into his closet, and there asked him how he liked such a picture? 'Sir, says Mr. Waller, my eyes are dim, and I know not whose it is.' The King answered, 'It is the Princess of Orange;' and says Mr. Waller, 'she is like the greatest woman in the world.' 'Whom do you call so, said the King,' 'Queen Elizabeth, said he.' 'I wonder, Mr. Waller, replied the King, you should think so; but I must confess, she had a wise council;' and Sir, said Mr. Waller, 'did you ever know a Fool chuse a wise one.'

Mr. Waller died of a dropsy October 21, 1687. Finding his distemper encrease, and having yielded all hopes of recovery, he ordered his son-in-law Dr. Peter Birch, to desire all his children to join with him, and give him the sacrament. He at the same time professed himself a believer in revealed religion with great earnestness, telling them, that he remembered when the duke of Buckingham, once talked profanely before King Charles, he told him, 'My lord, I am a great deal older than your grace, and I believe I have heard more arguments for atheism, than ever your grace did; but I have lived long enough to see, there was nothing in them, and so I hope will your grace.' It is said, that had Mr. Waller lived longer, he would have inclined to the revolution, which by the violent measures of James II. he could foresee would happen. He was interred in the church-yard of Beaconsfield, where a monument is erected to his memory, the inscriptions on it were written by Mr. Thomas Rymer.

He left several children behind him: He bequeathed his estate to his second son Edmund, his eldest, Benjamin, being so far from inheriting his father's wit, that he had not a common portion. Edmund, the second Son, used to be chosen member of Parliament for Agmondesham, and in the latter part of his life turned Quaker. William, the third son, was a merchant in London, and Stephen, the fourth, a civilian. Of the daughters, Mary was married to Dr. Peter Birch, prebendary of Westminster; another to Mr. Harvey of Suffolk, another to Mr. Tipping of Oxfordshire.

These are the most material circumstances in the life of Mr. Waller, a man whose wit and parts drew the admiration of the world upon him when he was living, and has secured him the applause of posterity. As a statesman, lord Clarendon is of opinion, he wanted steadiness, and even insinuates, that he was deficient in point of honour; the earl at least construes his timidity, and apparent cowardice, in a way not very advantageous to him.

All men have honoured him as the great refiner of English poetry, who restored numbers to the delicacy they had lost, and joined to melifluent cadence the charms of sense. But as Mr. Waller is unexceptionally the first who brought in a new turn of verse, and gave to rhime all the graces of which it was capable, it would be injurious to his fame, not to present the reader with the opinions of some of the greatest men concerning him, by which he will be better able to understand his particular excellencies, and will see his beauties in full glow before him. To begin with Mr. Dryden, who, in his dedication to the Rival Ladies, addressed to the earl of Orrery, thus characterizes Waller.

'The excellency and dignity of rhime were never fully known till Mr. Waller sought it: He first made writing easily an art; first shewed us to conclude the sense most commonly in distichs, which in the verses of those before him, runs on for so many lines together, that the reader is out of breath to overtake it.'

Voltaire, in his letters concerning the English nation, speaking of British poets, thus mentions Waller. 'Our author was much talked of in France. He had much the same reputation in London that Voiture had in Paris; and in my opinion deserved it better. Voiture was born in an age that was just emerging from barbarity; an age that was still rude and ignorant; the people of which aimed at wit, tho' they had not the least pretensions to it, and sought for points and conceits instead of sentiments. Bristol stones are more easily found than diamonds. Voiture born with an easy and frivolous genius, was the first who shone in this Aurora of French literature. Had he come into the world after those great genius's, who spread such glory over the age of Lewis XIV, he would either have been unknown, would have been despised, or would have corrected his stile. Waller, tho' better than Voiture, was not yet a finished poet. The graces breathe in such of Waller's works as are wrote in a tender strain; but then they are languid thro' negligence, and often disfigured with false thoughts. The English had not at this time attained the art of correct writing; but his serious compositions exhibit a strength and vigour, which could not have been expected from the softness and effeminacy of his other pieces.'

The anonymous author of the preface to the second part of our author's poems, printed in the year 1690, has given his character at large, and tells us; 'That Waller is a name that carries every thing in it that is either great, or graceful in poetry. He was indeed the parent of English verse, and the first who shewed us our tongue had beauty and numbers in it. The tongue came into his hands like a rough diamond; he polished it first, and to that degree, that artists since have admired the workmanship without pretending to mend it. He undoubtedly stands first in the list of refiners; and for ought I know the last too; for I question whether in Charles II's reign; the English did not come to its full perfection, and whether it had not had its Augustan age, as well as the Latin.' Thus far this anonymous author. If I may be permitted to give my opinion in so delicate a point as the reputation of Waller, I shall take the liberty to observe, that had he, in place of preceding, succeeded those great wits who flourished in the reign of Charles II, he could never have rose to such great reputation, nor would have deserved it: No small honour is due to him for the harmony which he introduced, but upon that chiefly does his reputation stand. He certainly is sometimes languid; he was rather a tender than a violent lover; he has not that force of thinking, that amazing reach of genius for which Dryden is renowned, and had it been his lot to have appeared in the reign of Queen Anne, I imagine, he would not have been ranked above the second class of poets. But be this as it may, poetry owes him the highest obligations for refining it, and every succeeding genius will be ready to acknowledge, that by copying Waller's strains, they have improved their own, and the more they follow him, the more they please.

Mr. Waller altered the Maid's Tragedy from Fletcher, and translated the first Act of the Tragedy of Pompey from the French of Corneille. Mrs. Katharine Philips, in a letter to Sir Charles Cotterell, ascribes the translation of the first act to our author; and observes, that Sir Edward Filmer did one, Sir Charles Sidley another, lord Buckhurst another; but who the fifth, says she, I cannot learn.

Mrs. Philips then proceeds to give a criticism on this performance of Waller's, shews some faults, and points out some beauties, with a spirit and candour peculiar to her.

The best edition of our author's works is that published by Mr. Fenton, London 1730, containing poems, speeches, letters, &c. In this edition is added the preface to the first edition of Mr. Waller's poems after the restoration, printed in the year 1664.

As a specimen of Mr. Waller's poetry, we shall give a transcript of his Panegyric upon Oliver Cromwell.

A Panegyric to my Lord Protector, of the present greatness and joint interest of his Highness and this Nation.

In the Year 1654.

> While with a strong, and yet a gentle hand
> You bridle faction, and our hearts command,
> Protect us from our selves, and from the foe,
> Make us unite, and make us conquer too;

Let partial spirits still aloud complain,
Think themselves injur'd that they cannot reign,
And own no liberty, but where they may
Without controul upon their fellows prey.

Above the waves as Neptune shew'd his face
To chide the winds, and save the Trojan race;
So has your Highness, rais'd above the rest,
Storms of Ambition tossing us represt.

Your drooping country, torn with civil hate,
Restor'd by you, is made a glorious state;
The feat of empire, where the Irish come,
And the unwilling Scotch, to fetch their doom.

The sea's our own, and now all nations greet,
With bending sails, each vessel of our fleet.
Your pow'r extends as far as winds can blow,
Or swelling sails upon the globe may go.

Heav'n, that hath plac'd this island to give law,
To balance Europe, and her states to awe,
In this conjunction doth on Britain smile;
The greatest leader, and the greatest isle.

Whether this portion of the world were rent
By the rude ocean from the Continent,
Or thus created, it was sure design'd
To be the sacred refuge of mankind.

Hither th' oppressed shall henceforth resort
Justice to crave, and succour at your court;
And then your Highness, not for our's alone,
But for the world's Protector shall be known.

Fame swifter than your winged navy flies
Thro' ev'ry land that near the ocean lies,
Sounding your name, and telling dreadful News
To all that piracy and rapine use.

With such a chief the meanest nation blest,
Might hope to lift her head above the rest:
What may be thought impossible to do
By us, embraced by the seas, and you?

Lords of the world's great waste, the ocean, we
Whole forests send to reign upon the sea,
And ev'ry coast may trouble or relieve;
But none can visit us without your leave.

Angels and we have this prerogative,
That none can at our happy seats arrive;
While we descend at pleasure to invade
The bad with vengeance, and the good to aid.

Our little world, the image of the great,
Like that, amidst the boundless ocean set,
Of her own growth hath all that nature craves,
And all that's rare, as tribute from the waves.

As Ægypt does not on the clouds rely,
But to the Nile owes more than to the sky;
So what our Earth and what our heav'n denies,
Our ever-constant friend the sea, supplies.

The taste of hot Arabia's spice we know,
Free from the scorching sun that makes it grow;
Without the worm in Persian silks we shine,
And without planting drink of ev'ry vine.

To dig for wealth we weary not our limbs.
Gold (tho' the heaviest Metal) hither swims:
Our's is the harvest where the Indians mow,
We plough the deep, and reap what others sow.

Things of the noblest kind our own soil breeds;
Stout are our men, and warlike are our steeds;
Rome (tho' her eagle thro' the world had flown)
Cou'd never make this island all her own.

Here the third Edward, and the Black Prince too,
France conq'ring Henry flourish'd, and now you;
For whom we staid, as did the Grecian state,
Till Alexander came to urge their fate.

When for more world's the Macedonian cry'd,
He wist not Thetys in her lap did hide
Another yet, a word reserv'd for you,
To make more great than that he did subdue.

He safely might old troops to battle lead
Against th' unwarlike Persian, and the Mede;
Whose hasty flight did from a bloodless field,
More spoils than honour to the visitor yield.

A race unconquer'd, by their clime made bold,
The Caledonians arm'd with want and cold,
Have, by a fate indulgent to your fame,
Been from all ages kept for you to tame.

Whom the old Roman wall so ill confin'd,
With a new chain of garrisons you bind:
Here foreign gold no more shall make them come,
Our English Iron holds them fast at home.

They that henceforth must be content to know
No warmer region than their hills of snow,
May blame the sun, but must extol your grace,
Which in our senate hath allow'd them place.

Preferr'd by conquest, happily o'erthrown,
Falling they rise, to be with us made one:
So kind dictators made, when they came home,
Their vanquish'd foes free citizens of Rome.

Like favour find the Irish, with like fate
Advanc'd to be a portion of our state:
While by your valour, and your bounteous mind,
Nations, divided by the sea, are join'd.

Holland, to gain your friendship, is content
To be our out-guard on the continent:
She from her fellow-provinces wou'd go,
Rather than hazard to have you her foe.

In our late fight, when cannons did diffuse
(Preventing posts) the terror and the news;
Our neighbour princes trembled at their roar:
But our conjunction makes them tremble more.

Your never-failing sword made war to cease,
And now you heal us with the acts of peace
Our minds with bounty and with awe engage,
Invite affection, and restrain our rage.

Less pleasure take brave minds in battles won,
Than in restoring such as are undone:
Tygers have courage, and the rugged bear,
But man alone can whom he conquers, spare.

To pardon willing; and to punish, loath;
You strike with one hand, but you heal with both.
Lifting up all that prostrate lye, you grieve
You cannot make the dead again to live.

When fate or error had our Age mis-led,
And o'er this nation such confusion spread;
The only cure which cou'd from heav'n come down,
Was so much pow'r and piety in one.

One whose extraction's from an ancient line,
Gives hope again that well-born men may shine:
The meanest in your nature mild and good,
The noble rest secured in your blood.

Oft have we wonder'd, how you hid in peace
A mind proportion'd to such things as these;
How such a ruling sp'rit you cou'd restrain,
And practise first over your self to reign.

Your private life did a just pattern give
How fathers, husbands, pious sons shou'd live;
Born to command, your princely virtues slept
Like humble David's while the flock he kept:

But when your troubled country call'd you forth,
Your flaming courage, and your matchless worth
Dazling the eyes of all that did pretend,
To fierce contention gave a prosp'rous end.

Still as you rise, the state, exalted too,
Finds no distemper while 'tis chang'd by you;
Chang'd like the world's great scene, when without noise
The rising sun night's vulgar lights destroys.

Had you, some ages past, this race of glory
Run, with amazement we shou'd read your story;
But living virtue, all atchievements past,
Meets envy still to grapple with at last.

This Cæsar found, and that ungrateful age,
With losing him, went back to blood and rage.
Mistaken Brutus thought to break their yoke,
But cut the bond of union with that stroke.

That sun once set, a thousand meaner stars
Gave a dim light to violence and wars,
To such a tempest as now threatens all,
Did not your mighty arm prevent the fall.

If Rome's great senate cou'd not wield that sword
Which of the conquer'd world had made them lord,
What hope had our's, while yet their pow'r was new,
To rule victorious armies, but by you?

You, that had taught them to subdue their foes,
Cou'd order teach, and their high sp'rits compose:
To ev'ry duty you'd their minds engage,
Provoke their courage, and command their rage.

So when a lion shakes his dreadful mane,
And angry grows; if he that first took pain
To tame his youth, approach the haughty beast,
He bends to him, but frights away the rest.

As the vext world, to find repose, at last
Itself into Augustus' arms did cast:
So England now doth, with like toil opprest,
Her weary head upon your bosom rest.

Then let the muses, with such notes as these,
Instruct us what belongs unto our peace;
Your battles they hereafter shall indite,
And draw the image of our Mars in fight;

Tell of towns storm'd, of armies overcome,
Of mighty kingdoms by your conduct won,
How, while you thunder'd, clouds of dust did choak
Contending troops, and seas lay hid in smoke.

Illustrious acts high raptures do infuse,
And ev'ry conqueror creates a muse;
Here in low strains your milder deeds we sing,
But there, my lord, we'll bays and olive bring,

To crown your head; while you in triumph ride
O'er vanquish'd nations, and the sea beside:
While all your neighbour princes unto you,
Like Joseph's sheaves, pay reverence and bow.

Footnotes:

1. The ancient seat of the Sydneys family in Kent; now in the possession of William Perry, esq; whose lady is niece to the late Sydney, earl of Leicester. A small, but excellent poem upon this delightful seat, was published by an anonymous hand, in 1750, entitled, Penshurst. See Monthly Review, vol. II. page 331.

2. Life, p. 8, 9.

3. History of the Rebellion, Edit. Oxon. 1707, 8vo.

John Ogilby

This poet, who was likewise an eminent Geographer and Cosmographer, was born near Edinburgh in the year 1600[1]. His father, who was of an ancient and genteel family, having spent his estate, and being prisoner in the King's Bench for debt, could give his son but little education at school; but our author, who, in his early years discovered the most invincible industry, obtained a little knowledge in the Latin grammar, and afterwards so much money, as not only to procure his father's discharge from prison, but also to bind himself apprentice to Mr. Draper a dancing master in Holbourn, London. Soon after, by his dexterity in his profession, and his complaisant behaviour to his master's employers, he obtained the favour of them to lend him as much money as to buy out the remaining part of his time, and set up for himself; but being afterwards appointed to dance in the duke of Buckingham's great Masque, by a false step, he strained a vein in the inside of his leg, which ever after occasioned him to halt. He afterwards taught dancing to the sisters of Sir Ralph Hopton, at Wytham in Somersetshire, where, at leisure, he learned to handle the pike and musket. When Thomas earl of Strafford became Lord Lieutenant of Ireland, he was retained in his family to teach the art of dancing, and being an excellent penman, he was frequently employed by the earl to transcribe papers for him.

In his lordship's family it was that he first gave proofs of his inclination to poetry, by translating some of Æsop's Fables into English verse, which he communicated to some learned men, who understood Latin better than he, by whose assistance and advice he published them. He was one of the troop of guards belonging to the earl, and composed an humourous piece entitled the Character of a Trooper. About the time he was supported by his lordship, he was made master of the revels for the kingdom of Ireland, and built a little theatre for the representation of dramatic entertainments, in St. Warburgh's street in Dublin: but upon the breaking out of the rebellion in that kingdom, he was several times in great danger of his life, particularly when he narrowly escaped being blown up in the castle of Rathfarnam. About the time of the conclusion of the war in England, he left Ireland, and being shipwrecked, came to London in a very necessitous condition. After he had made a short stay in the metropolis, he travelled on foot to Cambridge, where his great industry, and love of learning, recommended him to the notice of several scholars, by whose assistance he became so compleat a master of the Latin tongue, that in 1646 he published an English translation of Virgil, which was printed in large 8vo. and dedicated to William marquis of Hereford. He reprinted it at London 1654 in fol. with this title; The Works of Publius Virgilius Maro, translated and adorned with Sculptures, and illustrated with Annotations; which, Mr. Wood tells us, was the fairest edition, that till then, the English press ever produced. About the year 1654 our indefatigable author learned the Greek language, and in four year's time published in fol. a translation of Homer's Iliad, adorned with excellent sculptures, illustrated with Annotations, and addressed to King Charles II. The same year he published the Bible in a large fol. at Cambridge, according to the translation set forth by the special command of King James I. with the Liturgy and Articles of the Church of England, with Chorographical Sculptures. About the year 1662 he went into Ireland, then having obtained a patent to be made master of the revels there, a place which Sir William Davenant sollicited in vain. Upon this occasion he built a theatre at Dublin, which cost him 2000 l. the former being ruined during the troubles. In 1664 he published in London, in fol. a translation of Homer's Odyssey, with Sculptures, and Notes. He afterwards wrote two heroic poems, one entitled the Ephesian Matron, the other the Roman Slave, both dedicated to Thomas earl of Ossory. The next work he composed was an Epic Poem in 12 Books, in honour of King Charles I. but this was entirely lost in the fire of London in September 1666, when Mr. Ogilby's house in White Fryars was burnt down, and his whole fortune, except to the value of five pounds, destroyed. But misfortunes seldom had any irretrievable consequences to Ogilby, for by his insinuating address, and most astonishing industry, he was soon able to repair whatever loss he sustained by any cross accident. It was not long till he fell on a method of raising a fresh sum of money. Procuring his house to be rebuilt, he set up a printing-office, was appointed his Majesty's Cosmographer and Geographic Printer, and printed many great works translated and collected by himself and his assistants, the enumeration of which would be unnecessary and tedious.

This laborious man died September 4, 1676, and was interred in the vault under part of the church in St. Bride's in Fleet-street. Mr. Edward Philips in his Theatrum Poetarum stiles him one of the prodigies, from producing, after so late an initiation into literature, so many large and learned volumes, as well in verse as in prose, and tells us, that his Paraphrase upon Æsop's Fables, is generally confessed to have exceeded whatever hath been done before in that kind.

As to our author's poetry, we have the authority of Mr. Pope to pronounce it below criticism, at least his translations; and in all probability his original epic poems which we have never seen, are not much superior to his translations of Homer and Virgil. If Ogilby had not a poetical genius, he was notwithstanding a man of parts, and made an amazing proficiency in literature, by the force of an unwearied application. He cannot be sufficiently commended for his virtuous industry, as well as his filial piety, in procuring, in so early a time of life, his father's liberty, when he was confined in a prison.

Ogilby seems indeed to have been a good sort of man, and to have recommended himself to the world by honest means, without having recourse to the servile arts of flattery, and the blandishments of falshood. He is an instance of the astonishing efficacy of application; had some more modern poets been blessed with a thousandth part of his oeconomy and industry, they needed not to have lived in poverty, and died of want. Although Ogilby cannot be denominated a genius, yet he found means to make a genteel livelihood by literature, which many of the sons of Parnassus, blessed with superior powers, curse as a very dry and unpleasing soil, but which proceeds more from want of culture, than native barrenness.

Footnote:

1. Athen Oxon. vol. ii. p. 378.

Wilmot, Earl of Rochester

It is an observation founded on experience, that the poets have, of all other men, been most addicted to the gratifications of appetite, and have pursued pleasure with more unwearied application than men of other characters. In this respect they are indeed unhappy, and have ever been more subject to pity than envy. A violent love of pleasure, if it does not destroy, yet, in a great measure, enervates all other good qualities with which a man may be endowed; and as no men have ever enjoyed higher parts from nature, than the poets, so few, from this unhappy attachment to pleasure, have effected so little good by those amazing powers. Of the truth of this observation, the nobleman, whose memoirs we are now to present to the reader, is a strong and indelible instance, for few ever had more ability, and more frequent opportunities, for promoting the interests of society, and none ever prostituted the gifts of Heaven to a more inglorious purpose. Lord Rochester was not more remarkable for the superiority of his parts, than the extraordinary debauchery of his life, and with his dissipations of pleasure, he suffered sometimes malevolent principles to govern him, and was equally odious for malice and envy, as for the boundless gratifications of his appetites.

This is, no doubt, the character of his lordship, confirmed by all who have transmitted any account of him: but if his life was supremely wicked, his death was exemplarily pious; before he approached to the conclusion of his days, he saw the follies of his former pleasures, he lived to repent with the severest contrition, and charity obliges all men to believe that he was as sincere in his protestations of penitence, as he had been before in libertine indulgence. The apparent sorrow he felt, arising from the stings and compunctions of conscience, entitle him to the reader's compassion, and has determined us to represent his errors with all imaginable tenderness; which, as it is agreeable to every benevolent man, so his lordship has a right to this indulgence, since he obliterated his faults by his penitence, and became so conspicuous an evidence on the side of virtue, by his important declarations against the charms of vice.

Lord Rochester was son of the gallant Henry lord Wilmot, who engaged with great zeal in the service of King Charles I. during the civil wars, and was so much in favour with Charles II. that he entrusted his person to him, after the unfortunate battle of Worcester, which trust he discharged with so much fidelity and address, that the young King was conveyed out of England into France, chiefly by his care, application and vigilance. The mother of our author was of the ancient family of the St. Johns in Wiltshire, and has been celebrated both for her beauty and parts.

In the year 1648, distinguished to posterity, by the fall of Charles I. who suffered on a scaffold erected before the window of his own palace, our author was born at Dichley, near Woodstock, in the same county, the scene of many of his pleasures, and of his death. His lordship's father had the misfortune to reap none of the rewards of suffering loyalty, for he died in 1660, immediately before the restoration, leaving his son as the principal part of his inheritance, his titles, honours, and the merit of those extraordinary services he had done the crown; but though lord Wilmot left his son but a small estate, yet he did not suffer in his education by these means, for the oeconomy of his mother supplied that deficiency, and he was educated suitable to his quality. When he was at school (it is agreed by all his biographers) he gave early instances of a readiness of wit; and those shining parts which have since appeared with so much lustre, began then to shew themselves: he acquired the Latin to such perfection, that, to his dying day, he retained a great relish for the masculine firmness, as well as more elegant beauties of that language, and was, says Dr. Burnet, 'exactly versed in those authors who were the ornaments of the court of Augustus, which he read often with the peculiar delight which the greatest wits have often found in those studies.' When he went to the university, the general joy which over-ran the nation upon his Majesty's return, amounted to something like distraction, and soon spread a very malignant influence through all ranks of life. His lordship tasted the pleasures of libertinism, which then broke out in a full tide, with too acute a relish, and was almost overwhelmed in the abyss of wantonness. His tutor was Dr. Blandford, afterwards promoted to the sees of Oxford and Worcester, and under his inspection he was committed to the more immediate care of Phinehas Berry, fellow of Wadham College, a man of learning and probity, whom his lordship afterwards treated with much respect, and rewarded as became a great man; but notwithstanding the care of his tutor, he had so deeply engaged in the dissipations of the general jubilee, that he could not be prevailed upon to renew his studies, which were totally lost in the joys more agreeable to his inclination. He never thought of resuming again the pursuit of knowledge, 'till the fine address of his governor, Dr. Balfour, won him in his travels, by degrees, to those charms of study, which he had through youthful levity forsaken, and being seconded by reason, now more strong, and a more mature taste of the pleasure of learning, which the Dr. took care to place in the most agreeable and advantageous light, he became enamoured of knowledge, in the pursuit of which he often spent those hours he sometimes stole from the witty, and the fair. He returned from his travels in the 18th year of his age, and appeared at court with as great advantage as any young nobleman ever did. He had a graceful and well proportioned person, was master of the most refined breeding, and possessed a very obliging and easy manner. He had a vast vivacity of thought, and a happy flow of expression, and all who conversed with him entertained the highest opinion of his understanding; and 'tis indeed no wonder he was so much caressed at a court which abounded with men of wit, countenanced by a merry prince, who relished nothing so much as brilliant conversation.

Soon after his lordship's return from his travels, he took the first occasion that offered, to hazard his life in the service of his country.

In the winter of the year 1665 he went to sea, with the earl of Sandwich, when he was sent out against the Dutch East India fleet, and was in the ship called the Revenge, commanded by Sir Thomas Tiddiman, when the attack was made on the port of Bergen in Norway, the Dutch Ships having got into that port. It was, says Burnet, 'as desperate an attempt as ever was made, and during the whole action, the earl of Rochester shewed as brave and resolute a courage as possible. A person of honour told me he heard the lord Clifford, who was in the same ship, often magnify his courage at that time very highly; nor did the rigour of the season, the hardness of the voyage, and the extreme danger he had been in, deter him from running the like the very next occasion; for the summer following he went to sea again, without communicating his design to his nearest relations. He went aboard the ship commanded by Sir Edward Spragge, the day before the great sea-fight of that year; almost all the volunteers that went in that ship were killed. During the action, Sir Edward Spragge not being satisfied with the behaviour of one of the captains, could not easily find a person that would undertake to venture through so much danger to carry his command to the captain; this lord offered himself to the service, and went in a little boat, through all the shot, and delivered his message, and returned back to Sir Edward, which was much commended by all that saw it.' These are the early instances of courage, which can be produced in favour of lord Rochester, which was afterwards impeached, and very justly, for in many private broils, he discovered a timid pusillanimous spirit, very unsuitable to those noble instances of the contrary, which have just been mentioned.

The author of his life prefixed to his works, which goes under the name of M. St. Evremond, addressed to the Duchess of Mazarine, but which M. Maizeau asserts not to be his, accounts for it, upon the general observation of that disparity between a man and himself, upon different occasions. Let it suffice, says he, 'to observe, that we differ not from one another, more than we do from ourselves at different times.' But we imagine another, and a stronger reason may be given, for the cowardice which Rochester afterwards discovered in private broils, particularly in the affair between him and the earl of Mulgrave, in which he behaved very meanly[1]. The courage which lord Rochester shewed in a naval engagement, was in the early part of his life, before he had been immersed in those labyrinths of excess and luxury, into which he afterwards sunk. It is certainly a true observation, that guilt makes cowards; a man who is continually subjected to the reproaches of conscience, who is afraid to examine his heart, lest it should appear too horrible, cannot have much courage: for while he is conscious of so many errors to be repented of, of so many vices he has committed, he naturally starts at danger, and flies from it as his greatest enemy. It is true, courage is sometimes constitutional, and there have been instances of men, guilty of every enormity, who have discovered a large share of it, but these have been wretches who have overcome all sense of honour, been lost to every consideration of virtue, and whose courage is like that of the lion of the desart, a kind of ferocious impulse unconnected with reason. Lord Rochester had certainly never overcome the reproaches of his conscience, whose alarming voice at last struck terror into his heart, and chilled the fire of the spirits.

Since his travels, and naval expeditions, he seemed to have contracted a habit of temperance, in which had he been so happy as to persevere, he must have escaped that fatal rock, on which he afterwards split, upon his return to court, where love and pleasure kept their perpetual rounds, under the smiles of a prince, whom nature had fitted for all the enjoyments of the most luxurious desires. In times so dissolute as these, it is no wonder if a man of so warm a constitution as Rochester, could not resist the too flattering temptations, which were heightened by the participation of the court in general. The uncommon charms of Rochester's conversation, induced all men to court him as a companion, tho' they often paid too dear for their curiosity, by being made the subject of his lampoons, if they happened to have any oddities in their temper, by the exposing of which he could humour his propensity to scandal. His pleasant extravagancies soon became the subject of general conversation, by which his vanity was at once flattered, and his turn of satire rendered more keen, by the success it met with.

Rochester had certainly a true talent for satire, and he spared neither friends nor foes, but let it loose on all without discrimination. Majesty itself was not secure from it; he more than once lampooned the King, whose weakness and attachment to some of his mistresses, he endeavoured to cure by several means, that is, either by winning them from him, in spite of the indulgence and liberality they felt from a royal gallant, or by severely lampooning them and him on various occasions; which the King, who was a man of wit and pleasure, as well as his lordship, took for the natural sallies of his genius, and meant rather as the amusements of his fancy, than as the efforts of malice; yet, either by a too frequent repetition, or a too close and poignant virulence, the King banished him from the court for a satire made directly on him; this satire consists of 28 stanzas, and is entitled The Restoration, or the History of the Insipids; and as it contains the keenest reflexions against the political conduct, and private character of that Prince, and having produced the banishment of this noble lord, we shall here give it a place, by which his lordship's genius for this kind of writing will appear.

The RESTORATION, or The History of INSIPIDS, a Lampoon.

I.

Chaste, pious, prudent, Charles the second,
The miracle of thy restoration,
May like to that of quails be reckon'd,
Rain'd on the Israelitish nation;
The wish'd for blessing from Heaven sent,
Became their curse and punishment.

II.

The virtues in thee, Charles, inherent,
Altho' thy count'nance be an odd piece,
Prove thee as true a God's Vicegerent,
As e'er was Harry with his cod-piece:
For chastity, and pious deeds,
His grandsire Harry Charles exceeds.

III.

Our Romish bondage-breaker Harry,
Espoused half a dozen wives.
Charles only one resolv'd to marry,
And other mens he never ——;
Yet has he sons and daughters more
Than e'er had Harry by threescore.

IV.

Never was such a faith's defender;
He like a politic Prince, and pious,
Gives liberty to conscience tender,
And does to no religion tie us;
Jews, Christians, Turks, Papists, he'll please us
With Moses, Mahomet, or Jesus.

V.

In all affairs of church or state
He very zealous is, and able,
Devout at pray'rs, and sits up late
At the cabal and council-table.
His very dog, at council-board,
Sits grave and wise as any lord.

VI.

Let Charles's policy no man flout,
The wisest Kings have all some folly;
Nor let his piety any doubt;
Charles, like a Sov'reign, wise and holy,
Makes young men judges of the bench,
And bishops, those that love a wench.

VII.

His father's foes he does reward,
Preserving those that cut off's head;
Old cavaliers, the crown's best guard,
He lets them starve for want of bread.
Never was any King endow'd
With so much grace and gratitude.

VIII.

Blood, that wears treason in his face,
Villain compleat in parson's gown,
How much is he at court in grace,
For stealing Ormond and the crown!
Since loyalty does no man good,
Let's steal the King, and out-do Blood.

IX.

A Parliament of knaves and sots
(Members by name you must not mention)
He keeps in pay, and buys their votes,
Here with a place, there with a pension:
When to give money he can't cologue 'em,
He does with scorn prorogue, prorogue 'em.

X.

But they long since, by too much giving,
Undid, betray'd, and sold the nation,
Making their memberships a living,
Better than e'er was sequestration.
God give thee, Charles, a resolution
To damn the knaves by dissolution.

XI.

Fame is not grounded on success,
Tho' victories were Cæsar's glory;
Lost battles make not Pompey less,
But left him stiled great in story.
Malicious fate does oft devise
To beat the brave, and fool the wise.

XII.

Charles in the first Dutch war stood fair
To have been Sov'reign of the deep,
When Opdam blew up in the air,
Had not his Highness gone to sleep:
Our fleet slack'd sails, fearing his waking,
The Dutch had else been in sad taking.

XIII.

The Bergen business was well laid,
Tho' we paid dear for that design;
Had we not three days parling staid,
The Dutch fleet there, Charles, had been thine:
Tho' the false Dane agreed to fell 'em,
He cheated us, and saved Skellum.

XIV.

Had not Charles sweetly chous'd the States,
By Bergen-baffle grown more wise;
And made 'em shit as small as rats,
By their rich Smyrna fleet's surprise:
Had haughty Holmes, but call'd in Spragg,
Hans had been put into a bag.

XV.

Mists, storms, short victuals, adverse winds,
And once the navy's wise division,
Defeated Charles's best designs,
'Till he became his foes derision:
But he had swing'd the Dutch at Chatham,
Had he had ships but to come at 'em.

XVI.

Our Black-Heath host, without dispute,
(Rais'd, put on board, why? no man knows)
Must Charles have render'd absolute
Over his subjects, or his foes:
Has not the French King made us fools,
By taking Maestricht with our tools?

XVII.

But Charles, what could thy policy be,
To run so many sad disasters;
To join thy fleet with false d'Estrees
To make the French of Holland masters?
Was't Carewell, brother James, or Teague,
That made thee break the Triple League?

XVIII.

Could Robin Viner have foreseen
The glorious triumphs of his master;
The Wool-Church statue Gold had been,
Which now is made of Alabaster.
But wise men think had it been wood,
'Twere for a bankrupt King too good.

XIX.

Those that the fabric well consider.
Do of it diversly discourse;
Some pass their censure on the rider,
Others their judgment on the horse.
Most say, the steed's a goodly thing,
But all agree, 'tis a lewd King.

XX.

By the lord mayor and his grave coxcombs,
Freeman of London, Charles is made;
Then to Whitehall a rich Gold box comes,
Which was bestow'd on the French jade[2]:
But wonder not it should be so, sirs,
When Monarchs rank themselves with Grocers.

XXI.

Cringe, scrape no more, ye city-fops,
Leave off your feasting and fine speeches;
Beat up your drums, shut up your shops,
The courtiers then will kiss your breeches.
Arm'd, tell the Popish Duke that rules,
You're free-born subjects, not French mules.

XXII.

New upstarts, bastards, pimps, and whores,
That, locust-like, devour the land,
By shutting up th'Exchequer-doors,
When there our money was trapann'd,
Have render'd Charles's restoration
But a small blessing to the nation.

XXIII.

Then, Charles, beware thy brother York,
Who to thy government gives law;
If once we fall to the old sport,
You must again both to Breda;
Where, spite of all that would restore you,
Grown wise by wrongs, we should abhor you.

XXIV.

If, of all Christian blood the guilt
Cries loud of vengeance unto Heav'n,
That sea by treach'rous Lewis spilt,
Can never be by God forgiv'n:
Worse scourge unto his subjects, lord!
Than pest'lence, famine, fire, or sword.

XXV.

That false rapacious wolf of France,
The scourge of Europe, and its curse,
Who at his subjects cries does dance,
And studies how to make them worse;
To say such Kings, Lord, rule by thee,
Were most prodigious blasphemy.

XXVI.

Such know no law, but their own lust;
Their subjects substance, and their blood,
They count it tribute due and just,
Still spent and spilt for subjects good.
If such Kings are by God appointed,
The devil may be the Lord's anointed.

XXVII.

Such Kings! curs'd be the pow'r and name,
Let all the world henceforth abhor 'em;
Monsters, which knaves sacred proclaim,
And then, like slaves, fall down before 'em.
What can there be in Kings divine?
The most are wolves, goats, sheep, or swine.

XXVIII.

Then farewel, sacred Majesty,
Let's pull all brutish tyrants down;
Where men are born, and still live free,
There ev'ry head doth wear a crown:
Mankind, like miserable frogs,
Prove wretched, king'd by storks and dogs.

Much about this time the duke of Buckingham was under disgrace, for things of another nature, and being disengaged from any particular attachment in town, he and lord Rochester resolved, like Don Quixote of old, to set out in quest of adventures; and they met with some that will appear entertaining to our readers, which we shall give upon the authority of the author of Rochester's Life, prefixed to his works. Among many other adventures the following was one:

There happened to be an inn on New-market road to be lett, they disguised themselves in proper habits for the persons they were to assume, and jointly took this inn, in which each in his turn officiated as master; but they soon made this subservient to purposes of another nature.

Having carefully observed the pretty girls in the country with whom they were most captivated, (they considered not whether maids, wives, or widows) and to gain opportunities of seducing them, they invited the neighbours, who had either wives or daughters, to frequent feasts, where the men were plied hard with good liquor, and the women sufficiently warmed to make but as little resistance as would be agreeable to their inclinations, dealing out their poison to both sexes, inspiring the men with wine, and other strong liquors, and the women with love; thus they were able to deflower many a virgin, and alienate the affections of many a wife by this odd stratagem; and it is difficult to say, whether it is possible for two men to live to a worse purpose.

It is natural to imagine that this kind of life could not be of long duration. Feasts so frequently given, and that without any thing to pay, must give a strong suspicion that the inn-keepers must soon break, or that they were of such fortune and circumstances, as did not well suit the post they were in.— This their lordships were sensible of, but not much concerned about it, since they were seldom found long to continue in the same sort of adventures, variety being the life of their enjoyments. It was besides, near the time of his Majesty's going to Newmarket, when they designed, that the discovery of their real plots, should clear them of the imputation of being concerned in any more pernicious to the government. These two conjectures meeting, they thought themselves obliged to dispatch two important adventures, which they had not yet been able to compass.—There was an old covetous miser in the neighbourhood, who notwithstanding his age, was in possession of a very agreeable young wife. Her husband watched her with the same assiduity he did his money, and never trusted her out of his sight, but under the protection of an old maiden sister, who never had herself experienced the joys of love, and bore no great benevolence to all who were young and handsome. Our noble inn-keepers had no manner of doubt of his accepting a treat, as many had done, for he loved good living with all his heart, when it cost him nothing; and except upon these occasions he was the most temperate and abstemious man alive; but then they could never prevail with him to bring his wife, notwithstanding they urged the presence of so many good wives in the neighbourhood to keep her company. All their study was then how to deceive the old sister at home, who was set as a guardian over that fruit which the miser could neither eat himself, nor suffer any other to taste; but such a difficulty as this was soon to be overcome by such inventions. It was therefore agreed that lord Rochester should be dressed in woman's cloaths, and while the husband was feasting with my lord duke, he should make trial of his skill with the old woman at home. He had learned that she had no aversion to the bottle when she could come secretly and conveniently at it. Equipped like a country lass, and furnished with a bottle of spiritous liquors, he marched to the old miser's house. It was with difficulty he found means to speak with the old woman, but at last obtained the favour; where perfect in all the cant of those people, he began to tell the occasion of his coming, in hopes she would invite him to come in, but all in vain; he was admitted no further that the porch, with the house door a-jar: At last, my lord finding no other way, fell upon this expedient. He pretended to be taken suddenly ill, and tumbled down upon the threshold. This noise brings the young wife to them, who with much trouble persuades her keeper to help her into the house, in regard to the decorum of her sex, and the unhappy condition she was in. The door had not been long shut, till our imposter by degrees recovers, and being set on a chair, cants a very religious thanksgiving to the good gentlewoman for her kindness, and observed how deplorable it was to be subject to such fits, which often took her in the street, and exposed her to many accidents, but every now and then took a sip of the bottle, and recommended it to the old benefactress, who was sure to drink a hearty dram. His lordship had another bottle in his pocket qualified with a Opium, which would sooner accomplish his desire, by giving the woman a somniferous dose, which drinking with greediness, she soon fell fast asleep.

His lordship having so far succeeded, and being fired with the presence of the young wife, for whom he had formed this odd scheme, his desires became impetuous, which produced a change of colour, and made the artless creature imagine the fit was returning. My lord then asked if she would be so charitable as to let him lie down on the bed; the good-natured young woman shewed him the way, and being laid down, and staying by him at his request, he put her in mind of her condition, asking about her husband, whom the young woman painted in his true colours, as a surly, jealous old tyrant. The rural innocent imagining she had only a woman with her, was less reserved in her behaviour and expressions on that account, and his lordship soon found that a tale of love would not be unpleasing to her. Being now no longer able to curb his appetite, which was wound up beyond the power of restraint, he declared his sex to her, and without much struggling enjoyed her.

He now became as happy as indulgence could make him; and when the first transports were over, he contrived the escape of this young adultress from the prison of her keeper. She hearkened to his proposals with pleasure, and before the old gentlewoman was awake, she robbed her husband of an hundred and fifty pieces, and marched off with lord Rochester to the inn, about midnight.

They were to pass over three or four fields before they could reach it, and in going over the last, they very nearly escaped falling into the enemy's hands; but the voice of the husband discovering who he was, our adventurers struck down the field out of the path, and for the greater security lay down in the grass. The place, the occasion, and the person that was so near, put his lordship in mind of renewing his pleasure almost in sight of the cuckold. The fair was no longer coy, and easily yielded to his desires. He in short carried the girl home and then prostituted her to the duke's pleasure, after he had been cloyed himself. The old man going home, and finding his sitter asleep, his wife fled, and his money gone, was thrown into a state of madness, and soon hanged himself. The news was soon spread about the neighbourhood, and reached the inn, where both lovers, now as weary of their purchase as desirous of it before, advised her to go to London, with which she complied, and in all probability followed there the trade of prostitution for a subsistence.

The King, soon after this infamous adventure, coming that way, found them both in their posts at the inn, took them again into favour, and suffered them to go with him to Newmarket. This exploit of lord Rochester is not at all improbable, when his character is considered; His treachery in the affair of the miser's wife is very like him; and surely it was one of the greatest acts of baseness of which he was ever guilty; he artfully seduced her, while her unsuspecting husband was entertained by the duke of Buckingham; he contrived a robbery, and produced the death of the injured husband; this complicated crime was one of those heavy charges on his mind when he lay on his death-bed, under the dreadful alarms of his conscience.

His lordship's amours at court made a great noise in the world of gallantry, especially that which he had with the celebrated Mrs. Roberts, mistress to the King, whom she abondoned for the possession of Rochester's heart, which she found to her experience, it was not in her power long to hold. The earl, who was soon cloyed with the possession of any one woman, tho' the fairest in the world, forsook her. The lady after the first indignation of her passion subsided, grew as indifferent, and considered upon the proper means of retrieving the King's affections. The occasion was luckily given her one morning while she was dressing: she saw the King coming by, she hurried, down with her hair disheveled, threw herself at his feet, implored his pardon, and vowed constancy for the future. The King, overcome with the well-dissembled agonies of this beauty, raised her up, took her in his arms, and protested no man could see her, and not love her: he waited on her to her lodging, and there compleated the reconciliation. This easy behaviour of the King, had, with many other instances of the same kind, determined my lord Hallifax to assert, "That the love of King Charles II, lay as much as any man's, in the lower regions; that he was indifferent as to their constancy, and only valued them for the sensual pleasure they could yield."

Lord Rochester's frolics in the character of a mountebank are well known, and the speech which he made upon the occasion of his first turning itinerant doctor, has been often printed; there is in it a true spirit of satire, and a keenness of lampoon, which is very much in the character of his lordship, who had certainly an original turn for invective and satirical composition.

We shall give the following short extract from this celebrated speech, in which his lordship's wit appears pretty conspicuous.

"If I appear (says Alexander Bendo) to any one like a counterfeit, even for the sake of that chiefly ought I to be construed a true man, who is the counterfeit's example, his original, and that which he employs his industry and pains to imitate and copy. Is it therefore my fault if the cheat, by his wit and endeavours, makes himself so like me, that consequently I cannot avoid resembling him? Consider, pray, the valiant and the coward, the wealthy merchant and the bankrupt; the politician and the fool; they are the same in many things, and differ but in one alone. The valiant man holds up his hand, looks confidently round about him, wears a sword, courts a lord's wife, and owns it; so does the coward. One only point of honour, and that's courage, which (like false metal, one only trial can discover) makes the distinction. The bankrupt walks the exchange, buys bargains, draws bills, and accepts them with the richest, whilst paper and credit are current coin; that which makes the difference is real cash, a great defect indeed, and yet but one, and that the last found out, and still till then the least perceived.—Now for the politician; he is a grave, deliberating, close, prying man: Pray are there not grave, deliberating, close, prying fools? If therefore the difference betwixt all these (tho' infinite in effect) be so nice in all appearance, will you yet expect it should be otherwise between the false physician, astrologer, &c. and the true? The first calls himself learned doctor, sends forth his bills, gives physic and council, tells, and foretells; the other is bound to do just as much. It is only your experience must distinguish betwixt them, to which I willingly submit myself."

When lord Rochester was restored again to the favour of King Charles II, he continued the same extravagant pursuits of pleasure, and would even use freedoms with that Prince, whom he had before so much offended; for his satire knew no bounds, his invention was lively, and his execution sharp.

He is supposed to have contrived with one of Charles's mistress's the following stratagem to cure that monarch of the nocturnal rambles to which he addicted himself. He agreed to go out one night with him to visit a celebrated house of intrigue, where he told his Majesty the finest women in England were to be found. The King made no scruple to assume his usual disguise and accompany him, and while he was engaged with one of the ladies of pleasure, being before instructed by Rochester how to behave, she pick'd his pocket of all his money and watch, which the king did not immediately miss. Neither the people of the house, nor the girl herself was made acquainted with the quality of their visitor, nor had the least suspicion who he was. When the intrigue was ended, the King enquired for Rochester, but was told he had quitted the house, without taking leave. But into what embarassment was he thrown when upon searching his pockets, in order to discharge the reckoning, he found his money gone; he was then reduced to ask the favour of the Jezebel to give him credit till tomorrow, as the gentleman who came in with him had not returned, who was to have pay'd for both. The consequence of this request was, he was abused, and laughed at; and the old woman told him, that she had often been served such dirty tricks, and would not permit him to stir till the reckoning was paid, and then called one of her bullies to take care of him. In this ridiculous distress stood the British monarch; the prisoner of a bawd, and the life upon whom the nation's hopes were fixed, put in the power of a ruffian. After many altercations the King at last proposed, that she should accept a ring which he then took off his finger, in pledge for her money, which she likewise refused, and told him, that as she was no judge of the value of the ring, she did not chuse to accept such pledges. The King then desired that a Jeweller might be called to give his opinion of the value of it, but he was answered, that the expedient was impracticable, as no jeweller could then be supposed to be out of bed. After much entreaty his Majesty at last prevailed upon the fellow, to knock up a jeweller and shew him the ring, which as soon as he had inspected, he stood amazed, and enquired, with eyes fixed upon the fellow, who he had got in his house? to which he answered, a black-looking ugly son of a w— —, who had no money in his pocket, and was obliged to pawn his ring. The ring, says the jeweller, is so immensely rich, that but one man in the nation could afford to wear it; and that one is the King. The jeweller being astonished at this accident, went out with the bully, in order to be fully satisfied of so extraordinary an affair; and as soon as he entered the room, he fell on his knees, and with the utmost respect presented the ring to his Majesty. The old Jezebel and the bully finding the extraordinary quality of their guest, were now confounded, and asked pardon most submissively on their knees. The King in the best natured manner forgave them, and laughing, asked them, whether the ring would not bear another bottle.

Thus ended this adventure, in which the King learned how dangerous it was to risk his person in night-frolics; and could not but severely reprove Rochester for acting such a part towards him; however he sincerely resolved never again to be guilty of the like indiscretion.

These are the most material of the adventures, and libertine courses of the lord Rochester, which historians and biographers have transmitted to posterity; we shall now consider him as an author.

He seems to have been too strongly tinctured with that vice which belongs more to literary people, than to any other profession under the fun, viz. envy. That lord Rochester was envious, and jealous of the reputation of other men of eminence, appears abundantly clear from his behaviour to Dryden, which could proceed from no other principle; as his malice towards him had never discovered itself till the tragedies of that great poet met with such general applause, and his poems were universally esteemed. Such was the inveteracy he shewed to Mr. Dryden, that he set up John Crown, an obscure man, in opposition to him, and recommended him to the King to compose a masque for the court, which was really the business of the poet laureat; but when Crown's Conquest of Jerusalem met with as extravagant success as Dryden's Almanzor's, his lordship then withdrew his favour from Crown, as if he would be still in contradiction to the public. His malice to Dryden is said to have still further discovered itself, in hiring ruffians to cudgel him for a satire he was supposed to be the author of, which was at once malicious, cowardly, and cruel: But of this we shall give a fuller account in the life of Mr. Dryden.

Mr. Wolsely, in his preface to Valentinian, a tragedy, altered by lord Rochester from Fletcher, has given a character of his lordship and his writings, by no means consistent with that idea, which other writers, and common tradition, dispose us to form of him.

'He was a wonderful man, says he, whether we consider the constant good sense, and agreeable mirth of his ordinary conversation, or the vast reach and compass of his inventions, and the amazing depth of his retired thoughts; the uncommon graces of his fashion, or the inimitable turns of his wit, the becoming gentleness, the bewitching softness of his civility, or the force and fitness of his satire; for as he was both the delight, the love, and the dotage of the women, so was he a continued curb to impertinence, and the public censure of folly; never did man stay in his company unentertained, or leave it uninstructed; never was his understanding biassed, or his pleasantness forced; never did he laugh in the wrong place, or prostitute his sense to serve his luxury; never did he stab into the wounds of fallen virtue, with a base and a cowardly insult, or smooth the face of prosperous villany, with the paint and washes of a mercenary wit; never did he spare a sop for being rich, or flatter a knave for being great. He had a wit that was accompanied with an unaffected greatness of mind, and a natural love to justice and truth; a wit that was in perpetual war with knavery, and ever attacking those kind of vices most, whose malignity was like to be the most dissusive, such as tended more immediately to the prejudice of public bodies; and were a common nusance to the happiness of human kind. Never was his pen drawn but on the side of good sense, and usually employed like the arms of the ancient heroes, to stop the progress of arbitrary oppression, and beat down the brutishness of headstrong will: to do his King and country justice, upon such public state thieves as would beggar a kingdom to enrich themselves: these were the vermin whom to his eternal honour his pen was continually pricking and goading; a pen, if not so happy in the success, yet as generous in the aim, as either the sword of Theseus, or the club of Hercules; nor was it less sharp than that, or less weighty than this. If he did not take so much care of himself as he ought, he had the humanity however, to wish well to others; and I think I may truly affirm he did the world as much good by a right application of satire, as he hurt himself by a wrong pursuit of pleasure.'

In this amiable light has Mr. Wolsely drawn our author, and nothing is more certain, than that it is a portraiture of the imagination, warmed with gratitude, or friendship, and bears but little or no resemblance to that of Rochester; can he whose satire is always levelled at particular persons, be said to be the terror of knaves, and the public foe of vice, when he himself has acknowledged that he satirized only to gratify his resentment; for it was his opinion, that writing satires without being in a rage, was like killing in cold blood. Was his conversation instructive whose mouth was full of obscenity; and was he a friend to his country, who diffused a dangerous venom thro' his works to corrupt its members? in which, it is to be feared he has been but too successful. Did he never smooth the face of prosperous villainy, as, Mr. Wolsely expresses it, the scope of whose life was to promote and encourage the most licentious debauchery, and to unhinge all the principles of honour?—Either Mr. Wolsely must be strangely mistaken? or all other writers who have given us accounts of Rochester must be so; and as his single assertions are not equal to the united authorities of so many, we may reasonably reject his testimony as a deviation from truth.

We have now seen these scenes of my lord Rochester's life, in which he appears to little advantage; it is with infinite pleasure we can take a view of the brighter side of his character; to do which, we must attend him to his death-bed. Had he been the amiable man Mr. Wolsely represents him, he needed not have suffered so many pangs of remorse, nor felt the horrors of conscience, nor been driven almost to despair by his reflexions on a mispent life.

Rochester lived a profligate, but he died a penitent. He lived in defiance of all principles; but when he felt the cold hand of death upon him, he reflected on his folly, and saw that the portion of iniquity is, at last, sure to be only pain and anguish.

Dr. Burnet, the excellent bishop of Sarum (however he may be reviled by a party) with many other obligations conferred upon the world, has added some account of lord Rochester in his dying moments. No state policy in this case, can well be supposed to have biased him, and when there are no motives to falsehood, it is somewhat cruel to discredit assertions. The Dr. could not be influenced by views of interest to give this, or any other account of his lordship; and could certainly have no other incentive, but that of serving his country, by shewing the instability of vice, and, by drawing into light an illustrious penitent, adding one wreath more to the banners of virtue.

Burnet begins with telling us, that an accident fell out in the early part of the Earl's life, which in its consequences confirmed him in the pursuit of vicious courses.

"When he went to sea in the year 1665, there happened to be in the same ship with him, Mr. Montague, and another gentleman of quality; these two, the former especially, seemed persuaded that they mould never return into England. Mr. Montague said, he was sure of it; the other was not so positive. The earl of Rochester and the last of these entered into a formal engagement, not without ceremonies of religion, that if either of them died, he should appear and give the other notice of the future state, if there was any. But Mr. Montague would not enter into the bond. When the Day came that they thought to have taken the Dutch fleet in the port of Bergen, Mr. Montague, tho' he had such a strong presage in his mind of his approaching death, yet he bravely stayed all the while in the place of the greatest danger. The other gentleman signalized his courage in the most undaunted manner, till near the end of the action; when he fell on a sudden into such a trembling, that he could scarce stand: and Mr. Montague going to him to hold him up, as they were in each other; arms, a cannon ball carried away Mr. Montague's belly, so that he expired in an hour after."

The earl of Rochester told Dr. Burnet, that these presages they had in their minds, made some impression on him that there were separate beings; and that the soul either by a natural sagacity, or some secret notice communicated to it, had a sort of divination. But this gentleman's never appearing was a snare to him during the rest of his life: Though when he mentioned this, he could not but acknowledge, it was an unreasonable thing for him to think that beings in another state were not under such laws and limits that they could not command their motion, but as the supreme power should order them; and that one who had so corrupted the natural principles of truth as he had, had no reason to expect that miracles should be wrought for his conviction.

He told Dr. Burnet another odd presage of approaching death, in lady Ware, his mother-in-law's family. The chaplain had dreamed that such a day he should die; but being by all the family laughed out of the belief of it, he had almost forgot it, till the evening before at supper; there being thirteen at table, according to an old conceit that one of the family must soon die; one of the young ladies pointed to him, that he was the person. Upon this the chaplain recalling to mind his dream, fell into some disorder, and the lady Ware reproving him for his superstition, he said, he was confident he was to die before morning; but he being in perfect health, it was not much minded. It was saturday night, and he was to preach next day. He went to his chamber and set up late as it appeared by the burning of his candle; and he had been preparing his notes for his sermon, but was found dead in his bed next morning.

These things his lordship said, made him incline to believe that the soul was of a substance distinct from matter; but that which convinced him of it was, that in his last sickness, which brought him so near his death, when his spirits were so spent he could not move or stir, and did not hope to live an hour, he said his reason and judgment were so clear and strong, that from thence he was fully persuaded, that death was not the dissolution of the soul, but only the separation of it from matter. He had in that sickness great remorse for his past life; but he afterwards said, they were rather general and dark horrors, than any conviction of transgression against his maker; he was sorry he had lived so as to waste his strength so soon, or that he had brought such an ill name upon himself; and had an agony in his mind about it, which he knew not well how to express, but believed that these impunctions of conscience rather proceeded from the horror of his condition, than any true contrition for the errors of his life.

During the time Dr. Burnet was at lord Rochester's house, they entered frequently into conversation upon the topics of natural and reveal'd religion, which the Dr. endeavoured to enlarge upon and explain in a manner suitable to the condition of a dying penitent; his lordship expressed much contrition for his having so often violated the laws of the one, against his better knowledge, and having spurned the authority of the other in the pride of wanton sophistry. He declared that he was satisfied of the truth of the christian religion, that he thought it the institution of heaven, and afforded the most natural idea of the supreme being, as well as the most forcible motives to virtue of any faith professed amongst men.

'He was not only satisfied (says Dr. Burnet) of the truth of our holy religion, merely as a matter of speculation, but was persuaded likewise of the power of inward grace, of which he gave me this strange account. He said Mr. Parsons, in order to his conviction, read to him the 53d chapter of the prophesies of Isaiah, and compared that with the history of our Saviour's passion, that he might there see a prophesy concerning it, written many ages before it was done; which the Jews that blasphemed Jesus Christ still kept in their hands as a book divinely inspired. He said, as he heard it read, he felt an inward force upon him, which did so enlighten his mind and convince him, that he could resist it no longer, for the words had an authority which did shoot like rays or beams in his mind, so that he was not only convinced by the reasonings he had about it, which satisfied his understanding, but by a power, which did so effectually constrain him that he ever after firmly believed in his Saviour, as if he had seen him in the clouds.'

We are not quite certain whether there is not a tincture of enthusiasm in this account given by his lordship, as it is too natural to fly from one extreme to another, from the excesses of debauchery to the gloom of methodism; but even if we suppose this to have been the case, he was certainly in the safest extreme; and there is more comfort in hearing that a man whose life had been so remarkably profligate as his, should die under such impressions, than quit the world without one pang for past offences.

The bishop gives an instance of the great alteration of his lordship's temper and dispositions (from what they were formerly) in his sickness. 'Whenever he happened to be out of order, either by pain or sickness, his temper became quite ungovernable, and his passions so fierce, that his servants were afraid to approach him. But in this last sickness he was all humility, patience, and resignation. Once he was a little offended with the delay of a servant, who he thought made not haste enough, with somewhat he called for, and said in a little heat, that damn'd fellow.' Soon after, says the Dr. I told him that I was glad to find his stile so reformed, and that he had so entirely overcome that ill habit of swearing, only that word of calling any damned which had returned upon him was not decent; his answer was, 'O that language of fiends, which was so familiar to me, hangs yet about me, sure none has deserved more to be damned than I have done; and after he had humbly asked God pardon for it, he desired me to call the person to him that he might ask him forgiveness; but I told him that was needless, for he had said it of one who did not hear it, and so could not be offended by it. In this disposition of mind, continues the bishop, all the while I was with him four days together; he was then brought so low that all hope of recovery was gone. Much purulent matter came from him with his urine, which he passed always with pain, but one day with inexpressible torment; yet he bore it decently, without breaking out into repinings, or impatient complaints. Nature being at last quite exhausted, and all the floods of life gone, he died without a groan on the 26th of July 1680, in the 33d year of his age. A day or two before his death he lay much silent, and seemed extremely devout in his contemplations; he was frequently observed to raise his eyes to heaven, and send forth ejaculations to the searcher of hearts, who saw his penitence, and who, he hoped, would forgive him.'

Thus died lord Rochester, an amazing instance of the goodness of God, who permitted him to enjoy time, and inclined his heart to penitence. As by his life he was suffered to set an example of the most abandoned dissoluteness to the world; so by his death, he was a lively demonstration of the fruitlessness of vicious courses, and may be proposed as an example to all those who are captivated with the charms of guilty pleasure.

Let all his failings now sleep with him in the grave, and let us only think of his closing moments, his penitence, and reformation. Had he been permitted to have recovered his illness, it is reasonable to presume he would have been as lively an example of virtue as he had ever been of vice, and have born his testimony in favour of religion.

He left behind him a son named Charles, who dying on the 12th of November, was buried by his father on the 7th of December following: he also left behind him three daughters. The male line ceasing, Charles II. conferred the title of earl of Rochester on Lawrence viscount Killingworth, a younger son of Edward earl of Clarendon.

We might now enumerate his lordship's writings, of which we have already given some character; but unhappily for the world they are too generally diffused, and we think ourselves under no obligations to particularize those works which have been so fruitful of mischief to society, by promoting a general corruption of morals; and which he himself in his last moments wished he could recal, or rather that he never had composed.

Footnotes:

1. See the Life of Sheffield Duke of Buckingham.

2. The Duchess of Portsmouth.

George Villiers, Duke of Buckingham

Son and heir of George, duke, marquis, and earl of Buckingham, murdered by Felton in the year 1628. This nobleman was born at Wallingford-House in the parish of St. Martin's in the Fields on the 30th of January 1627, and baptized there on the 14th of February following, by Dr. Laud, then bishop of Bath and Wells, afterwards archbishop of Canterbury.

Before we proceed to give any particulars of our noble author's life, we must entreat the reader's indulgence to take a short view of the life of his grace's father, in which, some circumstances extremely curious will appear; and we are the more emboldened to venture upon this freedom, as some who have written this life before us, have taken the same liberty, by which the reader is no loser; for the first duke of Buckingham was a man whose prosperity was so instantaneous, his honours so great, his life so dissipated, and his death so remarkable, that as no minister ever enjoyed so much power, so no man ever drew the attention of the world more upon him. No sooner had he returned from his travels, and made his first appearance at court, than he became a favourite with King James, who, (says Clarendon) 'of all wise men he ever knew, was most delighted and taken with handsome persons and fine cloaths.'

He had begun to be weary of his favourite the earl of Somerset, who was the only one who kept that post so long, without any public reproach from the people, till at last he was convicted of the horrid conspiracy against the life of Sir Thomas Overbury, and condemned as a murderer. While these things were in agitation, Villiers appeared at court; he was according to all accounts, the gayest and handsomest man in his time, of an open generous temper, of an unreserved affability, and the most engaging politeness.

In a few days he was made cup-bearer to the King, by which he was of course to be much in his presence, and so admitted to that conversation with which that prince always abounded at his meals. He had not acted five weeks on this stage, to use the noble historian's expression, till he mounted higher, being knighted, and made gentleman of the bed-chamber, and knight of the most noble order of the garter, and in a short time a baron, a viscount, an earl, a marquis, and lord high-admiral of England, lord warden of the cinque ports, master of the horse, and entirely disposed all the favours of the King, acting as absolutely in conferring honours and distinctions, as if he himself had wore the diadem.

We find him soon after making war or peace, according to humour, resentment, or favour. He carried the prince of Wales into Spain to see the Infanta, who was proposed to him as a wife; and it plainly enough appears, that he was privy to one intrigue of prince Charles, and which was perhaps the only one, which that prince, whom all historians, whether friends or enemies to his cause; have agreed to celebrate for chastity, and the temperate virtues. There is an original letter of prince Charles to the duke, which was published by Mr. Thomas Hearne, and is said once to have belonged to archbishop Sancroft. As it is a sort of curiosity we shall here insert it,

"STENNY,

"I have nothing now to write to you, but to give you thankes both for the good councell ye gave me, and for the event of it. The King gave mee a good sharpe potion, but you took away the working of it by the well relished comfites ye sent after it. I have met with the partie, that must not be named, once alreddie, and the culler of wryting this letter shall make mee meet with her on saturday, although it is written the day being thursday. So assuring you that the bus'ness goes safely onn, I rest

"Your constant friend

"CHARLES.

"I hope you will not shew the King this letter, but put it in the safe custody of mister Vulcan."

It was the good fortune of this nobleman to have an equal interest with the son as with the father; and when prince Charles ascended the throne, his power was equally extensive, and as before gave such offence to the House of Commons and the people, that he was voted an enemy to the realm, and his Majesty was frequently addressed to remove him from his councils. Tho' Charles I. had certainly more virtues, and was of a more military turn than his father, yet in the circumstance of doating upon favourites, he was equally weak. His misfortune was, that he never sufficiently trusted his own judgment, which was often better than that of his servants; and from this diffidence he was tenacious of a minister of whose abilities he had a high opinion, and in whose fidelity he put confidence.

The duke at last became so obnoxious, that it entered into the head of an enthusiast, tho' otherwise an honest man, one lieutenant Felton, that to assassinate this court favourite, this enemy of the realm, would be doing a grateful thing to his country by ridding it of one whose measures in his opinion, were likely soon to destroy it.—

The fate of the duke was now approaching, and it is by far the most interesting circumstance in his life.

We shall insert, in the words of the noble historian, the particular account of it.

'John Felton, an obscure man in his own person, who had been bred a soldier, and lately a lieutenant of foot, whose captain had been killed on the retreat at the Isle of Ree, upon which he conceived that the company of right ought to have been conferred upon him; and it being refused him by the duke of Buckingham, general of the army, had given up his commission and withdrawn himself from the army. He was of a melancholic nature, and had little conversation with any body, yet of a gentleman's family in Suffolk, of a good fortune, and reputation. From the time that he had quitted the army he resided at London; when the House of Commons, transported with passion and prejudice against the duke, had accused him to the House of Peers for several misdemeanors and miscarriages, and in some declarations had stiled him the cause of all the evils the kingdom suffered, and an enemy to the public.

'Some transcripts of such expressions, and some general invectives he met with amongst the people, to whom this great man was not grateful, wrought so far upon this melancholic gentleman, that he began to believe he should do God good service if he killed the duke. He chose no other instrument to do it than an ordinary knife, which he bought of a common cutler for a shilling, and thus provided, he repaired to Portsmouth, where he arrived the eve of St. Bartholomew. The duke was then there, in order to prepare and make ready the fleet and the army, with which he resolved in a few days to transport himself to the relief of Rochelle, which was then besieged by cardinal Richelieu, and for the relief whereof the duke was the more obliged, by reason that at his being at the Isle of Ree, he had received great supplies of victuals, and some companies of their garrison from the town, the want of both which they were at this time very sensible of, and grieved at.

'This morning of St. Bartholomew, the duke had received letters, in which he was advertised, that Rochelle had relieved itself; upon which he directed that his breakfast might be speedily made ready, and he would make haste to acquaint the King with the good news, the court being then at Southwick, about five miles from Portsmouth. The chamber in which he was dressing himself was full of company, and of officers in the fleet and army. There was Monsieur de Soubize, brother to the duke de Rohan, and other French gentlemen, who were very sollicitous for the embarkation of the army, and for the departure of the fleet for the relief of Rochelle; and they were at that time in much trouble and and perplexity, out of apprehension that the news the duke had received that morning might slacken the preparations of the voyage, which their impatience and interest, persuaded them was not advanced with expedition; and so they held much discourse with the duke of the impossibility that his intelligence could be true, and that it was contrived by the artifice and dexterity of their enemies, in order to abate the warmth and zeal that was used for their relief, the arrival of which relief, those enemies had much reason to apprehend; and a longer delay in sending it, would ease them of that terrible apprehension; their forts and works towards the sea, and in the harbour being almost finished.

'This discourse, according to the natural custom of that nation, and by the usual dialect of that language, was held with such passion and vehemence, that the standers-by who understood not French, did believe they were angry, and that they used the duke rudely. He being ready, and informed that his breakfast was ready, drew towards the door, where the hangings were held up; and in that very passage turning himself to speak with Sir Thomas Fryer, a colonel of the army, who was then speaking near his ear, he was on a sudden struck over his shoulder upon the breast with a knife; upon which, without using any other words, than that the villain has killed me, and in the same moment pulling out the knife himself, he fell down dead, the knife having pierced his heart. No man had ever seen the blow, or the man who gave it; but in the confusion they were in, every man made his own conjecture, and declared it as a thing known, most agreeing, that it was done by the French, from the angry discourse they thought they had heard from them, and it was a kind of miracle, that they were not all killed that instant: The sober sort that preserved them from it, having the same opinion of their guilt, and only reserving them for a more judicial examination, and proceeding.

'In the crowd near the door, there was found upon the ground a hat, in the inside whereof, there was sewed upon the crown a paper, in which were writ four or five lines of that declaration made by the House of Commons, in which they had stiled the duke an enemy to the kingdom; and under it a short ejaculation towards a prayer. It was easily enough concluded, that the hat belonged to the person who had committed the murder, but the difficulty remained still as great, who that person should be; for the writing discovered nothing of the name; and whosoever it was, it was very natural to believe, that he was gone far enough not to be found without a hat. In this hurry, one running one way, another another way, a man was seen walking before the door very composedly without a hat; whereupon one crying out, here's the fellow that killed the duke, upon which others run thither, every body asking which was he; to which the man without the hat very composedly answered, I am he. Thereupon some of those who were most furious suddenly run upon the man with their drawn swords to kill him; but others, who were at least equally concerned in the loss and in the sense of it, defended him; himself with open arms very calmly and chearfully exposing himself to the fury and swords of the most enraged, as being very willing to fall a sacrifice to their sudden anger, rather than be kept for deliberate justice, which he knew must be executed upon him.

'He was now enough known, and easily discovered to be that Felton, whom we mentioned before, who had been a lieutenant in the army; he was quickly carried into a private room by the persons of the best condition, some whereof were in authority, who first thought fit, so far to dissemble, as to mention the duke only grievously wounded, but not without hopes of recovery. Upon which Felton smiled, and said, he knew well enough he had given him a blow that had determined all their hopes. Being then asked at whose instigation he had performed that horrid, wretched act, he answered them with a wonderful assurance, That they should not trouble themselves in that enquiry; that no man living had credit or power enough with him to have engaged or disposed him, to such an action, that he had never entrusted his purpose or resolution to any man; that it proceeded from himself, and the impulse of his own conscience, and that the motives thereunto will appear if his hat were found. He spoke very frankly of what he had done, and bore the reproaches of them that spoke to him, with the temper of a man who thought he had not done amiss. But after he had been in prison some time, where he was treated without any rigour, and with humanity enough; and before and at his tryal, which was about four months after, at the King's Bench, he behaved himself with great modesty, and wonderful repentance; being as he said convinced in his conscience that he had done wickedly, and asked pardon of the King and Duchess, and all the Duke's servants, whom he acknowledged he had offended, and very earnestly besought the judges that he might have his hand struck off, with which he had performed that impious act before he should be put to death.'

This is the account lord Clarendon gives in the first volume of his history, of the fall of this great favourite, which serves to throw a melancholy veil over the splendor of his life, and demonstrates the extreme vanity of exterior pomp, and the danger those are exposed to who move on the precipice of power. It serves to shew that of all kind of cruelty, that which is the child of enthusiasm is the word, as it is founded upon something that has the appearance of principles; and as it is more stedfast, so does it diffuse more mischief than that cruelty which flows from the agitations of passion: Felton blindly imagined he did God service by assassination, and the same unnatural zeal would perhaps have prompted him to the murder of a thousand more, who in his opinion were enemies to their country.

The above-mentioned historian remarks, that there were several prophecies and predictions scattered about, concerning the duke's death; and then proceeds to the relation of the most astonishing story we have ever met with.

As this anecdote is countenanced by so great a name, I need make no apology for inserting it, it has all the evidence the nature of the thing can admit of, and is curious in itself.

'There was an officer in the King's wardrobe in Windsor-Castle of a good reputation for honesty and discretion, and then about the age of fifty years, or more. This man had been bred in his youth in a school in the parish where Sir George Villiers the father of the Duke lived, and had been much cherished and obliged in that season of his age, by the said Sir George, whom afterwards he never saw. About six months before the miserable end of the duke of Buckingham, about midnight, this man, being in his bed at Windsor, where his office was, and in very good health, there appeared to him, on the side of his bed, a man of very venerable aspect, who fixing his eyes upon him, asked him, if he knew him; the poor man half dead with fear, and apprehension, being asked the second time, whether he remembered him, and having in that time called to his memory, the presence of Sir George Villiers, and the very cloaths he used to wear, in which at that time he used to be habited; he answered him, That he thought him to be that person; he replied, that he was in the right, that he was the same, and that he expected a service from him; which was, that he should go from him to his son the duke of Buckingham, and tell him, if he did not somewhat to ingratiate himself to the people, or at least, to abate the extreme malice they had against him, he would be suffered to live but a short time, and after this discourse he disappeared, and the poor man, if he had been at all waking, slept very well till the morning, when he believed all this to be a dream, and considered it no otherwise.

'Next night, or shortly after, the same person appeared to him again in the same place, and about the same time of the night, with an aspect a little more severe than before; and asking him whether he had done as he required him? and perceiving he had not, he gave him very severe reprehensions, and told him, he expected more compliance from him; and that if he did not perform his commands, he should enjoy no peace of mind, but should be always pursued by him: Upon which he promised to obey him.

'But the next morning waking exceedingly perplexed with the lively representation of all that had passed, he considered that he was a person at such a distance from the duke, that he knew not how to find any admittance into his presence, much less any hope to be believed in what he should say, so with great trouble and unquietness he spent some time in thinking what he should do. The poor man had by this time recovered the courage to tell him, That in truth he had deferred the execution of his commands, upon considering how difficult a thing it would be for him to get access to the duke, having acquaintance with no person about him; and if he could obtain admission to him, he would never be able to persuade him that he was sent in such a manner, but he should at best be thought to be mad, or to be set on and employed by his own or the malice of other men to abuse the duke, and so he should be sure to be undone. The person replied, as he had done before, that he should never find rest, till he should perform what he required, and therefore he were better to dispatch it; that the access to his son was known to be very easy; and that few men waited long for him, and for the gaining him credit, he would tell him two or three particulars, which he charged him never to mention to any person living, but to the duke himself; and he should no sooner hear them, but he would believe all the rest he should say; and so repeating his threats he left him.

'In the morning the poor man more confirmed by the last appearance, made his journey to London, where the court then was. He was very well known to Sir Ralph Freeman, one of the masters of the requests, who had married a lady that was nearly allied to the duke, and was himself well received by him. To him this man went; and tho' he did not acquaint him with all the particulars, he said enough to him to let him see there was somewhat extraordinary in it, and the knowledge he had of the sobriety and discretion of the man, made the more impression on him. He desired that by his means he might be brought to the duke, to such a place, and in such a manner as should be thought fit; affirming, that he had much to say to him; and of such a nature as would require much privacy, and some time and patience in the hearing. Sir Ralph promised he would speak first to the duke of him, and then he should understand his pleasure, and accordingly on the first opportunity he did inform him of the reputation and honesty of the man, and then what he desired, and all he knew of the matter. The duke according to his usual openness and condescension told him, that he was the next day, early, to hunt with the King; that his horses should attend him to Lambeth Bridge, where he would land by five o'Clock in the morning, and if the man attended him there at that hour, he would walk and speak with him as long as should be necessary. Sir Ralph carried the man with him next morning, and presented him to the duke at his landing, who received him courteously, and walked aside in conference near an hour, none but his own servants being at that hour near the place, and they and Sir Ralph at such a distance, that they could not hear a word, though the duke sometimes spoke, and with great commotion, which Sir Ralph the more easily perceived, because he kept his eyes always fixed upon the duke; having procured the conference, upon somewhat he knew, there was of extraordinary; and the man told him in his return over the water, that when he mentioned those particulars, which were to gain him credit, the substance whereof he said he durst not impart to him, the duke's colour changed, and he swore he could come by that knowledge only by the devil, for that those particulars were known only to himself, and to one person more, who, he was sure, would never speak of it.

'The duke pursued his purpose of hunting, but was observed to ride all the morning with great pensiveness, and in deep thoughts, without any delight in the exercise he was upon, and before the morning was spent, left the field, and alighted at his mother's lodgings at Whitehall, with whom he was shut up for the space of two or three hours, the noise of their discourse frequently reaching the ears of those who attended in the next rooms and when the duke left her, his countenance appeared full of trouble, with a mixture of anger: a countenance that was never before observed in him in any conversation with her, towards whom he had a profound reverence, and the countess herself was, at the duke's leaving her, found overwhelmed in tears, and in the highest agony imaginable; whatever there was of all this, it is a notorious truth, that when the news of the duke's murder (which happened within a few months) was brought to his mother, she seemed not in the least degree surprized, but received it as if she had foreseen it, nor did afterwards express such a degree of sorrow, as was expected from such a mother, for the loss of such a son.'

This is the representation which lord Clarendon gives of this extraordinary circumstance, upon which I shall not presume to make any comment; but if ever departed spirits were permitted to interest themselves with human affairs, and as Shakespear expresses it, revisit the glimpses of the moon, it seems to have been upon this occasion: at least there seems to be such rational evidence of it, as no man, however fortified against superstition, can well resist.

But let us now enter upon the life of the son of this great man; who, if he was inferior to his father as a statesman, was superior in wit, and wanted only application to have made a very great figure, even in the senate, but his love of pleasure was immoderate, which embarrassed him in the pursuit of any thing solid or praise-worthy.

He was an infant when his father's murder was perpetrated, and received his early education from several domestic tutors, and was afterwards sent to the university of Cambridge: when he had finished his course there, he travelled with his brother lord Francis, under the care of William Aylesbury, esquire. Upon his return, which was after the breaking out of the civil wars, he was conducted to Oxford, and presented to his Majesty, then there, and entered into Christ Church. Upon the decline of the King's cause, the young duke of Buckingham attended Prince Charles into Scotland, and was present in the year 1651 at the battle of Worcester, where he escaped beyond sea, and was soon after made knight of the garter. He came afterwards privately into England, and, November 19, 1657, married Mary, the daughter and heir of Thomas lord Fairfax, by whose interest he recovered all or most of his estate, which he had lost before. After the restoration, at which time he is said to have possessed an estate of 20,000 l. per annum, he was made one of the lords of the King's bed-chamber, and of the privy council, lord lieutenant of Yorkshire, and, at last, master of the horse.

In the year 1666, being discovered to have maintained secret correspondence by letters, and other transactions, tending to raise mutinies among some of his Majesty's forces, and stir up sedition among his people, and to have carried on other traiterous designs and practices, he absconded, upon which a proclamation was issued the same year for apprehending him. Mr. Thomas Carte, in his Life of the Duke of Ormond[1], tells us, 'that the duke's being denied the post of president of the North, was probably the reason of his disaffection to the King; and, that just before the recess of the Parliament, one Dr. John Heydon was taken up for treasonable practices, in sowing a sedition in the navy, and engaging persons in a conspiracy to seize the Tower. The man was a pretender to great skill in astrology, but had lost much of his reputation, by prognosticating the hanging of Oliver to his son Richard Cromwel and Thurloe, who came to him in disguise, for the calculation of nativities, being dressed like distressed cavaliers. He was for that put into prison, and continued in confinement sixteen months, whilst Cromwel outlived the prediction four years. This insignificant fellow was mighty great with the duke of Buckingham, who, notwithstanding the vanity of the art, and the notorious ignorance of the professor of it, made him cast not only his own, but the King's nativity; a matter of dangerous curiosity, and condemned by a statute which could only be said to be antiquated, because it had not for a long time been put in execution. This fellow he had likewise employed, among others, to excite the seamen to mutiny, as he had given money to other rogues to put on jackets to personate seamen, and to go about the country begging in that garb, and exclaiming for want of pay, while the people oppressed with taxes, were cheated of their money by the great officers of the crown. Heydon pretended to have been in all the duke's secrets, for near four years past, and that he had been all that time designing against the King and his government, that his grace thought the present reason favourable for the execution of his design, and had his agents at work in the navy and in the kingdom, to ripen the general discontents of the people, and dispose them to action, that he had been importuned by him to head the first party he could get together, and engage in an insurrection, the duke declaring his readiness to appear and join in the undertaking, as soon as the affair was begun. Some to whom Heydon unbosomed himself, and had been employed by him to carry letters to the duke of Buckingham, discovered the design. Heydon was taken up, and a serjeant at arms sent with a warrant by his Majesty's express order to take up the duke, who, having defended his house by force, for some time at least, found means to escape. The King knew Buckingham to be capable of the blackest designs, and was highly incensed at him for his conduct last sessions, and insinuating that spirit into the Commons, which had been so much to the detriment of the public service. He could not forbear expressing himself with more bitterness against the duke, than was ever dropped from him upon any other occasion. When he was sollicited in his behalf, he frankly said, that he had been the cause of continuing the war, for the Dutch would have made a very low submission, had the Parliament continued their first vigorous vote of supplying him, but the duke's cabals had lessened his interest both abroad and at home, with regard to the support of the war. In consequence of this resentment, the King put him out of the privy council, bedchamber, and lieutenancy of York, ordering him likewise to be struck out of all commissions. His grace absconding, a proclamation was issued out, requiring his appearance, and surrender of himself by a certain day.'

Notwithstanding this appearance of resentment against him, yet Charles, who was far from being of an implacable temper, took Buckingham again into favour, after he had made an humble submission; he was restored to his place in the council, and in the bedchamber in 1667, and seemed perfectly confirmed in the good graces of the King, who was, perhaps, too much charmed with his wit to consider him as an enemy.

In the year 1670, the duke was supposed to be concerned in Blood's attempt on the life of the duke of Ormond. This scheme was to have conveyed that nobleman to Tyburn, and there to have hanged him; for which purpose he was taken out of his coach in St. James's Street, and carried away by Blood and his son beyond Devonshire House, Piccadilly, but then rescued. Blood afterwards endeavoured to steal the crown out of the Tower, but was seized; however, he was not only pardoned, but had an estate of five hundred pounds a year given him in Ireland, and admitted into an intimacy with the King. The reason of Blood's malice against the duke of Ormond was, because his estate at Sorney was forfeited for his treason in the course of government, and must have been done by any lord lieutenant whatever. This, together with the instigation of some enemy of the duke of Ormond's at court, wrought upon him so, that he undertook the assassination. Mr. Carte supposes, that no man was more likely to encourage Blood in this attempt, than the duke of Buckingham, who, he says was the most profligate man of his time, and had so little honour in him, that he would engage in any scheme to gratify an irregular passion. The duke of Ormond had acted with some severity against him, when he was detected in the attempt of unhinging the government, which had excited so much resentment, as to vent itself in this manner. Mr. Carte likewise charges the duchess of Cleveland with conspiring against Ormond, but has given no reasons why he thinks she instigated the attempt. The duchess was cousin to the duke of Buckingham, but it appears in the Annals of Gallantry of those times, that she never loved him, nor is it probable she engaged with him in so dangerous a scheme.

That Buckingham was a conspirator against Ormond, Mr. Carte says, there is not the least doubt; and he mentions a circumstance of his guilt too strong to be resisted. That there were reasons to think him the person who put Blood upon the attempt of the duke of Ormond, (says he) 'cannot well be questioned, after the following relation, which I had from a gentleman (Robert Lesly of Glaslough, in the county of Monaghan, esquire) whose veracity and memory, none that knew him, will ever doubt, who received it from the mouth of Dr. Turner, bishop of Ely. The earl of Ossory came in one day, not long after the affair, and seeing the duke of Buckingham standing by the King, his colour rose, and he spoke to this effect; My lord, I know well, that you are at the bottom of this late attempt of Blood's upon my father, and therefore I give you fair warning, if my father comes to a violent end by sword or pistol, or the more secret way of poison, I shall not be at a loss to know the first author of it; I shall consider you as the assassin; I shall treat you as such, and wherever I meet you, I shall pistol you, though you stood behind the King's chair, and I tell it you in his Majesty's presence, that you may be sure I shall keep my word.' I know not whether this will be deemed any breach of decorum to the King, in whose presence it was said, but, in my opinion, it was an act of spirit and resentment worthy of a son, when his father's life was menaced, and the villain (Blood) who failed in the attempt, was so much courted, caressed, and in high favour immediately afterwards.

In June 1671, the duke was installed chancellor of the university of Cambridge, and the same year was sent ambassador to the King of France;

who being pleased with his person and errand, entertained him very nobly for several days together; and upon his taking leave, gave him a sword and belt set with Pearls and Diamonds, to the value of 40,000 pistoles. He was afterwards sent to that King at Utrecht in June 1672, together with Henry earl of Arlington, and George lord Hallifax. He was one of the cabal at Whitehall, and in the beginning of the session of Parliament, February 1672, endeavoured to cast the odium of the Dutch war from himself, upon lord Arlington, another of the cabal. In June 1674, he resigned the chancellorship of Cambridge. About this time he became a great favourer of the Nonconformists. February 16, 1676, his grace, and James earl of Salisbury, Anthony earl of Shaftsbury, and Philip lord Wharton, were committed to the Tower by order of the House of Lords, for a contempt, in refusing to retract what they had said the day before, when the duke, immediately after his Majesty had ended his speech to both Houses, endeavoured to shew from law and reason, that the long prorogation was nulled, and the Parliament was consequently dissolved.

The chief of our author's works is,

The Rehearsal, a Comedy, first acted on December 7, 1671. It is said that the duke was assisted in writing this play, by his Chaplain Dr. Thomas Sprat, Martin Clifford, esquire, master of the Charterhouse, and Mr. Samuel Butler, author of Hudibras. Jacob, in his Lives of the Poets, observes, 'that he cannot exactly learn when his grace began this piece; but this much, says he, we may certainly gather from the plays ridiculed in it, that it was before the end of 1663, and finished before 1664, because it had been several times rehearsed, the players were perfect in their parts, and all things in readiness for its acting, before the great plague in 1665, and that then prevented it, for what was then intended, was very different from what now appears. In that he called his poet Bilboa, by which name Sir Robert Howard was the person pointed at. During this interval, many plays were published, written in heroic rhime, and on the death of Sir William Davenant 1669, whom Mr. Dryden succeeded in the laurel, it became still in greater vogue; this moved the duke to change the name of his poet, from Bilboa to Bayes.'

This character of Bayes is inimitably drawn; in it the various foibles of poets (whether good, bad or indifferent) are so excellently blended as to make the most finished picture of a poetical coxcomb: 'Tis such a master-piece of true humour as will ever last, while our English tongue is understood, or the stage affords a good comedian to play it. How shall I now avoid the imputation of vanity, when I relate, that this piece, on being revived (when I[2] first appeared in the part of Bayes) at the Theatre-Royal in Covent-Garden in the year 1739, was, in that one season (continued to 1740) played upwards of forty nights, to great audiences, with continued mirthful applause. As this is a truth, I give it to the candid; and let the relation take its chance, though it should not be thought by some (who may not abound in good nature) that I only mean by this, to pay due regard to the merit of the piece, though it speaks for itself; for, without extraordinary merit in the writing, it could never have gained such an uncommon run, at the distance of fourscore years from its being first written, when most of those pieces were forgot which it particularly satirises; or, if remembered, they were laughed into fame by the strong mock-parodies with which this humorous piece of admirable burlesque abounds.

Mr. Dryden, in revenge for the ridicule thrown on him in this piece, exposed the duke under the name of Zimri in his Absalom and Achitophel. This character, drawn by Dryden, is reckoned a masterpiece; it has the first beauty, which is truth; it is a striking picture, and admirably marked: We need make no apology for inserting it here; it is too excellent to pass unnoticed.

> In the first rank of these did Zimri stand:
> A man so various that he seemed to be
> Not one, but all mankind's epitome.
> Stiff in opinions, always in the wrong;
> Was every thing by starts, and nothing long;
> But, in the course of one revolving moon,
> Was Chymist, fidler, statesman, and buffoon:
> Then all for women, painting, rhiming, drinking;
> Besides ten thousand freaks that died in thinking.
> Blest madman, who could every hour employ,
> In something new to wish, or to enjoy!
> Railing, and praising were his usual themes,
> And both, to shew his judgment, in extremes;
> So over violent, or over civil,
> That every man with him was God, or devil.
> In squandering wealth was his peculiar art;
> Nothing went unrewarded but desert.
> Beggar'd by fools, whom still he found too late,
> He had his jest, and they had his estate.
> He laught himself from court, then sought relief,
> By forming parties, but could ne'er be chief.
> Thus wicked, but in will, of means bereft,
> He left not faction, but of that was left.

It is allowed by the severest enemies of this nobleman, that he had a great share of vivacity, and quickness of parts, which were particularly turned to ridicule; but while he has been celebrated as a wit, all men are silent as to other virtues, for it is no where recorded, that he ever performed one generous disinterested action in his whole life; he relieved no distressed merit; he never shared the blessing of the widow and fatherless, and as he lived a profligate, he died in misery, a by-word and a jest, unpitied and unmourned.

He died April 16, 1687, Mr. Wood says, at his house in Yorkshire, but Mr. Pope informs us, that he died at an inn in that county, in very mean circumstances. In his Epistle to lord Bathurst, he draws the following affecting picture of this man, who had possessed an estate of near 50,000 l. per annum, expiring,

> In the worst inn's worst room, with mat half hung
> The floors of plaister, and the walls of dung,
> On once a flock-bed, but repair'd with straw,
> With tape-ty'd curtains, never meant to draw,
> · The George and Garter dangling from that bed,
> Where tawdry yellow, strove with dirty red,
> Great Villiers lies—alas! how chang'd from him
> That life of pleasure, and that foul of whim!
> Gallant and gay, in Cliveden's proud alcove,
> The bow'r of wanton Shrewsbury[3] and love;
> Or just as gay in council, in a ring
> Of mimick'd statesmen and their merry king.
> No wit to flatter left of all his store!
> No fool to laugh at, which he valued more;
> There, victor of his health, of fortune, friends,
> And fame, this lord of useless thousands ends.
> His grace's fate, sage Cutler could foresee,
> And well (he thought) advised him, 'live like me.'
> As well, his grace replied, 'like you, Sir John!
> That I can do, when all I have is gone:'

Besides the celebrated Comedy of the Rehearsal, the duke wrote the following pieces;

1.   An Epitaph on Thomas, Lord Fairfax, which has been often reprinted.

2.   A Short Discourse upon the Reasonableness of Men's having a Religion or Worship of God. This Piece met with many Answers, to which, the Duke wrote Replies.

3.   A Demonstration of the above Duty.

4. Several Poems, particularly, Advice to a Painter to draw my Lord Arlington. Timon, a Satire on several Plays, in which he was assisted by the Earl of Rochester; a Consolatory Epistle to Julian Secretary to the Muses; upon the Monument; upon the Installment of the Duke of Newcastle; the Rump-Parliament, a Satire; the Mistress; the Lost Mistress; a Description of Fortune.

5. Several Speeches.

Footnotes:

1. B. vi. vol. ii. p. 347.

2. T.C.

3. The countess of Shrewsbury, a woman abandoned to gallantries. The earl her husband was killed by the duke of Buckingham; and it has been said that, during the combat, she held the duke's horses in the habit of a page.

Matthew Smith, Esquire

(The following Account of this Gentleman came to our Hands too late to be inserted in the Chronological Series.)

This gentleman was the son of John Smith, an eminent Merchant at Knaresborough in the county of York, and descended from an ancient family of that name, seated at West-Herrington and Moreton House in the county pal. of Durham. Vide Philpot's Visitation of Durham, in the Heralds Office, page 141.

He was a Barrister at Law, of the Inner-Temple, and appointed one of the council in the North, the fifteenth of King Charles I. he being a Loyalist, and in great esteem for his eminence and learning in his profession; as still further appears by his valuable Annotations on Littleton's Tenures he left behind him in manuscript. He also wrote some pieces of poetry, and is the author of two dramatical performances.

1.   The Country Squire, or the Merry Mountebank, a Ballad Opera of one Act.

2.   The Masquerade du Ciel, a Masque, which was published the year that he died, 1640, by John Smith of Knaresborough, Esq; (eldest son and heir to this Matthew, by Anne his wife, daughter of Henry Roundell, esq; who dedicated it to the Queen. He was a person of the greatest loyalty, and very early addicted to arms, which made him extreamly zealous and active during the civil wars, in joining with the Royalists, particularly at the battle of Marston-Moor 1644, when he personally served under Prince Rupert, for which he and his family were plundered and sequestered. He also fined twice for Sheriff, to avoid the oaths in those days.)

Thomas Otway

This excellent poet was not more remarkable for moving the tender passions, than for the variety of fortune, to which he was subjected. We have some where read an observation, that the poets have ever been the least philosophers, and were always unhappy in a want of firmness of temper, and steadiness of resolution: of the truth of this remark, poor Mr. Otway is a lively instance; he never could sufficiently combat his appetite of extravagance and profusion, to live one year in a comfortable competence, but was either rioting in luxurious indulgence, or shivering with want, and exposed to the insolence and contempt of the world. He was the son of Mr. Humphry Otway, rector of Wolbeding in Sussex, and was born at Trottin in that county, on March 3, 1651. He received his education at Wickeham school, near Winchester, and became a commoner of Christ Church in Oxford, in the beginning of the year 1669. He quitted the university without a degree, and retired to London, though, in the opinion of some historians, he went afterwards to Cambridge, which seems very probable, from a copy of verses of Mr. Duke's to him, between whom subsisted a sincere friendship till the death of Mr. Otway. When our poet came to London, the first account we hear of him, is, that he commenced player, but without success, for he is said to have failed in want of execution, which is so material to a good player, that a tolerable execution, with advantage of a good person, will often supply the place of judgment, in which it is not to be supposed Otway was deficient.

Though his success as an actor was but indifferent, yet he gained upon the world by the sprightliness of his conversation, and the acuteness of his wit, which, it seems, gained him the favour of Charles Fitz Charles, earl of Plymouth, one of the natural sons of King Charles II. who procured him a cornet's Pommission in the new raised English forces designed for Flanders. All who have written of Mr. Otway observe, that he returned from Flanders in very necessitous circumstances, but give no account how that reverse of fortune happened: it is not natural to suppose that it proceeded from actual cowardice, or that Mr. Otway had drawn down any disgrace upon himself by misbehaviour in a military station. If this had been the case, he wanted not enemies who would have improved the circumstance, and recorded it against him, with a malicious satisfaction; but if it did not proceed from actual cowardice, yet we have some reason to conjecture that Mr. Otway felt a strong disinclination to a military life, perhaps from a consciousness that his heart failed him, and a dread of misbehaving, should he ever be called to an engagement; and to avoid the shame of which he was apprehensive in consequence of such behaviour, he, in all probability, resigned his commission, which could not but disoblige the earl of Plymouth, and expose himself to necessity. What pity is it, that he who could put such masculine strong sentiments into the mouth of such a resolute hero as his own Pierre, should himself fail in personal courage, but this quality nature withheld from him, and he exchanged the chance of reaping laurels in the field of victory, for the equally uncertain, and more barren laurels of poetry. The earl of Rochester, in his Session of the Poets, has thus maliciously recorded, and without the least grain of wit, the deplorable circumstances of Otway.

> Tom Otway came next, Tom Shadwell's dear Zany,
> And swears for heroics he writes best of any;
> Don Carlos his pockets so amply had filled,
> That his mange was quite cured, and his lice were all killed.
> But Apollo had seen his face on the stage,   }
> And prudently did not think fit to engage   }
> The scum of a playhouse, for the prop of an age.   }

Mr. Otway translated out of French into English, the History of the Triumvirate; the First Part of Julius Cæsar, Pompey and Crassus, the Second Part of Augustus, Anthony and Lepidus, being a faithful collection from the best historians, and other authors, concerning the revolution of the Roman government, which happened under their authority, London 1686 in 8vo. Our author finding his necessities press, had recourse to writing for the stage, which he did with various success: his comedy has been blamed for having too much libertinism mixed with it; but in tragedy he made it his business, for the most part, to observe the decorum of the stage. He has certainly followed nature in the language of his tragedy, and therefore shines in the passionate parts more than any of our English poets. As there is something familiar and domestic in the fable of his tragedy, he has little pomp, but great energy in his expressions; for which reason, though he has admirably succeeded in the tender and melting parts of his tragedies, he sometimes falls into too great a familiarity of phrase in those, which, by Aristotle's rule, ought to have been raised and supported by the dignity of expression. It has been observed by the critics, that the poet has founded his tragedy of Venice Preservcd, on so wrong a plot, that the greatest characters in it are those of rebels and traitors. Had the hero of this play discovered the same good qualities in defence of his country, that he shewed for his ruin and subversion, the audience could not enough pity and admire him; but as he is now represented, we can only say of him, what the Roman historian says of Catiline, that his fall would have been glorious (si pro Patria sic concidisset) had he so fallen, in the service of his country.

Mr. Charles Gildon, in his Laws of Poetry, stiles Mr. Otway a Poet of the first Magnitude, and tells us, and with great justice, that he was perfect master of the tragic passions, and draws them every where with a delicate and natural simplicity, and therefore never fails to raise strong emotions in the soul. I don't know of a stronger instance of this force, than in the play of the Orphan; the tragedy is composed of persons whose fortunes do not exceed the quality of such as we ordinarily call people of condition, and without the advantage of having the scene heightened by the importance of the characters; his inimitable skill in representing the workings of the heart, and its affection, is such that the circumstances are great from the art of the poet, rather than from the figure of the persons represented. The whole drama is admirably wrought, and the mixture of passions raised from affinity, gratitude, love, and misunderstanding between brethren, ill usage from persons obliged slowly returned by the benefactors, keeps the mind in a continual anxiety and contrition. The sentiments of the unhappy Monimia are delicate and natural, she is miserable without guilt, but incapable of living with a consciousness of having committed an ill act, though her inclination had no part in it. Mrs. Barry, the celebrated actress, used to say, that in her part of Monimia in the Orphan, she never spoke these words, Ah! poor Castalio, without tears; upon which occasion Mr. Gildon observes, that all the pathetic force had been lost, if any more words had been added, and the poet would have endeavoured, in vain, to have heightened them, by the addition of figures of speech, since the beauty of those three plain simple words is so great by the force of nature, that they must have been weakened and obscured by 'the finest flowers of rhetoric.

The tragedy of the Orphan is not without great blemishes, which the writer of a criticism on it, published in the Gentleman's Magazine, has very judiciously and candidly shewn. The impetuous passion of Polydore breaks out sometimes in a language not sufficiently delicate, particularly in that celebrated passage where he talks of rushing upon her in a storm of love. The simile of the bull is very offensive to chaste ears, but poor Otway lived in dissolute times, and his necessity obliged him to fan the harlot-face of loose desire, in compliance to the general corruption. Monimia staying to converse with Polydor, after he vauntingly discovers his success in deceiving her, is shocking; had she left him abruptly, with a wildness of horror, that might have thrown him under the necessity of seeking an explanation from

Castalio, the scene would have ended better, would have kept the audience more in suspence, and been an improvement of the consequential scene between the brothers; but this remark is submitted to superior judges.

Venice Preferred is still a greater proof of his influence over our passions, and the faculty of mingling good and bad characters, and involving their fortunes, seems to be the distinguished excellence of this writer. He very well knew that nothing but distressed virtue can strongly touch us with pity, and therefore, in this play, that we may have a greater regard for the conspirators, he makes Pierre talk of redressing wrongs, and repeat all the common place of male contents.

> To see the sufferings of my fellow-creatures,
> And own myself a man: to see our senators
> Cheat the deluded people with a shew
> Of Liberty, which yet they ne'er must taste of!
> They say by them our hands are free from fetters,
> Yet whom they please they lay in basest bonds;
> Bring whom they please to infamy and sorrow;
> Drive us like wrecks down the rough tide of power
> Whilst no hold's left, to save us from destruction:
> All that bear this are villains, and I one,
> Not to rouse up at the great call of nature,
> And check the growth of these domestic spoilers,
> Who make us slaves, and tell us 'tis our charter.

Jaffier's wants and distresses, make him prone enough to any desperate resolution, yet says he in the language of genuine tenderness,

> But when I think what Belvidera feels,
> The bitterness her tender spirit tastes of,
> I own myself a coward: bear my weakness,
> If throwing thus my arms about thy neck,
> I play the boy, and blubber in thy bosom.

Jaffier's expostulation afterwards, is the picture of all who are partial to their own merit, and generally think a relish of the advantages of life is pretence enough to enjoy them.

> Tell me, why good Heaven
> Thou mad'st me what I am, with all the spirit,
> Aspiring thoughts, and elegant desires
> That fill the happiest man? ah rather why

Didst thou not form me, sordid as my fate,
Base minded, dull, and fit to carry burdens.

How dreadful is Jaffier's soliloquy, after he is engaged in the conspiracy.

I'm here; and thus the shades of night surround me,
I look as if all hell were in my heart,
And I in hell. Nay surely 'tis so with me;
For every step I tread, methinks some fiend
Knocks at my breast, and bids it not be quiet.
I've heard how desperate wretches like myself
Have wandered out at this dead time of night
To meet the foe of mankind in his walk:
Sure I'm so curst, that though of Heaven forsaken,
No minister of darkness, cares to tempt me.
Hell, hell! why sleep'st thou?

The above is the most awful picture of a man plunged in despair, that ever was drawn by a poet; we cannot read it without terror: and when it is uttered as we have heard it, from the late justly celebrated Booth, or those heart-affecting actors Garrick, and Barry, the flesh creeps, and the blood is chilled with horror.

In this play Otway catches our hearts, by introducing the episode of Belvidera. Private and public calamities alternately claim our concern; sometimes we could wish to see a whole State sacrificed for the weeping Belvidera, whose character and distress are so drawn as to melt every heart; at other times we recover again, in behalf of a whole people in danger. There is not a virtuous character in the play, but that of Belvidera, and yet so amazing is the force of the author's skill in blending private and public concerns, that the ruffian on the wheel, is as much the object of pity, as if he had been brought to that unhappy fate by some honourable action.

Though Mr. Otway possessed this astonishing talent of moving the passions, and writing to the heart, yet he was held in great contempt by some cotemporary poets, and was several times unsuccessful in his dramatic pieces. The merits of an author are seldom justly estimated, till the next age after his decease; while a man lives in the world, he has passion, prejudice, private and public malevolence to combat; his enemies are industrious to obscure his fame, by drawing into light his private follies; and personal malice is up in arms against every man of genius.

Otway was exposed to powerful enemies, who could not bear that he should acquire fame, amongst whom Dryden is the foremost. The enmity between Dryden and Otway could not proceed from jealousy, for what were Otway's, when put in the ballance with the amazing powers of Dryden? like a drop to the ocean: and yet we find Dryden declared himself his open enemy; for which, the best reason that can be assigned is, that Otway was a retainer to Shadwell, who was Dryden's aversion. Dryden was often heard to say, that Otway was a barren illiterate man, but 'I confess, says he, he has a power which I have not;' and when it was asked him, what power that was? he answered, 'moving the passions.' This truth was, no doubt, extorted from Dryden, for he seems not to be very ready in acknowledging the merits of his cotemporaries. In his preface to Du Fresnoy's Art of Painting, which he translated, he mentions Otway with respect, but not till after he was dead; and even then he speaks but coldly of him. The passage is as follows, 'To express the passions which are seated on the heart by outward signs, is one great precept of the painters, and very difficult to perform. In poetry the very same passions, and motions of the mind are to be expressed, and in this consists the principal difficulty, as well as the excellency of that art. This (says my author) is the gift of Jupiter, and to speak in the same Heathen language, is the gift of our Apollo, not to be obtained by pains or study, if we are not born to it; for the motions which are studied, are never so natural, as those which break out in the heighth of a real passion. Mr. Otway possessed this part as thoroughly as any of either the ancients or moderns. I will not defend every thing in his Venice Preserved, but I must bear this testimony to his memory, that the passions are truly touched in it, though, perhaps, there is somewhat to be desired, both in the grounds of them, and the heighth and elegance of expression; but nature is there, which is the greatest beauty.' Notwithstanding our admiration of Dryden, we cannot, without some indignation, observe, how sparing he is in the praises of Otway, who, considered as a tragic writer, was surely superior to himself. Dryden enchants us indeed with flow'ry descriptions, and charms us with (what is called) the magic of poetry; but he has seldom drawn a tear, and millions of radiant eyes have been witnesses for Otway, by those drops of pity which they have shed. Otway might be no scholar, but that, methinks, does not detract from the merit of a dramatist, nor much assist him in succeeding. For the truth of this we may appeal to experience. No poets in our language, who were what we call scholars, have ever written plays which delight or affect the audience. Shakespear, Otway and Southern were no scholars; Ben Johnson, Dryden and Addison were: and while few audiences admire the plays of the latter, those of the former are the supports of the stage.

After suffering many eclipses of fortune, and being exposed to the most cruel necessities, poor Otway died of want, in a public house on Tower-hill, in the 33rd year of his age, 1685. He had, no doubt, been driven to that part of the town, to avoid the persecution of his creditors and as he durst not appear much abroad to sollicit assistance, and having no means of getting money in his obscure retreat, he perished. It has been reported, that Mr. Otway, whom delicacy had long deterred from borrowing small sums, driven at last to the most grievous necessity ventured out of his lurking place, almost naked and shivering, and went into a coffee-house on Tower-hill, where he saw a gentleman, of whom he had some knowledge, and of whom he sollicited the loan of a shilling. The gentleman was quite shocked, to see the author of Venice Preserved begging bread, and compassionately put into his hand a guinea.

Mr. Otway having thanked his benefactor, retired, and changed the guinea to purchase a roll; as his stomach was full of wind by excess of fasting, the first mouthful choaked him, and instantaneously put a period to his days.

Who can consider the fate of this gentleman, without being moved to pity? we can forgive his acts of imprudence, since they brought him to so miserable an end; and we cannot but regret, that he who was endowed by nature with such distinguished talents, as to make the bosom bleed with salutary sorrow, should himself be so extremely wretched, as to excite the same sensations for him, which by the power of his eloquence and poetry, he had raised for imaginary heroes. We know, indeed, of no guilty part of Otway's life, other than those fashionable faults, which usually recommend to the conversation of men in courts, but which serve for excuses for their patrons, when they have not a mind to provide for them. From the example of Mr. Otway, succeeding poets should learn not to place any confidence in the promises of patrons; it discovers a higher spirit, and reflects more honour on a man to struggle nobly for independance, by the means of industry, than servilely to wait at a great man's gate, or to sit at his table, meerly to afford him diversion: Competence and independence have surely more substantial charms, than the smiles of a courtier, which are too frequently fallacious. But who can read Mr Otway's story, without indignation at those idols of greatness, who demand worship from men of genius, and yet can suffer them to live miserably, and die neglected?

The dramatic works of Mr. Otway are,

1.   Alcibiades, a Tragedy, acted at the Duke of York's Theatre, 1675, dedicated to Charles, Earl of Middlesex. The story of this play is taken from Cor. Nepos, and Plutarch's Life of Alcibiades.

2.   Titus and Berenice, a Tragedy, acted at the Duke's Theatre, 1677, dedicated to John, Earl of Rochester. This play consists of but three Acts, and is a translation from M. Racine into heroic verse; for the story see Suetonius, Dionysius, Josephus; to which is added the Cheats of Scapin, a Farce, acted the same year. This is a translation from Moliere, and is originally Terence's Phormio.

3.   Friendship in Fashion, a Comedy, acted at the Duke's Theatre, 1678, dedicated to the Earl of Dorset and Middlesex. This play was revived at the Theatre-Royal in Drury-Lane, 1749, and was damned by the audience, on account of the immorality of the design, and the obscenity of the dialogue.

4.   Don Carlos, Prince of Spain, a Tragedy, acted at the Duke of York's Theatre, 1679. This play, which was the second production of our author, written in heroic verse, was acted with very great applause, and had a run of thirty nights; the plot from the Novel called Don Carlos.

5.   The Orphan, or the Unhappy Marriage, a Tragedy, acted at the Duke of York's Theatre, 1680, dedicated to her Royal Highness the Duchess. It is founded on the History of Brandon, and a Novel called the English Adventurer. Scene Bohemia.

6.   The History and Fall of Caius Marius, a Tragedy, acted at the Duke's Theatre, 1680, dedicated to Lord Viscount Falkland. The characters of Marius Junior and Lavinia, are borrowed literally from Shakespear's Romeo and Juliet, which Otway has acknowledged in his Prologue.

7.   The Soldier's Fortune, a Comedy, acted at the Duke's Theatre, 1681. This play is dedicated to Mr. Bentley his Bookseller; for the copy money, as he tells us himself, see Boccace's Novels, Scarron's Romances.

8.   The Atheist, or the Second Part of the Soldier's Fortune, a Comedy, acted at the Duke of York's Theatre, 1684, dedicated to Lord Eland, the eldest son to the Marquis of Hallifax.

9.   Venice Preserved, or a Plot Discovered, a Tragedy, acted at the Duke's Theatre, 1685, dedicated to the Duchess of Portsmouth. Of this we have already given some account, and it is so frequently acted, that any enlargement would be impertinent. It is certainly one of the most moving plays upon the English stage; the plot from a little book, giving an account of the Conspiracy of the Spaniards against Venice.

Besides his plays, he wrote several poems, viz.

The Poet's Complaint to his Muse, or a Satire against Libels, London; 1680, in 4to.

Windsor Castle, or a Monument to King Charles the Second.

Miscellany Poems, containing a New Translation of Virgil's Eclogues, Ovid's Elegies, Odes of Horace, London 1864. He translated likewise the Epistle of Phædra to Hyppolitus, printed in the Translation of Ovid's Epistles, by several hands. He wrote the Prologue to Mrs. Bhon's City Heiress. Prefixed to Creechis Lucretius, there is a copy of verses written by Mr. Otway, in praise of that translation.

John Oldham

This eminent satyrical poet, was the son of the reverend Mr. John Oldham, a nonconformist minister, and grandson to Mr. John Oldham, rector of Nun-Eaton, near Tedbury in Gloucestershire. He was born at Shipton (where his father had a congregation, near Tedbury, and in the same county) on the 9th of August 1653. He was educated in grammar learning, under the care of his father, till he was almost fitted for the university; and to be compleatly qualified for that purpose, he was sent to Tedbridge school, where he spent about two years under the tuition of Mr. Henry Heaven, occasioned by the earnest request of alderman Yeats of Bristol, who having a son at the same school, was desirous that Mr. Oldham should be his companion, which he imagined would much conduce to the advancement of his learning. This for some time retarded Oldham in the prosecution of his own studies, but for the time he lost in forwarding Mr. Yeat's son, his father afterwards made him an ample amends. Mr. Oldham being sent to Edmund Hall in Oxford, was committed to the care of Mr. William Stephens: of which hall he became a bachelor in the beginning of June 1670. He was soon observed to be a good latin scholar, and chiefly addicted himself to the study of poetry, and other polite acquirements[1]. In the year 1674, he took the degree of bachelor of arts, but left the university before he compleated that degree by determination, being much against his inclination compelled to go home and live for some time with his father. The next year he was very much afflicted for the death of his dear friend, and constant companion, Mr. Charles Mervent, as appears by his ode upon that occasion. In a short time after he became usher to the free-school at Croyden in Surry. Here it was, he had the honour of receiving a visit from the earl of Rochester, the earl of Dorset, Sir Charles Sedley, and other persons of distinction, meerly upon the reputation of some verses which they had seen in manuscript. The master of the school was not a little surprized, at such a visit, and would fain have taken the honour of it to himself, but was soon convinced that he had neither wit nor learning enough to make a party in such company. This adventure was no doubt very happy for Mr. Oldham, as it encreased his reputation and gained him the countenance of the Great, for after about three years continuance at Croyden school, he was recommended by his good friend Harman Atwood, Esq; to Sir Edward Thurland, a judge, near

Rygate in the same county, who appointed him tutor to his two grandsons. He continued in this family till 1680. After this he was sometime tutor to a son of Sir William Hicks, a gentleman living within three or four miles of London, who was intimately acquainted with a celebrated Physician, Dr. Richard Lower, by whose peculiar friendship and encouragement, Mr. Oldham at his leisure hours studied physic for about a year, and made some progress in it, but the bent of his poetical genius was too strong to become a proficient in any school but that of the muses. He freely acknowledges this in a letter to a friend, written in July 1678.

> While silly I, all thriving arts refuse,   }
> And all my hopes, and all my vigour lose,   }
> In service of the worst of jilts a muse.   }
>   *   *   *   *   *   }
>
> Oft I remember, did wise friends dissuade,
> And bid me quit the trifling barren trade.
> Oft have I tryed (heaven knows) to mortify
> This vile and wicked bent of poetry;
> But still unconquered it remains within,
> Fixed as a habit, or some darling sin.
> In vain I better studies there would sow;
> Oft have I tried, but none will thrive or grow.
> All my best thoughts, when I'd most serious be,
> Are never from its foul infection free:
> Nay God forgive me when I say my prayers,
> I scarce can help polluting them with verse.
> The fab'lous wretch of old revers'd I seem,
> Who turn whatever I touch to dross of rhime.

Our author had not been long in London, before he was found out by the noblemen who visited him at Croyden, and who now introduced him to the acquaintance of Mr. Dryden. But amongst the Men of quality he was most affectionately caressed by William Earl of Kingston, who made him an offer of becoming his chaplain; but he declined an employment, to which servility and dependence are so necessarily connected. The writer of his life observes, that our author in his satire addressed to a friend, who was about to quit the university, and came abroad into the world, lets his friend know, that he was frighted from the thought of such an employment, by the scandalous sort of treatment which often accompanies it. This usage deters men of generous minds from placing themselves in such a station of life; and hence persons of quality are frequently excluded from the improving, agreeable conversation of a learned and obsequious friend. In this satire Mr. Oldham writes thus,

Some think themselves exalted to the sky,
If they light on some noble family.
Diet and horse, and thirty-pounds a year,
Besides the advantage of his lordship's ear.
The credit of the business and the state,
Are things that in a youngster's sense found great.
Little the unexperienced wretch does know,
What slavery he oft must undergo;
Who tho' in silken stuff, and cassoc drest,
Wears but a gayer livery at best.
When diner calls, the implement must wait,
With holy words to consecrate the meat;
But hold it for a favour seldom known,
If he be deign'd the honour to sit down.
Soon as the tarts appear, Sir Crape withdraw,
Those dainties are not for a spiritual maw.
Observe your distance, and be sure to stand
Hard by the cistern, with your cap in hand:
There for diversion you may pick your teeth,
Till the kind voider comes for your relief,
For meer board wages, such their freedom sell,
Slaves to an hour, and vassals to a bell:
And if th' employments of one day be stole,
They are but prisoners out upon parole:
Always the marks of slavery remain,
And they tho' loose, still drag about their chain.
And where's the mighty prospect after all,
A chaplainship serv'd up, and seven years thrall?
The menial thing, perhaps for a reward,   }
Is to some slender benefice prefer'd,   }
With this proviso bound that he must wed,   }
My lady's antiquated waiting maid,
In dressing only skill'd, and marmalade.
Let others who such meannesses can brook,
Strike countenance to ev'ry great man's look:
Let those, that have a mind, turn slave to eat,
And live contented by another's plate:
I rate my freedom higher, nor will I,
For food and rayment track my liberty.

But if I must to my last shift be put,
To fill a bladder, and twelve yards of gut,
Richer with counterfeited wooden leg,
And my right arm tyed up, I'll choose to beg.
I'll rather choose to starve at large, than be,
The gaudiest vassal to dependancy.

The above is a lively and animated description of the miseries of a slavish dependance on the great, particularly that kind of mortification which a chaplain must undergo. It is to be lamented, that gentlemen of an academical education should be subjected to observe so great a distance from those, over whom in all points of learning and genius they may have a superiority. Tho' in the very nature of things this must necessarily happen, yet a high spirit cannot bear it, and it is with pleasure we can produce Oldham, as one of those poets who have spurned dependence, and acted consistent with the dignity of his genius, and the lustre of his profession.

When the earl of Kingston found that Mr. Oldham's spirit was too high to accept his offer of chaplainship, he then caressed him as a companion, and gave him an invitation to his house at Holmes-Pierpont, in Nottinghamshire. This invitation Mr. Oldham accepted, and went into the country with him, not as a dependant but friend; he considered himself as a poet, and a clergyman, and in consequence of that, he did not imagine the earl was in the least degraded by making him his bosom companion. Virgil was the friend of Mæcenas, and shone in the court of Augustus, and if it should be observed that Virgil was a greater poet than Oldham, it may be answered, Mæcenas was a greater man than the Earl of Kingston, and the court of Augustus much more brilliant than that of Charles II.

Our author had not been long at the seat of this Earl, before, being seized with the small pox, he died December 9, 1683, in the 30th year of his age, and was interred with the utmost decency, his lordship attending as chief mourner, in the church there, where the earl soon after erected a monument to his memory.—Mr. Oldham's works were printed at London 1722, in two volumes 12mo. They chiefly consist of Satires, Odes, Translations, Paraphrases of Horace, and other authors; Elegiac Verses, Imitations, Parodies, Familiar Epistles, &c.—Mr. Oldham was tall of stature, the make of his body very thin, his face long, his nose prominent, his aspect unpromising, and satire was in his eye. His constitution was very tender, inclined to a consumption, and it was not a little injured by his study and application to learned authors, with whom he was greatly conversant, as appears from his satires against the Jesuits, in which there is discovered as much learning as wit. In the second volume of the great historical, geographical, and poetical Dictionary, he is stiled the Darling of the Muses, a pithy, sententious, elegant, and smooth writer: "His translations exceed the original, and his invention seems matchless. His satire against the Jesuits is of special note; he may be justly said to have excelled all the satirists of the age." Tho' this compliment in favour of Oldham is certainly too hyperbolical, yet he was undoubtedly a very great genius; he had treasured in his mind an infinite deal of knowledge, which, had his life been prolonged, he might have produced with advantage, for his natural endowments seem to have been very great: But he is not more to be reverenced as a Poet, than for that gallant spirit of Independence he discovered, and that magnanimity which scorned to stoop to any servile submissions for patronage: He had many admirers among his contemporaries, of whom Mr. Dryden professed himself one, and has done justice to his memory by some excellent verses, with which we shall close this account.

> Farewel too little, and too lately known,
> Whom I began to think, and call my own;
> For sure our souls were near allied, and thine
> Cast in the same poetic mould with mine.
> One common note on either lyre did strike,
> And knaves and tools were both abhorred alike.
> To the same goal did both our studies drive,
> The last set out, the soonest did arrive,
> Thus Nisus fell upon the slippery place,
> While his young friend perform'd and won the race.
> O early ripe! to thy abundant store,
> What could advancing age have added more?
> It might, what nature never gives the young,
> Have taught the numbers of thy native tongue.
> But satire needs not those, and wit will shine,
> Thro' the harsh cadence of a rugged line:
> A noble error, and but seldom made,
> When poets are by too much force betray'd.   }
> Thy gen'rous fruits, tho' gather'd e'er their prime,   }
> Still shewed a quickness; and maturing time   }

Once more, hail and farewel: Farewel thou young,
But ah! too short, Marcellus of our tongue;
Thy brows with ivy, and with laurels bound,
But fate, and gloomy night encompass thee around.

Footnote:

1. Life of Mr. Oldham, prefixed to his works, vol. i. edit.
Lond. 1722.

(Dillon) (Wentworth) Earl of Roscommon

This nobleman was born in Ireland during the lieutenancy of the earl of Strafford, in the reign of King Charles I. Lord Strafford was his godfather, and named him by his own surname. He passed some of his first years in his native country, till the earl of Strafford imagining, when the rebellion first broke out, that his father who had been converted by archbishop Usher to the Protestant religion, would be exposed to great danger, and be unable to protect his family, sent for his godson, and placed him at his own seat in Yorkshire, under the tuition, of Dr. Hall, afterwards bishop of Norwich; by whom he was instructed in Latin, and without learning the common rules of grammar, which he could never retain in his memory, he attained to write in that language with classical elegance and propriety, and with so much ease, that he chose it to correspond with those friends who had learning sufficient to support the commerce. When the earl of Strafford was prosecuted, lord Roscommon went to Caen in Normandy, by the advice of bishop Usher, to continue his studies under Bochart, where he is said to have had an extraordinary impulse of his father's death, which is related by Mr. Aubrey in his miscellany, 'Our author then a boy of about ten years of age, one day was as it were madly extravagant, in playing, getting over the tables, boards, &c. He was wont to be sober enough. They who observed him said, God grant this proves no ill luck to him. In the heat of this extravagant fit, he cries out my father is dead. A fortnight after news came from Ireland, that his father was dead. This account I had from Mr. Knowles who was his governor, and then with him, since secretary to the earl of Strafford; and I have heard his Lordship's relations confirm the same.'

The ingenious author of lord Roscommon's life, publish'd in the Gentleman's Magazine for the month of May, 1748, has the following remarks on the above relation of Aubrey's.

'The present age is very little inclined to favour any accounts of this sort, nor will the name of Aubrey much recommend it to credit; it ought not however to be omitted, because better evidence of a fact is not easily to be found, than is here offered, and it must be, by preserving such relations, that we may at least judge how much they are to be regarded. If we stay to examine this account we shall find difficulties on both sides; here is a relation of a fact given by a man who had no interest to deceive himself; and here is on the other hand a miracle which produces no effect; the order of nature is interrupted to discover not a future, but only a distant event, the knowledge of which is of no use to him to whom it is revealed. Between these difficulties what way shall be found? Is reason or testimony to be rejected? I believe what Osborne says of an appearance of sanctity, may be applied to such impulses, or anticipations. "Do not wholly slight them, because they may be true; but do not easily trust them, because they may be false."'

Some years after he travelled to Rome, where he grew familiar with the most valuable remains of antiquity, applying himself particularly to the knowledge of medals, which he gained in great perfection, and spoke Italian with so much grace and fluency, that he was frequently mistaken there for a native. He returned to England upon the restoration of King Charles the IId, and was made captain of the band of pensioners, an honour which tempted him to some extravagancies. In the gaieties of that age (says Fenton) he was tempted to indulge a violent passion for gaming, by which he frequently hazarded his life in duels, and exceeded the bounds of a moderate fortune. This was the fate of many other men whose genius was of no other advantage to them, than that it recommended them to employments, or to distinction, by which the temptations to vice were multiplied, and their parts became soon of no other use, than that of enabling them to succeed in debauchery.

A dispute about part of his estate, obliging him to return to Ireland, he resigned his post, and upon his arrival at Dublin, was made captain of the guards to the duke of Ormond.

When he was at Dublin he was as much as ever distempered with the same fatal affection for play, which engaged him in one adventure, which well deserves to be related. 'As he returned to his lodgings from a gaming table, he was attacked in the dark by three ruffians, who were employed to assassinate him. The earl defended himself with so much resolution, that he dispatched one of the aggressors, while a gentleman accidentally passing that way interposed, and disarmed another; the third secured himself by flight. This generous assistant was a disbanded officer of a good family and fair reputation; who by what we call partiality of fortune, to avoid censuring the iniquities of the times, wanted even a plain suit of clothes to make a decent appearance at the castle; but his lordship on this occasion presenting him to the duke of Ormond, with great importunity prevailed with his grace that he might resign his post of captain of the guards to his friend, which for about three years the gentleman enjoyed, and upon his death, the duke returned the commission to his generous benefactor.'[1]

His lordship having finished his affairs in Ireland, he returned to London, was made master of the horse to the dutchess of York, and married the lady Frances, eldest daughter of the earl of Burlington, and widow of colonel Courtnay.

About this time, in imitation of those learned and polite assemblies, with which he had been acquainted abroad; particularly one at Caen, (in which his tutor Bochartus died suddenly while he was delivering an oration) he began to form a society for refining and fixing the standard of our language. In this design, his great friend Mr. Dryden was a particular assistant; a design, says Fenton, of which it is much more easy to conceive an agreeable idea, than any rational hope ever to see it brought to perfection. This excellent design was again set on foot, under the ministry of the earl of Oxford, and was again defeated by a conflict of parties, and the necessity of attending only to political disquisitions, for defending the conduct of the administration, and forming parties in the Parliament. Since that time it has never been mentioned, either because it has been hitherto a sufficient objection, that it was one of the designs of the earl of Oxford, by whom Godolphin was defeated; or because the statesmen who succeeded him have not more leisure, and perhaps less taste for literary improvements. Lord Roscommon's attempts were frustrated by the commotions which were produced by King James's endeavours to introduce alterations in religion. He resolved to retire to Rome, alledging, 'it was best to sit next the chimney when the chamber smoaked.'

It will, no doubt, surprize many of the present age, and be a just cause of triumph to them, if they find that what Roscommon and Oxford attempted in vain, shall be carried into execution, in the most masterly manner, by a private gentleman, unassisted, and unpensioned. The world has just reason to hope this from the publication of an English Dictionary, long expected, by Mr. Johnson; and no doubt a design of this sort, executed by such a genius, will be a lasting monument of the nation's honour, and that writer's merit.

Lord Roscommon's intended retreat into Italy, already mentioned, on account of the troubles in James the IId's reign, was prevented by the gout, of which he was so impatient, that he admitted a repellent application from a French empyric, by which his distemper was driven up into his bowels, and put an end to his life, in 1684.

Mr. Fenton has told us, that the moment in which he expired, he cried out with a voice, that expressed the most intense fervour of devotion,

> My God! my father, and my friend!
> Do not forsake me, at my end.

Two lines of his own version of the hymn, Dies iræ, Dies illa.

The same Mr. Fenton, in his notes upon Waller, has given Roscommon a character too general to be critically just. 'In his writings, says he, we view the image of a mind, which was naturally serious and solid, richly furnished, and adorned with all the ornaments of art and science; and those ornaments unaffectedly disposed in the most regular and elegant order. His imagination might have probably been fruitful and sprightly, if his judgment had been less severe; but that severity (delivered in a masculine, clear, succinct stile) contributed to make him so eminent in the didactical manner, that no man with justice can affirm he was ever equalled by any of our nation, without confessing at the same time, that he is inferior to none. In some other kinds of writing his genius seems to have wanted fire to attain the point of perfection: but who can attain it?'

From this account of the riches of his mind, who would not imagine that they had been displayed in large volumes, and numerous performances? Who would not, after the perusal of this character, be surprized to find, that all the proofs of this genius, and knowledge and judgment, are not sufficient to form a small volume? But thus it is, that characters are generally written: We know somewhat, and we imagine the rest. The observation that his imagination would have probably been more fruitful and sprightly, if his judgment had been less severe; might, if we were inclined to cavil, be answer'd by a contrary supposition, that his judgment would have been less severe, if his imagination had been more fruitful. It is ridiculous to oppose judgment and imagination to each other; for it does not appear, that men have necessarily less of the one, as they have more of the other.

We must allow, in favour of lord Roscommon, what Fenton has not mentioned so distinctly as he ought, and what is yet very much to his honour, That he is perhaps the only correct writer in verse before Addison; and that if there are not so many beauties in his composition, as in those of some of his contemporaries, there are at least fewer faults. Nor is this his highest praise; for Mr. Pope has celebrated him as the only moral writer in Charles the IId's reign.

> Unhappy Dryden—in all Charles's days,
> Roscommon only boasts unspotted lays.

Mr. Dryden speaking of Roscommon's essay on translated verse, has the following observation: 'It was that, says he, that made me uneasy, till I tried whether or no I was capable of following his rules, and of reducing the speculation into practice. For many a fair precept in poetry, is like a seeming demonstration in mathematics: very specious in the diagram, but failing in mechanic operation. I think I have generally observed his instructions. I am sure my reason is sufficiently convinced both of their truth and usefulness; which in other words is to confess no less a vanity, than to pretend that I have at least in some places made examples to his rules.'

This declaration of Dryden will be found no more than one of those cursory civilities, which one author pays to another; and that kind of compliment for which Dryden was remarkable. For when the sum of lord Roscommon's precepts is collected, it will not be easy to discover how they can qualify their reader for a better performance of translation, than might might have been attained by his own reflexions.

They are however here laid down:

> 'Tis true composing is the nobler part,
> But good translation is no easy art:
> For tho' materials have long since been found,
> Yet both your fancy and your hands are bound;
> And by improving what was writ before,
> Invention labours less, but judgment more.
> Each poet with a different talent writes,
> One praises, one instructs, another bites.
> Horace did ne'er aspire to epic bays
> Nor lofty Maro stoop to lyric lays.
> Examine how your humour is inclin'd,
> And watch the ruling passion of your mind.
> Then seek a poet, who your way does bend.
> And chuse an author, as you chuse a friend.
> United by this sympathetic bond,
> You grow familiar, intimate, and fond;
> Your thoughts, your words, your stiles, your souls
> agree,
> No longer his interpreter, but he.
> Take then a subject, proper to expound
> *   *   *   *   *
> But moral, great, and worth a poet's voice,
> For men of sense, despise a trivial choice:
> And such applause, it must expect to meet
> As would some painter busy in the street;
> Take pains the genuine meaning to explore,

There sweat, there strain, tug the laborious oar:
Search every comment, that your care can find.
Some here, some there, may hit the poet's mind.
Yet, be not blindly guided by the throng,
The multitude is always in the wrong.
When things appear unnatural, or hard,
Consult your author, with himself compar'd.
Who knows what blessings Phæbus may bestow,
And future ages to your labours owe?
Such secrets are not easily found out,
But once discovered leave no room for doubt.
Truth stamps conviction in your ravish'd breast,
And peace and joy attend the glorious guest.
They who too faithfully on names insist;
Rather create, than dissipate the mist:
And grow unjust by being over nice,
(For superstition, virtue turns to vice)
Let Crassus ghost, and Labienus tell
How twice in Parthian plains their legions fell,
Since Rome hath been so jealous of her fame,
That few know Pacorus, or Monæses name.
And 'tis much safer to leave out than add   }
*   *   *   *   *   }
                                                            }
Abstruse and mystic thoughts, you must express,   }
With painful care, but seeming easiness;
For truth shines brightest, thro' the plainest dress,
Your author always will the best advise,
Fall when he falls, and when he rises, rise.

Nothing could have induced us to have laboured thro' so great a number of cold unspirited lines, but in order to shew, that the rules which my lord has laid down are meerly common place, and must unavoidably occur to the mind of the most ordinary reader. They contain no more than this; that the author should be suitable to the translator's genius; that he should be such as may deserve a translation; that he who intends to translate him, should endeavour to understand him; that perspicuity should be studied, and unusual or uncouth names, sparingly inserted; and that the stile of the original should be copied in its elevation and depression. These are the common-place rules delivered without elegance, or energy, which have been so much celebrated, but how deservedly, let our unprepossess'd readers judge.

Roscommon was not without his merit; he was always chaste, and sometimes harmonious; but the grand requisites of a poet, elevation, fire, and invention, were not given him, and for want of these, however pure his thoughts, he is a languid unentertaining writer.

Besides this essay on translated verse, he is the author of a translation of Horace's Art of poetry; with some other little poems, and translations published in a volume of the minor poets.

Amongst the MSS. of Mr. Coxeter, we found lord Roscommon's translation of Horace's Art of Poetry, with some sketches of alterations he intended to make; but they are not great improvements; and this translation, of all his lordship's pieces, is the most unpoetical.

Footnote:

1. Fenton.